Interpreting Christmas at Museums and Historic Sites

About the Organization

The American Association for State and Local History (AASLH) is a national history membership association headquartered in Nashville, Tennessee, that provides leadership and support for its members who preserve and interpret state and local history in order to make the past more meaningful to all people. AASLH members are leaders in preserving, researching, and interpreting traces of the American past to connect the people, thoughts, and events of yesterday with the creative memories and abiding concerns of people, communities, and our nation today. In addition to sponsorship of this book series, AASLH publishes History News magazine, a newsletter, technical leaflets and reports, and other materials; confers prizes and awards in recognition of outstanding achievement in the field; supports a broad education program and other activities designed to help members work more effectively; and advocates on behalf of the discipline of history. To join AASLH, go to www.aaslh.org or contact Membership Services, AASLH, 2021 21st Ave. South, Suite 320, Nashville, TN 37212.

About the Series

The American Association for State and Local History publishes the *Interpreting History* series in order to provide expert, in-depth guidance in interpretation for history professionals at museums and historic sites. The books are intended to help practitioners expand their interpretation to be more inclusive of the range of American history.

Books in this series help readers:

- quickly learn about the questions surrounding a specific topic,
- introduce them to the challenges of interpreting this part of history, and
- highlight best practice examples of how interpretation has been done by different organizations.

They enable institutions to place their interpretative efforts into a larger context, despite each having a specific and often localized mission. These books serve as quick references to practical considerations, further research, and historical information.

Titles in the Series

Interpreting Christmas at Museums and Historic Sites

Edited by
Kenneth C. Turino
and
Max A. van Balgooy

ROWMAN & LITTLEFIELD
Lanham • Boulder • New York • London

Published by Rowman & Littlefield
An imprint of The Rowman & Littlefield Publishing Group, Inc.
4501 Forbes Boulevard, Suite 200, Lanham, Maryland 20706
www.rowman.com

86-90 Paul Street, London EC2A 4NE

Alexandra Rasic, Andrew Jackson's Hermitage, Campbell House Museum, Carol M. Highsmith, David J. Murray, Hampton National Historic Site, Historic New England, James Dobson, Kenneth C. Turino, Laurence Perry, Library of Congress, Indianapolis Museum of Art at Newfields, Lindenwald, Louisiana State Museum, Max A. van Balgooy, National Archives and Records Administration, National Museum of African American History and Culture, National Park Service, National Trust for Places of Historic Interest or Natural Beauty, Ohio History Connection, Old Salem Museum and Gardens, Robert A. Wilson, and Strawbery Banke Museum.

Versions of "The Spirit of Christmas Past: A Hampton NHS Holiday Experience" by Gregory R. Weidman, "'Twas the Year before Christmas: Planning Your Event and Protecting Resources" by Laurel A. Racine, "Decorating for Christmas: Collaborating with Garden Clubs" by Lenora Henson, and "The Ghost of Christmas That Never Was: The Evolution of the Annual Holiday Event at Lindenwald" by James A. McKay and Patricia West previously appeared in "The Curator's Role in Crowd-Pleasing Events: Maintaining Safety, Accuracy, and Sanity in the Excitement of It All," *Collections* 10, no. 1 (March 1, 2014): 47–66.

British Library Cataloguing in Publication Information Available

Library of Congress Cataloging-in-Publication Data
Names: Turino, Kenneth, editor. | Balgooy, Max van, editor.
Title: Interpreting Christmas at museums and historic sites / Edited by Kenneth C. Turino and
    Max A. van Balgooy.
Description: Lanham, Maryland : Rowman & Littlefield Publishers, [2024] | Series:
    Interpreting history AASLH | Includes bibliographical references and index.
Identifiers: LCCN 2024015423 (print) | LCCN 2024015424 (ebook) | ISBN 9781538162934
    (cloth) | ISBN 9781538162941 (paperback) | ISBN 9781538162958 (epub)
Subjects: LCSH: Christmas—Social aspects. | Museums—Interpretive programs. | Museums—
    Social aspects. | Historic sites—Interpretive programs. | Historic sites—Social aspects.
Classification: LCC GT4985 .I57 2024 (print) | LCC GT4985 (ebook) | DDC
    394.2663—dc23/eng/20240411
LC record available at https://lccn.loc.gov/2024015423
LC ebook record available at https://lccn.loc.gov/2024015424

∞™ The paper used in this publication meets the minimum requirements of American National Standard for Information Sciences—Permanence of Paper for Printed Library Materials, ANSI/ NISO Z39.48-1992.

Contents

Introduction

Kenneth C. Turino and
Max A. van Balgooy

For many house museums, historic sites, historical societies, and museums, December—with its holidays, Christmas, Hanukkah, and Kwanzaa—can be the most visited times of the year (and most profitable). The Christmas tree stands proudly in the parlor, glistening with ornaments and surrounded by colorfully wrapped gifts, and carolers outside are singing "Away in a Manger" and "Jingle Bells." But are these scenes appropriate for every setting? A colonial farm in New England? A Spanish rancho in California? An antebellum plantation in Louisiana? An Italianate mansion in St. Louis? The Gilded Age home of a Jewish family in San Francisco? While these holidays are widely celebrated, not everyone observes these holidays in the same manner. Americans celebrate holidays for cultural, historical, religious, and social reasons, including the traditions of myriad ethnic groups that have settled in the United States over the centuries. These holidays hold a vital place in American culture, serving as moments for reflection, celebration, and bonding with others. History museums and historic sites offer ideal settings to experience and appreciate these rich traditions.

While this book focuses on Christmas, it is not a history of Christmas in America. Despite the significant social and economic impacts of Christmas both in the United States and globally, it is a topic often overlooked by scholars.[1] Even with the wealth of books and articles on national and regional Christmas celebrations, there remains ample room for further research on its history.

Likewise, interpreting Christmas is a vast subject that cannot be fully covered in a single volume. Nevertheless, we hope it can inspire ideas on how sites and museums can leverage this and other holidays to engage innovatively with their communities. For instance, El Museo del Barrio in New York City caters to the needs of its Puerto Rican and Latin American community through its exhibitions and programs. For nearly fifty years, the museum has hosted a Three Kings Day celebration. Held twelve days after Christmas on January 6, Three Kings Day, or the Feast of the Epiphany, commemorates the arrival of the three kings—Balthazar, Melchior, and Gaspar—in Bethlehem to worship the newborn Christ child. This day is a cherished holiday tradition in Spain, Puerto Rico, Mexico, and many Latin American countries.

As a profession, we value diversity and inclusion, so we have included Christmas celebrations in different regions of our country by different people over time. To expand the opportunities, we incorporate chapters on other holidays in December—Hanukkah and Kwanzaa specifically—as well as case studies of museums with events and programs that include these and other cultural traditions. We encourage all historical organizations to closely examine their communities and consider their unique ethnic and religious celebrations. While many historic sites are focused on a period of significance, it should not prevent them from broadening their interpretation to better represent the diversity of their communities. Our previous book *Reimagining Historic House Museums: New Approaches and Proven Solutions* focused on using new models for historic sites and museums to engage with their communities in a more relevant, inclusive, and creative manner.[2] Holidays offer yet another way to do this.

> Visitors trust museums to offer reliable glimpses into the past, and with history museums and historic sites forming the majority of museums in the United States, it is crucial that Christmas programs are presented accurately and meaningfully. The challenge lies in equipping staff and volunteers with the necessary knowledge and skills to successfully research, plan, and host Christmas events or activities and to expand these to include some of their communities' traditions. Christmas has continually evolved over time and will continue to do so. As public historians and museum professionals, it's our responsibility to adapt and evolve alongside it.

How to Use This Book

Board members, staff, and volunteers involved in the management, research, and interpretation at house museums, historic sites, history museums, and historical societies across the United States will find this book provides a wide range of perspectives on Christmas and offers practical guidance for planning, research, interpretation, and programming at historic sites or museums. Moreover, it will inspire fresh ideas and approaches to your programs and activities. For faculty and graduate students in public history, museum studies, and heritage studies programs, it provides a focused case study on interpretation and presentation of popular culture. The diverse disciplines and experiences of the authors provide a broad look into the public celebration of a major holiday—and they will not all agree with each other.

A key principle in this book is that there is no one-size-fits-all interpretation of Christmas for all history museums and historic sites in the United States. Every organization is unique, with its own collections, resources, audiences, community, mission, and goals. Effective interpretation involves finding the right mix for your situation.

We encourage you to start by identifying your goals for interpreting Christmas: What do you want your visitors to know, feel, or do as a result of participating in your event or program? If you are successful, what do visitors say to their friends and family? How do you want to improve or enhance the quality of life of your visitors or the community? What do you want to do better or differently? Or perhaps you have internal goals for attendance, membership, or income? Write them down and share them with others in your organization to ensure everyone is in agreement.

Next, reflect on your organization's mission, vision, values, and capacity as you start planning. Your Christmas event or program should align with your mission, advance your vision, reflect your values, and be sustainable. House museums should also consider the history of their site and the culture, faith, and traditions of former residents and neighbors. Not every family, nor every museum, should feel obligated to celebrate Christmas, even if it is popular or historically accurate.

Reinterpretation can seem daunting, but it becomes manageable by reducing the scope of work and breaking it down into phases. You do not have to accomplish everything in one year. Start small, perhaps by clarifying your goals and making small adjustments to your existing programs. Or you could focus on researching Christmas traditions in your region; conducting visitor research; reorganizing how your event is planned and implemented; or building a partnership with a part of the community whose holiday traditions you would like to include. Each year, you can build incrementally toward your goals.

Use this book to spark ideas about topics, methods, processes, and principles that will elevate your organization's interpretation of Christmas. While some ideas may be ready-to-use, others may need to be scaled, modified, adapted, combined, or rearranged to best fit your situation.[3]

Contents and Organization

Interpreting Christmas at Museums and Historic Sites is divided into four sections: Research, Different Traditions at Different Times and Places, Planning, and Public Programming.

The first section explores the process of researching Christmas in the nineteenth and twentieth centuries from different perspectives. House museums, historic sites, and historical societies, many of which are housed in historic buildings, will find this particularly useful for developing content and themes. The first chapter, "Creating a Merry Christmas" by Kenneth C. Turino, examines the history of Christmas through the elements that are most visible at house museums, such as the tree, decorations, and stockings. It is followed by a series of essays exploring research techniques and approaches. Max A. van Balgooy shares a four-part process for researching state and local history using Christmas in California as a case study in "I'm Dreaming of a Warm Christmas." In "Unwrapping the History of Christmas," Mary A. van Balgooy explores how a group of women in Boston used a national and international network of women committed to abolishing slavery and inadvertently shaped modern Christmas traditions. Her chapter emphasizes the often-overlooked roles of women and how museums and historic sites can offer a more nuanced history of Christmas. Curator Gregory R. Weidman describes research techniques and sources to re-create historically accurate period rooms for "Holidays at Hampton," an annual event at a National Historic Site in Maryland.

Christmas was celebrated differently at different times and places, and the next section provides several dramatic examples. Karen Trahan Leathem describes New Orleans's traditions at Christmas, focusing on *réveillon*, a family and religious tradition centered on food that contrasted with the boisterous public celebrations and revived in the 1980s to boost tourism. Many plantation tours focus predominantly on festive decorations of white, slaveholding families, often neglecting the stories of the enslaved. Emmanuel Dabney urges us to dispel romantic illusions about Christmas during slavery in "'Presented Me as a Christmas Gift.'" Erik Greenberg's "We're Getting a Rocket for Christmas!" examines the significance of Christmas gifts during the early Space Race and suggests ways museums might create exhibitions about historical Christmas gift-giving practices and how they connect to national issues. Andrew R. Dunn's "Christmas behind Barbed Wire" explores how Japanese American families during World War II balanced the preservation of their cultural heritage with the pressure to assimilate. Despite incarceration and adversity, maintaining traditions, especially at Christmas, offered a crucial link to their cultural identity and a display of patriotism.

We include two chapters that go beyond Christmas to consider holidays that also occur in December and how they might affect interpretation in museums and historic sites. These are not written to be comprehensive descriptions of these holidays nor intended to ignore other ethnicities, cultures, or traditions, but to highlight the value of diversity and inclusion in popular programs and events. Martha B. Katz-Hyman's "Not Everyone Celebrates Christmas" discusses the challenge faced by historic sites and museums during Christmas: attracting visitors while avoiding exclusion of non-Christian audiences. She suggests reevaluating holiday programming to reflect the diversity of the community, including the celebration of Hanukkah, a Jewish festival commemorating divine intervention and the miracle of the oil at the Temple in Jerusalem. Kelly Elaine Navies's "Kwanzaa: A Teachable Moment for All Ages" discusses Kwanzaa, a nonreligious holiday created by Dr. Maulana Karenga during the Black Power Movement and how the National Museum of African American History and Culture uses Kwanzaa's core principles to create dynamic educational programming highlighting African American culture.

The third section of the book focuses on the practical aspects of planning and programming. In "'Twas the Year before Christmas," Laurel A. Racine gives a curator's perspective, guiding readers on how to balance festive celebrations with the protection of resources through effective planning and training. Andrew W. Hahn, at Campbell House in St. Louis, discusses the importance of proper planning and collaboration with staff and volunteers for acquiring, installing, and storing Christmas decorations in "Decking the Halls." In "Decorating for Christmas," Lenora M. Henson discusses the Theodore Roosevelt Inaugural National Historic Site's annual "Victorian Christmas" event. The site collaborates with local garden clubs to decorate the historic home, requiring careful planning and cooperation to protect the historic resource while creating a festive atmosphere. In "The Ghost of Christmas That Never Was," James McKay and Patricia West discuss how strategic planning and evaluation at Lindenwald transformed their annual candlelight event into a "Winter Celebration" that resulted in the protection of resources, engaging historical presentation, and freshness for attendees. Susan Fletcher, Barbara Franco, and Melody Smith, members of the American Association of State and Local History's (AASLH) Religious History Affinity Group, address a delicate issue: religion. They have developed a set of best practices for navigating this potentially sensitive aspect of holiday programming.

Interpreting Christmas at Museums and Historic Sites concludes with an exploration of popular programs and events through examples from across the country and overseas. These chapters not only provide inspiration for various interpretive methods and formats, but also options when a historically accurate Christmas is not possible. In "Have Yourself a Merry Little Christmas Festival," Sandra Smith explores how museum and historic site festivals can build new traditions and attract audiences. By balancing consistency with novelty, these festivals can become successful annual events. In "Not a Twinkle Out of Place," Sara Bhatia discusses how living history museums, with their extensive grounds and facilities, can create multifaceted holiday experiences. The museums profiled—Old Salem Museum and Gardens, Strawbery Banke, and Conner Prairie—each offer unique Christmas celebrations, providing both financial benefits and opportunities to attract new visitors and donors. In "A Feast for the Senses," Katie Knowles discusses the evolution of Christmas programming at National Trust properties in England, Wales, and Northern Ireland. Moving toward year-round opening, these sites now offer creative, sensory experiences rooted in the history of each location, an approach that has significantly increased visitor numbers during the festive season. In "Joy to the World," Stacia Kuceyeski and Carla Mello discuss the Ohio History Connection's Cultural Traditions program, which features various holiday traditions celebrated in Ohio, including Christmas, Hanukkah, Chinese New Year, and Kwanzaa. The program enhances cultural competency and represents a diverse community, emphasizing the importance of authentic voices and cultural partnerships. In "A Christmas Card to the Community," Jeannie Giroir Luckett discusses how a holiday shopping event evolved into a weekend festival for a multigenerational audience, becoming a meaningful and enriching experience for West Baton Rouge, Louisiana. In "The Ghost of Christmas Yet to Come," Anna Altschwager argues for a shift in historical public programs to focus more on inclusivity and the future. She suggests that programs should prioritize guests and their experiences, creating spaces for their stories. Altschwager emphasizes the importance of understanding motivations, setting clear goals, and fostering earnest engagement within the team. She reminds us, "We do our work for people, so push inclusivity in new ways to make sure people can see themselves in everything we do. Let us do work for people, not about people. Let us be graceful and share space. Let us know that stories will surprise, challenge, and delight us."

To close the book, an extensive bibliography emphasizes books and articles on the history of Christmas in the United States published since 2000. Although it is not exhaustive, it provides a valuable starting point for historic sites, house museums, and historical societies looking to enhance their Christmas interpretations.

However, there's still a world of Christmas history waiting to be explored. From theater and music, to food and decorator show houses, to multi-site partnerships and Twelfth Night celebrations, there's plenty of ground to cover. Not to mention the untold Christmas stories of places like military forts or urban tenements, or regions such as the Northwest and the Rockies. So, if you are an expert in these areas, why not share your knowledge at conferences, on blogs, in webinars, or in publications like *History News*? Your insights could help paint a fuller picture of America's Christmas past.

Interpreting Christmas at Museums and Historic Sites would not have been possible without the generous contributions of all the authors as well as several people who served as reviewers, provided introductions, and shared resources including Rebecca Beit-Aharon,

Dorothy Clark, Elizabeth Eder, Bethany Hawkins, Chris Mathias, Jane Nylander, John Orna-Ornstein, Thomas Reitz, Cally Steussy, and Damion Thomas. We extend our thanks to Meg Bellevance and Sara Bhatia for their diligent work in assembling the extensive bibliography. Their efforts have provided invaluable resources for museum staff and greatly enriched this book. Additionally, we are especially grateful to Sara Bhatia for her meticulous help with the indexing, ensuring that the contents are easily accessible to our readers.

Notes

1. Leigh Eric Schmidt, *Consumer Rites: The Buying and Selling of American Holidays* (Princeton, NJ: Princeton University Press, 1995); Philip Hancock and Alf Rehn, "Organizing Christmas," *Organization* 18, no. 6 (November 2011): 737–45.
2. Kenneth C. Turino and Max A. van Balgooy, *Reimagining Historic House Museums: New Approaches and Proven Solutions* (Lanham, MD: Rowman & Littlefield, 2019).
3. There are several books to guide rethinking, including *Thinkertoys: A Handbook for Creative-Thinking Techniques, Second Edition* by Michael Michalko (Berkeley, CA: Ten Speed Press, 2006), and *Creativity in Museum Practice* by Linda Norris and Rainey Tisdale (Walnut Creek, CA: Left Coast Press, 2014).

Part I

RESEARCH

CHAPTER 1

Creating a Merry Christmas

Making a List and Checking It Twice

Kenneth C. Turino

THE HISTORY OF CHRISTMAS in America is a rich tapestry of traditions, shaped by a diverse array of religious, cultural, and historical factors that evolved over centuries. Christmas celebrations over time varied by region and cultural background. Today the celebration of Christmas is for many people the most important secular holiday of the year, while others cherish it as a religious observance. The holiday season is also big business, something not to be ignored as historic sites work to be sustainable. Many sites see some of their highest attendance at holiday events, programs, tours of their decorated sites, and in their shops. Navigating how to "do Christmas" at your historic house or historical society depends on your site, region, and your goals (making a list helps).

The Christmas we know today evolved in the nineteenth century. As this publication demonstrates, there are different traditions across the country based on patterns of settlement and reasons noted above. Historians Stephen Nissenbaum, author of *The Battle for Christmas* (1997), and Penne L. Restad, who wrote *Christmas in America: A History* (1996), established it was stories, books, and magazines that helped spread the celebration of the holiday.[1] National publications such as *Godey's Lady's Book*, also known as *Godey's Magazine and Lady's Book* (Philadelphia, 1830–1878); *Gleason's Pictorial Drawing-Room Companion*, later *Ballou's Pictorial Drawing Room Companion* (Boston, 1851–1859); and *Frank Leslie's Illustrated Newspaper*, later renamed *Leslie's Weekly* (New York, 1855–1922) were particularly influential in the nineteenth century. By the late 1800s, the prominence of national mail-order catalog shopping began to influence, and ultimately homogenize, how people across the United States celebrated Christmas especially in rural areas.[2]

Beginning with Montgomery Ward in 1872 and more importantly the Sears, Roebuck and Company catalog in 1888, mail-order catalogs began offering Christmas decorations, gifts, and food to celebrate the holidays.[3] Christmas continued (and continues) to evolve. Other periodicals would continue the tradition of championing current fads and trends associated with the holiday into the twentieth century. These included *Good Housekeeping* (1885–present); *The Ladies' Home Journal and Practical Housekeeper*, then called *Ladies' Home Journal* (1883–2016); and *The Saturday Evening Post* (1897 to the present with a hiatus 1969–1970), to name a few of the more influential. All are good sources for study. In addition to these national trendsetting publications, many regions, cities, and towns had local publications that offered helpful hints and household columns with instructions for celebrating the holiday, creating decorations, decorating the Christmas tree, and preparing a Christmas feast. J. F. Ingalls's *Ingalls Home and Art Magazine* (1887–1893) published in Lynn, Massachusetts, featured instruction on decorating for the holiday, including art and needlework lessons and other household tips. It even included three full pages for the novice hostess on how to carve a Christmas turkey![4]

Based on years of researching the Christmas holiday, this chapter should serve as a Christmas 101 lesson, a cheat sheet of sorts describing the major trappings of the holiday that most historic sites and historical societies need to understand in order to create an accurate holiday experience for whatever period or periods you are interpreting. Included here is a brief history and use of Christmas greenery including wreaths, the poinsettia, and the Christmas tree; Christmas tree decorations; wrapping paper; Christmas stockings; Christmas ephemera such as greeting cards, postcards, and gift books.

Christmas Greenery

The practice of using greenery to decorate houses at Christmas has its origins in both pagan and Christian traditions. Little documentation can be found for decorating anywhere in the eighteenth century. "The holidays in 18th-century Williamsburg were more low-key than we celebrate them today," says Joseph Beatty, Colonial Williamsburg's director of research and interpretive education. "People would go to church and have big meals and gather with families and friends. As far as decorations go, we are fairly confident that maybe a few people would put up a bit of greenery and hang mistletoe inside, as was English custom, but that was it."[5]

In the first half of the nineteenth century, you could find certain denominations decorating churches with greenery. Even in New England, where the Puritans once banned Christmas celebrations, greenery was seen as early as 1805. Dr. William Bentley of Salem, Massachusetts, wrote in his diary that year at Christmas that he attended King's Chapel in Boston and "the church was well ornamented."[6] In 1812, Bentley commented that for the first time "the display of pine boughs and the ready sale of them in the Streets, one of the relics of European superstition" did not take place, implying that the sale of greenery presumably for home use had happened in previous years. In the 1820s and 1830s, New Yorkers admired the holiday decorations in shop windows, which included evergreens.[7]

After 1850, many periodicals contained illustrations of holiday parties with doorways, mirrors, and paintings festooned with swags of holly and mistletoe hanging from the ceiling. What was used depended on what might be harvested locally, and later in the nineteenth century, available in shops. People often used natural materials to decorate their homes. Evergreen branches, such as holly, ivy, and mistletoe, were popular choices for wreaths and garlands. Other materials such as grasses or mosses were also used to add a touch of greenery to the home. A Winslow Homer (1836–1910) wood engraving published in *Harper's Weekly* in December 1858 shows people gathering evergreens in the countryside.[8] The article describes these as intended "for chapel or ball room."

Wreaths

Christmas wreaths have a history dating to ancient times. So, when did they become popular in America? It is a surprisingly difficult question to answer, as Christmas traditions are generally deep-rooted, undocumented, have been adapted and changed over time, and are riddled with regional differences and personal interpretations.

Christmas wreaths hung on doors or garlands used as decorative elements in homes during the holiday season in America is not well documented. Christmas wreaths were hung on doors or used along with garlands as decorative elements in homes during the holiday season in America by the mid-1830s. Rose Terry of Hartford, Connecticut, noted in her 1834 diary that the day before Christmas she purchased a wreath "of laurel, trailing pine, pine and evergreen."[9]

Sprigs of holly and other greenery could also decorate mantelpieces and ornament picture frames (see figure 1.3). What greenery you used depended on your location. An 1847 article, "Maize in Milk: A Christmas Story of the South" by William George Simms, describes myrtle, bamboo, holly, and cassina greens being used to ornament a Carolina plantation.[10] Greenery would become more elaborate as the century progressed. "The Christmas-Tree," another illustration by Winslow Homer in *Harper's Weekly* in December 1858, shows a holiday party for children in a home.[11] The tree stands out prominently, accompanied by a clearly visible wreath on the window. A painting, adorned at the top with holly and mistletoe, hangs on the wall and garlands drape a chandelier.

The Cottage Hearth was a popular nineteenth-century magazine (first published in 1855 in Boston, Massachusetts), known for its focus on literature, domestic advice, and women's interests. An article on Christmas decorations states, "Christmas decorations make the room seem cheery and homelike and in the work itself of preparing them, there is a positive pleasure." The article goes on to discuss the advantages of certain greens and describes making Christmas wreaths, "the best wreaths for Christmas are those made in a rope of evergreen sprigs."[12] Lizzie M. Corning recorded in her diary on Christmas Eve in 1862 and 1864 the making of wreaths for the windows of her family's house in Concord, New Hampshire.

Other magazines such as *Harper's Young People* and *The Ladies' Home Journal* gave instructions for making various wreaths. In the 1870s and 1880s, the *American Agriculturist* gave instructions for using evergreens to make a variety of decorations including a "Christmas Harp" and a "Lyre of Leaves."[13] For December 1881, the publication suggested an ornate lambrequin for windows or above a picture frame or mirror.

Over time, Christmas wreaths evolved and today come in various shapes, sizes, and styles, incorporating a wide range of materials and decorations, from traditional evergreens to artificial materials and ornaments.

Poinsettia

Poinsettias are one of the most popular potted plants in use during the holiday season in the United States and are widely used in homes, churches, and businesses as festive decorations. Originally found in red, they are available in various colors today, including white, pink, and marbled varieties.

Legend has it that Joel Roberts Poinsett, who was the U.S. ambassador to Mexico from 1825 to 1829, brought the poinsettia to America. It was said that Poinsett, an amateur botanist, sent cuttings or plants to his greenhouse at his home in South Carolina. Almost no evidence exists to support much of this story. According to *Chronica Horticulturae*, a publication of the International Society for Horticultural Science, "the facts are as follows. The plant is indeed endemic to Southern Mexico. Specimens were received in the United States in 1828 and were on display in the Philadelphia Horticultural Society's flower show in June 1829. Its arrival was associated with the name of Joel Roberts Poinsett."[14]

German botanist Karl Willdenow gave the plant the botanical name, *Euphorbia pulcherrima* in 1834. By 1836, Robert Graham in Edinburgh published his taxonomic findings and changed the name to *Poinsettia pulcherrima*. The common name comes from honoring Joel Poinsett's contributions to introducing the plant into the United States.

From its display in Philadelphia, poinsettias gained in popularity. In 1837 the *Horticultural Register and Gardner's Magazine* ran an article stating the poinsettia was "becoming much in repute."[15] Penne Restad writes that the plant "could be found in select greenhouses as early as the 1830s but in 1870 New York shops began selling them at Christmas."[16]

At this time, the plant was not the lush plant we know today but less dense and more leggy. An early use of the plant in a home is documented at Hampton, the Ridgely's family's home in Maryland, in 1848.[17] By the beginning of the twentieth century, the poinsettia was fully associated with the holiday.

Christmas Tree

The Christmas tree, thought to have originated in Germany, stands as the most prominent and frequently discussed piece of greenery in home decorations. Despite its German roots, the adoption of the Christmas tree as a popular tradition in Germany itself took some time. According to author Judith Flanders, "by the 1770s and 1780s, whether a small tree in a pot placed on a table, a fir tree tip hanging point upward, with the end sharpened and spearing an apple, or among Pietist (who advocated for the revival of the devotional ideal in the Lutheran Church) or evangelical communities, branches decorated with candles and sweets placed on wooden pyramid frames" were only then becoming an integral part of the German Christmas.[18]

While there are diverse claims about the origin of the Christmas tree in the United States, its promotion as a timeless tradition is only backed by documented evidence from the 1810s, specifically among German immigrants in Pennsylvania. The earliest known image of a Christmas tree is a sketch done by John Lewis Krimmel in the Pennsylvania countryside between 1812 and 1819.[19] Krimmel was a German painter who immigrated to Philadelphia.

The popularity of Christmas trees in America grew steadily, albeit slowly, due to a combination of factors. German immigrants introduced Christmas trees and propagated the tradition in their settlement areas. Additionally, Americans who witnessed this custom during visits to Germany and England brought the tradition back home.[20] Stephen Nissenbaum shows "it was by reading about [and seeing illustrations of] Christmas trees not witnessing them that many thousands of Americans learned about the custom."[21] Their popularization in America spread in magazines, books, and trade cards (see figure 1.1).[22] The first, likely a German story, "Christmas Eve; or The Conversion," was published in *The Athenaeum* (a Boston Unitarian magazine) in 1820.[23] It is interesting to note there is no mention of a

Figure 1.1.   This invitation (ca. 1885) to the Christmas Exhibition at Richard Schwarz's Toy Emporium in Boston shows that early Christmas trees were atop a table. Gifts were hung on the tree or, if too large, sat on the table or floor. The presents are unwrapped, a typical practice until the end of the nineteenth century. Courtesy of Historic New England.

Christmas tree in "A Visit from Saint Nicholas" (also known as "'Twas the Night before Christmas") published in 1823. In 1836, the first printed image of a tree appears as the frontispiece to *The Stranger's Gift*, published in Boston and written by German immigrant Herman Bokum.

It was at a local church fair or Sunday School that most people of the mid-nineteenth century probably encountered their first Christmas tree. Many of these fairs were sponsored by the Unitarians who promoted the Christmas tree and the idea of Christmas in their publications. Newspaper advertisements cordially invited people to view Christmas trees, often for an admission fee. One ad stated, "The Sabbath School connected with the M. E. Church Middlebury (Vermont) will celebrate Christmas Eve, December 24, with a Christmas Tree . . . A pleasant time is anticipated."[24]

British author Harriet Martineau describes a Christmas celebration in Cambridge, Massachusetts, on New Year's Eve in 1838: "The tree was the top of a young fir, planted in a tub, which was ornamented with moss."[25] Other possibilities for securing a tree included a wooden cross attached to the bottom of a tree and held down with stones; alternatively a tree could be put in a stone jug filled with sand. An article in *Godey's* from December 1860 describes "making a Christmas Tree" beginning with "[t]he square of green baize being tacked down, a large stone jar was placed in the middle of it, and in this the tree stood nobly erect. Damp sand was put around the stem till the large green tree stood firmly in its place. A flounce of green chintz round the jar concealed its stony ugliness, and over the top, round the tree, was a soft cushion of moss."[26] There appear to be no manufactured stands until the 1870s. In 1876, *Arthur's Lady's Home Magazine* suggested converting a Christmas tree stand into a flower stand.[27] Two separate patents were issued in that same year, 1876 to Philadelphians—Abram Mott and Hermann Albrecht—for Christmas tree stands.

As period illustrations show, early trees did not look like the full trees we are accustomed to today. Rather the branches were widely spaced to allow candles to be lit without starting a fire and leave ample space for ornamentation. One common safety practice described in *Godey's Lady's Book* was to have a bucket of water with a stick and a sponge in it placed near the Christmas tree. If the tree caught fire, people could quickly douse the flames with the sponge or throwing the water from the bucket.[28] This was a practical and essential safety measure to have on hand during the holiday season and one not often seen in historic house displays. Harriet Martineau writes, "The ornaments were so well hung on that no accident happened, except that one doll's petticoat caught fire. There was a sponge tied to the end of a stick to put out any supernumerary blaze, and no harm ensued."[29]

As the popularity of the holiday grew, Christmas tree sales spread first in cities and then through the countryside. Penne Restad writes that a farmer's wife from New Jersey was selling trees in 1840 and the *New York Tribune* carried advertisements for trees as early as 1843.[30] It was not until the 1870s that floor-to-ceiling trees become popular. These can be seen in many period illustrations and in photographs of the time. Christmas trees were often part of a more elaborate holiday display, including Nativity scenes and a *Putz* (a European-derived decoration that included a fenced scene with scale model buildings, figures of animals, and a crèche, placed beneath and surrounding the tree).[31]

When did Christmas trees become popular in your area? This depended on where you were. For example, the practice started slowly in South Dakota:

The mere reporting of a tree in the Dell Rapids residence of Albion Thome by the *Sioux Falls Independent* in 1874 indicates that it was probably one of the few in the area. Four years later, the *Dakota Pantagraph* mentioned a "private tree" in a Sioux Falls residence. By the late 1880s, the practice had caught on. Advertisements for Christmas trees began appearing in the newspapers, and the *Argus-Leader* reported that trees graced many homes.[32]

Many secondary sources cite the artificial Christmas tree made of green-dyed goose feathers as originating in Germany in the 1880s and 1890s. By 1911, the Sears, Roebuck and Co. catalog offered three sizes of feather trees for sale. A U.S. Patent application for an imitation Christmas tree was issued in 1882 to August Wengenroth from Troy, New York. The branches for this tree were covered with chenille, rather than feathers. We do not know if this Christmas tree ever made it into production. Real Christmas trees were still the norm in the early twentieth century. According to many written and online sources, the first bristle- or brush-style artificial tree was made by Addis Housewares Company of Great Britain in 1930. Chris Cascio, assistant curator of Patent Models at Hagley Museum and Library recently disproved this story in an article by examining patents and shows "that artificial trees were indeed made by machines developed in the 1950s by the American Brush Machinery Company to manufacture twisted wire brushes like those used to clean toilets."[33]

The design and materials used in artificial Christmas trees continued to evolve in the twentieth century. In the mid-twentieth century, aluminum Christmas trees, also known as tinsel trees, became trendy with America's interest in the Space Age and were manufactured into the 1970s.[34] These trees were made of aluminum branches and were often accompanied by mechanized color wheels featuring various tinted segments on a clear plastic wheel. When the wheel rotated, a light shone through the clear plastic, casting an array of colors throughout the tree's metallic branches to create a shimmering effect.[35]

Candles in metal holders were the most common method of lighting on nineteenth century Christmas trees. These came in a dizzying assortment of sizes and shapes; many were clipped on, some balanced with a counterweight. Not all families adorned their trees with lit candles, and with the onset of the twentieth century, the use of strings of electric lights on Christmas trees became increasingly common (see figure 1.2). According to historian Karal Ann Marling, electric lights were among the first manufactured items tailored especially to Christmas. General Electric began selling Christmas lights in 1901. Period photographs and advertisements show that these lights were not limited to the tree but could be hung from ceiling lamps and used to decorate the dinner table.[36] The bubble light, a significant innovation of the modern age, features a colored vial filled with liquid that is heated and lit by an incandescent light bulb. Carl W. Otis patented this design in 1944, and in 1946, NOMA, one of America's largest Christmas light manufacturers, introduced it to the market.[37]

Christmas Tree Decorations

Trees were decorated with toys (gifts), candy, fruit, ribbon, and garlands. The earliest ornaments were generally homemade, fashioned out of paper or fabric. Many magazines, like *Harper's Weekly* and *Godey's*, often ran articles with instructions for making these ornaments. In *Godey's* December 1874 issue, two pages were devoted to "easily made at home" decorations that included illustrations for items such as a Basket for Sweets, an Ornamental Pen-Wiper, and a Pincushion. In December 1880, *Godey's* had instructions on making paper chains. Another decoration that began to appear by midcentury was strings of popcorn (sometimes spaced with cranberries), dried apples, and cranberries.[38]

As they were not yet commonplace, these trees could dazzle people. Joseph Kidder of Manchester, New Hampshire, wrote in his journal in 1851, "Though the tree was thought scarcely more than a day yet it grew as if by magic and bore fruit in abundance in its season. There were nearly seventy different articles suspended from its evergreen branches, making a very beautiful and attractive appearance."[39]

The first glass ornaments for Christmas trees in America appear in the mid-1860s as imports from Germany. These early glass ornaments were typically handblown and hand-painted. They came in a variety of sizes and shapes and were considered delicate and valuable decorations.[40] These ornaments were sold individually; it was only later in the century that sets of ornaments were sold. Entrepreneur F. W. Woolworth, and founder of the retail

Figure 1.2.   Early in the 1900s, insurance companies, local fire companies, and the National Fire Protection Association actively encouraged the use of electric lights in place of candles on Christmas trees. This brochure (ca. 1905) by the Edison Decorative & Miniature Lamp Department in Harrison, New Jersey, promoted lighting not just for the tree; the back of the brochure shows lights hanging from the ceiling to decorate a dinner table. Courtesy of Historic New England.

store that bore his name, visited Germany and began importing glass ornaments in a variety of shapes to sell in his "Five-and-Dimes" known for their low-priced merchandise in the 1890s.

These ornaments caught on and became widely popular. Max Eckhardt, a German immigrant who had his own business selling ornaments in the 1920s acted as a representative for Woolworth's. As war in Europe began, Eckhardt worked with the Corning Glass Company of Corning, New York, to produce the first American-made glass ornaments in December 1939. These ornaments filled a void when shipping embargoes on Germany began and ornament production in Europe ceased. These ornaments sold for a few cents under the name Shiny Brite and reached their zenith of popularity in the 1950s.[41] These, like the early ornaments, were passed down by families and can be found in many museum collections.

Depending on the historical periods represented in a historic house museum or a historical society collection, Christmas tree decorations are not confined to glass ornaments. Handcrafted items have remained popular and are still in use today. While some individuals preferred a single decorating style, historical records from the nineteenth and early twentieth centuries reveal that trees were often adorned with a mix of homemade and store-bought items. Decorations could include ornaments made from materials like paper, cardboard, cotton batting, celluloid, plastic, and metal. These ornaments were either homemade, crafted by individuals or families as part of cottage industries, or produced in factories.

From the late nineteenth century through the mid-twentieth century, Christmas tree decorations made in Germany, Poland, Czechoslovakia (now the Czech Republic), Italy, Hong Kong, Japan, the United States, and many other countries, might include the following:

- gold/silver and/or painted pressed paper flat and three-dimensional ornaments known as Dresdens (ornaments made in the shape of all types of animals, household objects, or vehicles);
- paper cornucopia candy containers decorated with paper scrap and Dresden trim;
- wax ornaments frequently made in the shape of an angel;
- wire- or tinsel-wrapped glass ornaments;
- silver tinsel garland, tinsel ornaments, and single-strand tinsel;
- garlands and bells made from honeycomb tissue paper;
- pressed metal and woven wire baskets to hold candy;
- pressed or spun cotton and cotton batting ornaments often with attached paper scrap;
- glass ornaments with spun glass attachments such as wings on birds and angels;
- glass bead ornaments known as Gablonz; and
- mass-produced celluloid and plastic ornaments.

Each of these types of Christmas ornaments were popular during a range of years; remember that they often were (and are) saved and passed down through a family, so ornaments made decades ago may be appropriate in a later period. There are numerous publications written primarily for the collectors' market about ornaments and their history.[42]

Wrapping Paper

Gift-wrapping did not become the norm until the end of the nineteenth century. Up until that time, Santa carried his bag filled with unwrapped presents. Gifts were placed in stockings or hung from or placed in the Christmas tree. If they were too big to hang on the tree, they were placed beneath it. This tradition persisted well into the 1890s, as evidenced by numerous illustrations from popular periodicals, trade cards, Christmas cards, and photographs from that era.

According to historian Karal Ann Marling, wrapped packages, specifically for adults, are first mentioned in "The Christmas Tree," a story published in *Godey's* in December 1860. Marling differentiates between wrapped packages and what we know as Christmas wrapping paper for gifts. She describes wrapped packages as "simple white paper of slightly irregular shape, held together with straight pins, sealing wax, or both." In the 1870s and 1880s, packages rapidly became "prettier, tidier, and more fashionable."[43]

By 1900, the Christmas tree was surrounded with gifts wrapped in mostly white tissue. Later, by about 1910 these presents might have a wide satin ribbon, a sprig of holly, or holly seals as seen in period illustrations and descriptions in Christmas stories and accounts.

Christmas gift boxes, in all shapes and sizes, covered with paper printed with images of holly appear at the end of the 1800s and first decade of the 1900s. These boxes, commonly known as holly boxes, became widely popular. The Dennison Manufacturing Company, founded in Maine and later based in Framingham, Massachusetts, played a significant role in popularizing Christmas stickers, boxes, and wrappings for sale in the United States during the late nineteenth and early twentieth centuries. Dennison produced holly stickers to adorn white wrapping paper and then boxes and introduced ready-made Christmas gift wrap. The wrappings consisted of holly tissue paper, first advertised for sale in 1908, in the same pattern as found on the boxes. Later, Dennison began producing a wide range of decorative paper and ribbons specifically designed for Christmas. The company offered various patterns, colors, and designs, catering to different tastes and preferences. Dennison's products made it much easier for people to wrap their gifts in an attractive and festive manner, which contributed to the popularization of Christmas wrappings.[44]

The holly motif on wrapping paper would succumb to the introduction of French envelope linings printed in colorful patterns. This happened by chance in 1917–1918, when Joyce Hall ran out of Christmas wrappings in his shop in Kansas City, Missouri. Hall used what he had on hand: paper used in French envelope linings. This was a huge hit and from then on, Christmas wrapping papers would come in a wide range of colors and patterns. Hall would go on to found Hallmark Cards and produce a variety of papers, tags, seals, ribbons, and of course greeting cards.[45]

Christmas Stockings

The origin of Christmas stockings is steeped in myth, potentially stemming from a Dutch ritual where children leave their shoes out on St. Nicholas Eve, December 5. It can be confidently stated that by the 1820s, stockings were being hung either by the bedside or the fireplace, a tradition that gained popularity even before the Christmas tree did.

The first illustration of a Christmas stocking in all likelihood is in *The Children's Friend. Number III: A New-Year's Present, to the Little Ones from Five to Twelve. Part III.* This twelve-page illustrated poem published anonymously in 1821 from New York was intended as a gift book for children (more on gift books to come). The illustration depicts hanging stockings next to the children's bed with Santa Claus filling them with gifts for good boys and girls. The text included "But where I found children naughty . . . I left a long black birchen rod switch." The more well-known "An Account of a Visit from St. Nicholas," written in 1823 by New Yorker Clement C. Moore, mentions this custom twice: "the stockings were hung by the chimney with care" and "[h]e spoke not a word but went straight to his work, and filled all the stockings." Note that there is no mention of a Christmas tree in either poem. Numerous accounts in diaries and letters point to the kinds of gifts filling stockings. Rose Terry of Hartford found in her stocking in 1834 "a dollar bill, a quarter of a dollar, a book and a paper of raisins," and concluded, "I think Saint Nicholas was very generous."[46] Not all children received treats, Marion Harland received a "wicked looking rod" in her stocking."[47]

Businesses were quick to take advantage of the need for gifts to fill stockings. Advertisements abounded such as Clapp's confectionery in Lynn, Massachusetts, which obliged with

Figure 1.3.   Thomas Nast's "Christmas 1863," in *Harper's Weekly*, January 3, 1863, features holiday celebrations in three panels titled "Eve," "Furlough," and "Morning." The "Morning" panel shows children opening presents and retrieving stockings that hang above the fireplace. Courtesy of Historic New England.

"a large stock of Sugar Toys and confectioneries, shellbarks, chestnuts, fresh baked Peanuts with Pears, Apples, Dates, and Figs."[48]

Throughout the nineteenth century, illustrations are found depicting Christmas stockings (see figure 1.3). Illustrations can also be seen on trade cards and postcards of the late nineteenth century.

By the 1870s there was a competition of sorts between the Christmas stocking and Christmas tree as to which would be best for gifts. The fact is that both were used. This gives you some leeway in decorating your historic home. A *New York Times* article from December 26, 1883, argues in favor of the revival of the Christmas stocking, calling it "a thing of beauty" and the Christmas tree "a rootless and lifeless corpse" and "filling all nervous people with a dread of fire."[49] Christmas stockings were generally stockings one had on hand, or foot to be more precise, not specialty items. These ranged in size as seen in the numerous illustrations available. It was only later that businesses began selling items specifically made and marketed as Christmas stockings. Sears began selling Christmas stockings in their general catalog in 1910 and you could even buy them filled with treats.

Christmas Ephemera

Historical societies and historic houses may boast extensive collections of Christmas cards, postcards, and trade cards that illustrate various aspects of holiday celebrations. You might even find letters to Santa in your archives. For instance, Historic New England's (HNE), library and archives holds a letter from Stephen Phillips of Chestnut Street in Salem, Massachusetts, in which he asks Santa for several items, including a carriage for his pony. That carriage is now a part of HNE's Phillips House museum's collection. These letters (which can often be tied to collections items as in this case) lend themselves to seasonal displays and/or for use in public presentations.

The early history of the Christmas card is well documented. Sir Henry Cole commissioned his friend, artist John Calcott Horsley, to design the first such card and had it printed in London in 1843. That card featured an illustration of a raucous crowd bordered on either side by scenes of charity.[50] In America, the earliest known cards show a family domestic scene with a black servant carrying a tray, the center flanked by food and drink all under a draped garland. These cards are circa 1849–1853, one for individual use and the other advertised the Albany, New York, department store Pease's Great Variety Store in the Temple of Fancy.[51]

The Christmas card took several decades to become a cornerstone of holiday celebrations. Louis Prang of Boston is recognized for his role in popularizing the Christmas card in America. Starting in 1875, Prang used the chromolithography technique to create multicolor prints. These early cards (1875–1879) were small (slightly larger than business cards) and strikingly secular. They were illustrated with butterflies, robin eggs, blueberries, or apple blossoms—not with the Christmas imagery we associate with cards today. They contained a simple greeting such as "Merry Christmas and a Happy New Year." Prang created a number of distinctive lines of cards moving on to larger formats in the late 1870s, often with fringe, finding these improved sales. He held annual design competitions starting in 1880, which

Figure 1.4. The Christmas card of the Turino Family of Stoneham, Massachusetts, about 1958 was typical of the period with musical notes to popular Christmas carols and an image of the family's firstborn son seated by an imitation Christmas tree. Mario Ciroli, a professional photographer and the godfather of the young boy, took the image. Courtesy of Kenneth C. Turino.

attracted major artists.[52] These cards, as well as later examples, often reflected contemporary design and imagery.

It was not until the 1880s that what we think of as traditional Christmas imagery—holly with red berries, ivy, ribbons, Christmas bells, snow-covered churches, or a home's hearth—were common. Christmas cards then and now can reflect the period they were created. Often they harken to a romantic past, but they do give museums and historical societies the opportunity to look at the changing world of fashion, design, and lifestyles of the period.

Although Boston and Rhode Island were important centers of early American Christmas card production, many communities had their own manufactories. This may offer great opportunity for research and making connections to your community. For example, the small town of Northford (now North Branford), Connecticut, became nationally known for Christmas cards. "During 1871, the Stevens brothers of Northford experimented with highly ornamental Christmas cards, which met with great success. Their cards, glittering and trimmed with fringe, satisfied the Victorian taste for elaborate decoration. So successful were the Stevens Brothers that about twenty-five competitors opened in the Northford area."[53]

Another popular type of Christmas greeting was the postcard. These had the advantage of costing less than Christmas cards and were cheaper to mail. The late nineteenth century saw the rise of the postcard as a popular means of communication—think of them as the text message of their time—and Christmas-themed postcards began to appear at the same time. Thousands of seasonal images were printed on postcards. Ken Ames claims, "More notable for the future of Christmas cards is the fact that Christmas postcards articulate a distinctive seasonal imagery."[54]

Until 1907, messages were not permitted on the address side of a postcard, but once that restriction was lifted, the sending and collecting of postcards became a huge pastime in the United States.

Another type of postcard that began to be produced during this time is the "real photo" postcard. Images on "real photo" postcards, made by printing a negative on photographically sensitive postcard paper, were often taken using a Kodak "postcard camera" beginning in 1903. The camera used 3½ by 5½ inch film—the same size as a standard postcard. These "real photo" postcards were often produced by amateur photographers and printed in either home darkrooms or by special request of companies such as Kodak. "Real photo" postcards with Christmas imagery such as children with toys next to the family Christmas tree, or visits to see Santa Claus in a local department store were there from the beginning. The popularity of sending postcards of all types and images waned in the 1920s as the desire to send quick written messages inexpensively was overtaken with the popularity of the telephone.

Posed photo Christmas cards, mailed in an envelope, became popular after World War II (see figure 1.4). At this time, and continuing to the present day, the cards commonly featured a family portrait or the portrait of a child or children. They might also capture a house, hearth, the family pet, or advertise a business. Some were formal, some humorous. Cards were usually printed with the phrase "Merry Christmas," "Season's Greetings," or some variant of holiday greeting and contained stylized designs of holly, houses, or musical notes from a Christmas carol.[55]

By the 1960s, with improvements in printing technology, the color photo Christmas card came to dominate the market. Often these photographs were not seasonal. As stated in an Eastman Kodak advertisement from 1967, "It could be a snapshot you took over the Fourth. Or one of the whole family on vacation. Or just the baby alone. The important thing is that it'll make an unusual—and unusually appealing—Christmas card."[56] These photo Christmas cards continue to be popular to the present day.

Gift Books

An often overlooked item that many historical societies and historic sites may have in their collections are gift books. These books, given as presents, can provide insights into the evolving attitudes toward gift giving, the commercialization of Christmas, and graphic design. Purchasing a beautifully bound edition signified not only the buyer's social status but also the esteem in which they held the intended recipient. "Books were on the cutting edge of a commercial Christmas, making up more than half of the earliest items advertised as Christmas gifts," observes historian Stephen Nissenbaum.[57]

With the introduction of the *Atlantic Souvenir* in 1825, publishers introduced a new literary genre known as the gift book, which were sold across the nation. These special editions, many ornate, were beautifully designed and were intended for various age groups from *St. Nicholas's Book* for children to *Literary Gem*, *Flowers of Loveliness*, and *Affection's Gift* for adults. Books might consist entirely of poetry, while others could be a compilation of stories, poetry, and essays, and still others were humorous. These books were specifically designed to be sold and used as gifts.

Gift books were not simply used for amusement but also to instruct and promote causes. In 1853, the Rochester Ladies' Anti-Slavery Society published an abolitionist gift book, *Autographs for Freedom*, an anthology of literature designed to help "sweep away from this otherwise happy land, the great sin of SLAVERY" and includes "The Heroic Slave," the only published fiction of Frederick Douglass.

An article in the *New York Times*, gives an overview of the history of gift books, and concludes, "By the early 20th century, the ornate gift books of the Victorian era had fallen out of fashion, as the rise of wood pulp paper made books as a whole much more affordable. But books as gifts never faded in popularity, no matter the circumstances."[58]

Practical Steps for Application

When I became director (for fourteen years) of a local historical society in Lynn, Massachusetts, now the Lynn Museum and Historical Society, we, like many other museums at Christmas, decorated our building for tours, sponsored an open house with children's activities, and held parties for our volunteers and members. It was one of the busiest times of the year for us and in our gift shop. In fact, we had the best sales of the year!

The staff and I sought to present a more accurate portrayal of the holiday celebration over time in the four period rooms in our historic structure. These rooms ranged from the late eighteenth century through the 1880s. With the assistance of volunteers, we mined our library and archives: the city's newspapers (the first published in the 1820s), magazines, diaries, letters, family records/books, scrapbooks, and court records. We also examined related material in our county (Essex) as well as in local, regional, and national publications. In addition, we looked at the material culture in our collection finding specific artifacts, ephemera, and stories associated with Christmas gifts.

This led us in the 1850s parlor to use a tabletop tree to display collections of our artifacts placed on the tree or the table including toys not normally on view. These included gift books and a doll that Annie Jenkins recalled receiving in the 1860s: "She was sitting under a big tree, laden with presents—what other presents I had I do not remember—the only [one] of any importance was my beautiful dolly."[59] In the 1880s bedroom we displayed a homemade stocking filled with treats allowing us to discuss that custom.

The ephemera in our collection was also significant in helping us create small case exhibitions during the holiday season in our museum wing. These included trade and Christmas cards, postcards, menus, other ephemera, ornaments, and related material. Ken Ames calls most exhibitions of this kind particularly with the vast numbers of Christmas cards and for a variety of other reasons "modest" but shows the value in doing more expansive explorations through exhibitions.[60] Doing all this allowed us to present accurate displays in our period rooms as well as seasonal displays, even if modest, in our museum annex making good use of the photograph and ephemera collections.

The society, in an ongoing effort, collected more recent and contemporary materials representative of the diverse peoples that called Lynn home. For example, with the December holidays, we sought out photographs showing different traditions and collected material that gave voice to the different cultural traditions that made up varied December holidays such as Hanukkah, Kwanzaa, and those closely related like Three Kings Day (the Feast of the Epiphany), which takes place in January. We also gathered images such as the city's annual Santa Claus parade, the downtown decked out in holiday lights, shop window displays, family celebrations, and community events.

Our research also informed various programs, including illustrated lectures on the history of Christmas and diverse aspects of holiday celebrations. These presentations, which I continue to deliver in various forms, served as the inspiration for this book. One of the most popular holiday programs (it had a decade-long run) was a Victorian Christmas dinner. Using menus in our collection, cookbooks, and accounts of meals in diaries (special occasion meals are often noted), volunteers prepared an authentic meal with the requisite turkey and all the fixings. Held in a nineteenth-century church hall decked out in greenery, this proved immensely popular as well as profitable. Food is a big part of holiday celebrations and offers many opportunities to engage visitors. As Sandra Oliver writes, "[T]he wonderful and important thing about food is that all your visitors—no matter what age, background, or gender—understand food on some level." And it can "be used as an entry point for introducing more complicated themes and ideas."[61] Holiday food-centered programs offer a great way to celebrate different cultures.

Our research also allowed us to publish articles in our newsletters, the local newspaper, area magazines, and to discuss the holiday on local radio stations. Members were grateful to learn how the people that make up their city celebrated Christmas over time. Our archivist/librarian Diane Shephard and I authored a chapter on the evolution of the Christmas holiday in an anthology, *No Race of Imitators: Lynn and Her People*. We also published a version in the Victorian Society in America's *Nineteenth Century* magazine, a national publication.

I hope this basic primer on Christmas traditions and the example of how one historical society researched and made use of these traditions will help historic sites expand and enliven their interpretation, better engage with members and their community, and even expand their reach regionally and even nationally. As museums move to tell more complete stories and broaden our interpretation, we need to find ways to celebrate the distinct traditions of the people that make up our community. Celebrating holidays, especially Christmas, is one way to do this.

Notes

1. Stephen Nissenbaum, *The Battle for Christmas* (New York: Vintage Books, 1997), 177–95; Penne L. Restad, *Christmas in America, A History* (New York: Oxford University Press, 1995), 63–66.
2. Jeanine Head Miller, "Rural America Shops by Mail" (Dearborn, MI: The Henry Ford, April 8, 2019), https://www.thehenryford.org/explore/blog/rural-america-shops-by-mail/.
3. These and other historical mail-order catalogs are available online.
4. Laura Willis Lathrop, "Domestic Helps for the Home," *Ingalls Home and Art Magazine* (December 1890): 84.
5. Jura Koncius, "The History of Williamsburg's Beloved (But Not So Colonial) Holiday Decorations," *Washington Post*, December 20, 2017.
6. William Bentley, *The Dairy of William Bentley, Volume 3* (Gloucester, MA: Peter Smith, 1962), 206.
7. Karal Ann Marling, *Merry Christmas! Celebrating America's Greatest Holiday* (Cambridge: Harvard University Press, 2000), 86–87; Restad, *Christmas in America*, 33.
8. Winslow Homer, *Harper's Weekly, Volume II* (December 25, 1858).
9. Rose Terry Cooke Diary, Wednesday Morning, December 24, 1834, MS 77458a, volume 1, Connecticut Historical Society.
10. Restad, *Christmas in America*, 77.
11. Homer, *Harper's Weekly, Volume II*.
12. *The Cottage Hearth* 2, no. 12 (1875): 311.
13. *American Agriculturist* (December 1879): 510.
14. Judith M. Taylor, Roberto G. Lopez, Christopher J. Currey, and Jules Janick, "The Poinsettia: History and Transformation," *Chronica Horticulturae* 51, no. 3 (2011): 23–28.
15. Kenneth L. Ames, *American Christmas Cards 1900–1960* (New Haven: Yale University Press, 2011), 82.
16. Restad, *Christmas in America*, 120.
17. See chapter 4, this volume, "The Spirit of Christmas Past: A Hampton NHS Holiday Experience."
18. Judith Flanders, *Christmas: A Biography* (New York: St. Martin's Press, 2017), 88.
19. John Lewis Krimmel Sketchbooks, Joseph Downs Collection of Manuscripts and Printed Ephemera, Winterthur Museum, Garden, and Library (Delaware).
20. Restad, *Christmas in America*, 59–61.
21. Nissenbaum, *The Battle for Christmas*, 177.
22. Marling, *Merry Christmas!*, 164–70.
23. Nissenbaum, *The Battle for Christmas*, 197–98.
24. *The Middlebury Register*, December 15, 1874, p. 2.
25. Harriot Martineau, *Retrospect of Western Travel, Vol. 2* (New York: Charles Lohman, 1838), 178–79.
26. Lizzie M'Intyre, "The Christmas Tree," *Godey's Lady's Book and Magazine* 60 (December 1860): 505–6.
27. "A Wee Bit Garden," *Arthur's Lady's Home Magazine* (1876): 44.
28. Randall M. Miller, ed. *The Greenwood Encyclopedia of Daily Life in America, Vol. 2* (New York: Bloomsbury Publishing, 2008), 186.
29. Martineau, *Retrospect of Western Travel*, 178–79.

30. Restad, *Christmas in America*, 63.
31. Marling, *Merry Christmas!* 67–70.
32. Tommy R. Thompson, "Angels and Dollars: One Hundred Years of Christmas in Sioux Falls," *South Dakota History* 26, no. 4 (1997): 197.
33. Chris Cascio, "It Just Doesn't Addis Up: Trimming the Legend of the Toilet Brush Christmas Tree," *Research and Collections News* (blog), Hagley Museum, November 20, 2023, https://www.hagley.org/ru/librarynews/it-just-doesnt-addis-trimming-legend-toilet-brush-christmas-tree.
34. See chapter 7, this volume, "We're Getting a Rocket for Christmas!: Gift-Giving and the Space Race."
35. Sarah Archer, *Midcentury Christmas: Holiday Fads, Fancies, and Fun from 1945–1970* (New York: Countryman Press, 2016), 94–107.
36. Marling, *Merry Christmas!*, 54–58.
37. Archer, *Midcentury Christmas*, 84.
38. Tom Reitz, "Popcorn: Fun for Christmas," *The Glow* 43, no. 4 (August 2022): 10–16.
39. Joseph Kidder, "A Manuscript Diary from January 1st 1851 to December 31st 1851," Manuscripts Collection, The Manchester Historic Association, Manchester, New Hampshire.
40. Restad, *Christmas in America*, 112–13.
41. Archer, *Midcentury Christmas*, 84.
42. Publications that offer an overview of types of Christmas tree ornaments include Robert Brenner, *Christmas Revisited* (West Chester, PA: Schiffer Publishing Ltd., 1986); Phillip V. Snyder, *The Christmas Tree Book* (New York: Viking Press, 1976); and Margaret Whitmyer and Kenn Whitmyer, *Christmas Collectibles, Second Edition* (Paducah, KY: Collector Books, 1994).
43. For a fuller discussion of the evolution of wrapping, bundles, and packages, see Marling, *Merry Christmas!*, 7–10.
44. Marling, *Merry Christmas!*, 23–25.
45. Marling, *Merry Christmas!*, 30–32.
46. Rose Terry Cooke Diary, Friday Morning, December 26, 1834, MS 77458a, volume 1, Connecticut Historical Society.
47. Restad, *Christmas in America*, 55.
48. *Lynn Record*, December 23, 1861, p. 3.
49. *New York Times*, December 26, 1883, p. 4.
50. George Bundy, *The History of the Christmas Card* (London: Rockcliff, c.1954; Detroit: Omnigraphics, 1992), 7–11.
51. Bundy, *The History of the Christmas Card*, 80.
52. Bundy, *The History of the Christmas Card*, 74–81.
53. Karen DePauw, "Sending Season's Greetings: Christmas Cards in Connecticut," ConnecticutHistory.org, December 20, 2022, https://connecticuthistory.org/sending-seasons-greetings-christmas-cards-in-connecticut/.
54. Ames, *American Christmas Cards*, 46.
55. For more information see Ames, *American Christmas Cards*, 193–203, and Kenneth Turino, "A Lens on Christmas Cards," *Historic New England* (Fall 2018): 28–30.
56. *Life* (November 10, 1967): 66.
57. Nissenbaum, *The Battle for Christmas*, 140.
58. Jennifer Harlan, "How a Good Book Became the 'Richest' of Holiday Gifts," *New York Times Book Review*, December 2, 2022.

59. Diane Shephard and Kenneth C. Turino, "The Evolution of a Holiday: Christmas in Lynn, Massachusetts, from the Seventeenth to the Nineteenth Centuries," in *No Race of Imitators,* ed. Elizabeth Hope Cushing (Lynn, MA: The Lynn Historical Society, 1992), 37.

60. Ames, *American Christmas Cards*, 12–14.

61. Sandra Oliver, "Interpreting Food History," *History News Technical Leaflet* #97 (Nashville: American Association for State and Local History, Spring 1997).

CHAPTER 2

I'm Dreaming of a Warm Christmas

Researching California (and Other Local Places)

Max A. van Balgooy

WHEN YOU ARE part of a small- to medium-sized history organization, pursuing research and interpretation can be a daunting task if you are juggling multiple responsibilities with limited resources. As a result, we often stick to familiar routines, including our beloved Christmas traditions in house museums and historic sites. We decorate a sparkling tree in the parlor, leave out cookies for Santa, display a grand roast-beef dinner for twelve, and hang a welcoming wreath on the front door. Sure, many visitors love it and return every year, but are they missing out on more meaningful stories? Are other organizations in town doing the same programming, diluting your impact? Are visitors not returning because of a "been there/done that" experience?

At the Homestead Museum in Southern California, I faced these challenges in creating meaningful and engaging events during December. English or German Christmas traditions were not widely practiced in California before statehood in 1850—it was colonized by the Spanish—and there were few sources available in the local public library. Second, I was preparing two historic houses for Christmas in three different periods so I needed details. What kind of tree? How was it decorated in 1870 compared to 1920? Did the family even use a tree in the 1840s? Finally, I was not only responsible for research, but also planning the holiday events and activities, designing the furnishings and decorations, preparing the publicity, and training staff and volunteers to lead tours. How could I leverage my research and interpretation to improve and enhance my program planning and publicity as well?

Start by recognizing that every historic site and history museum is distinctive because it is in a different community with its own history and culture. Local events, people, and places are usually more meaningful because they are familiar to visitors. There's nothing quite as effective as saying this happened *here*. Your community may be changing, and Christmas events may offer new residents a fun way to learn about local history. By providing a focused local perspective on the holiday, uncovering stories that are new and surprising to your audiences, your museum becomes more distinctive. It also provides an interpretive advantage: Christmas did not just happen, it happened here in a unique and special way. Second, the research process can help make connections to United States history, raising the level of significance of the people and events in your community and contributing to a national identity.

I follow a research process consisting of four major steps: collecting, connecting, choosing, and contributing. I will describe the special techniques for researching the local history of Christmas emphasizing "collecting" and "connecting" and allowing other chapters in this book to address "choosing" and "contributing" in more detail. While this process looks like a linear start-to-finish path, it is iterative and loops around considerably—the important idea is that you know where you are and what you need to do next.

I will also be harnessing the power of place, focusing on California. This state's history is often overlooked in national narratives yet holds surprising stories and connections to the rest of the United States. Other chapters in this book will explore research from different perspectives, including objects, period rooms, gender, and religion.

Further, I will demonstrate how linking local, state, and national histories can enrich our understanding. State and national histories offer a broader context for local events and figures, making it easier for visitors, especially tourists, to find personal relevance. Local history, on the other hand, breathes life into abstract events, offering a tangible, emotional connection to the past, right where visitors stand.

I assume you are already familiar with this research process, but if not, I recommend starting with *Nearby History, Fourth Edition* (2019) by David Kyvig, Myron Marty, and Larry Cebula; or *A Pocket Guide to Writing in History, Tenth Edition* (2020) by Mary Lynn Rampolla. If you have mastered the fundamentals, you might be interested in more advanced techniques described in *The Craft of Research, Fourth Edition* (2016) by Wayne C. Booth et al.; *Deep Work* (2016) by Cal Newport; *Building a Second Brain* (2022) by Tiago Forte; or *How to Take Smart Notes, Second Edition* (2022) by Sönke Ahrens.

Collecting

The first step in the research process is collecting information about your topic—which assumes you have a topic and a clear sense of its boundaries. Most researchers enjoy exploring the sources and jump right in, but this leads down lots of rabbit holes and dead ends, which can be incredibly distracting and time-wasting. A little is okay, but to stay focused and productive, guide your work with a research scope.

For history organizations, the scope of a topic can be most easily defined by time and geography. You cannot tackle everything, everywhere, always. Is it December 25, December, or winter? Are you researching the nineteenth century, 1870s, or 1876? Are the physical boundaries your community, your state, or your region? You can also define your scope as a question, such as "How was Christmas celebrated in Los Angeles before 1850?" or "How should I furnish the parlor in 1876?" You can adjust your research scope as you learn more about your topic, but at the start, these parameters will help you be more effective.

Historical research is all about the sources. If they are not available or do not survive, your ability to develop an understanding of the past will be limited. The most common place to start is with the resources you already have at hand, so begin by reviewing books and articles, collections catalogs, and research files about Christmas at your museum or local library.

Recent books and articles on the history of Christmas are the most helpful to understand what others have already uncovered and identify potential sources or research methods in the bibliography and footnotes. The bibliography at the end of this book, for example, may be a gateway into your topic. Develop your own annotated bibliography listing relevant books and articles along with notes on their value and significance (or gaps and biases!) for easy reference.

Based on your research scope, your initial research will reveal what is well covered or the gaps in knowledge, sources that are basic foundations or have been overlooked. Second, you will likely be faced with two challenges: too much information or too little.

If the amount of information is overwhelming, bring the materials together to get the big picture. Begin simply with a "project box" (or drawer or folder) where all the information is collected and organized in one place. Without a project box, your research becomes scattered on a desk, in an office, in a library, in folders, on your computer, or as photos on your phone, where it can be easily misplaced or forgotten. Bringing it all together in the same place increases your ability to find information. Like the annotated bibliography, create an annotated list of sources and collections to identify strengths and weaknesses, then review your research scope to determine the next steps. What paths are still open and which have closed off? Which are most promising, and which will require more time and effort? With a list of priorities, you can develop a work plan, remembering it does not all have to be done this year and can be completed in phases.

If you encounter an extraordinary assortment of potential archival material related to Christmas, such as journals, letters, or receipts, it may be better to tackle those later when you have developed a basic understanding of your topic. That will help you more easily spot the significance of an event, person, or object that might have been ignored early in your research. Otherwise, you lose the forest for the trees. Second, navigating a collection is time consuming, especially if it has not been cataloged or lacks a finding aid. Even with those research tools in hand, start out with sources that are much easier to find and explore. Someone may have already tackled the subject—there's no need to reinvent the wheel.

If there is little to no information on Christmas, do not stop your research at this point. It may require being more imaginative about the sources available or looking at sources in a new way. Your project box may consist of empty folders, but it will provide a reminder of the information you need and provide an immediate place to collect it over time. Other chapters in this book provide strategies for researching special topics.

After creating the project box, quote, paraphrase, or summarize the ideas and information culled from sources to find patterns and make connections. This is traditionally done on three-by-five-inch cards so they can be manually sorted and organized. In the twenty-first century, digital technology can help with the management of disparate notes, documents, and quotations. Scanning the documents as PDFs and storing them together in the same folder on your computer is akin to a folder in the project box, but you now can easily carry documents with you for reference, make copies as a backup and to share with others, and with the right computer application, search for keywords or organize them chronologically or with tags. Evernote is perhaps the easiest program for managing and storing your digital documents in the cloud, but advanced researchers may benefit from the features found in DEVONthink, Obsidian, Roam Research, Scrivener, or Zotero.[1]

Next, move your research on Christmas from history books and articles to historic documents for your region. *Nearby History* points out that "documents can often be the most direct and reliable link with an earlier day, preserving eyewitness observations, capturing sights and sounds, or tabulating conditions of the time."[2] Most likely you have already explored many of these, but its chapter 4 provides a good overview of the process for finding and interpreting books, articles, theses, dissertations, newspapers, government documents, directories, and maps.

A. Newspapers

Newspapers are particularly useful for Christmas research because you can easily focus on a specific geography and time period. As you scan the newspaper, also look for advertising and social news to round out your picture of the past. Do not forget to search a week or two after the holiday as weekly newspapers continue to report on community events. Do search newspapers outside of your state or city. You may discover that a newspaper in another part of the United States reported on events in your state or city, and learn the following:

- what products are exported and enjoyed during Christmas. On December 21, 1875, the *Chicago Daily Tribune* advertised Winter Nellis pears from California for the holidays.
- how Americans might have viewed holidays on the western frontier. On January 26, 1871, the *Manitowoc [Wisconsin] Tribune*, printed Bret Harte's story about Christmas in California. On February 22, 1849, the *Glasgow [Missouri] Weekly Times*, reported that they received news "from San Francisco, Alta California dated on Christmas day" that a "desperate state of affairs exists in California. Murders, robberies, etc., were hourly occurrences. Twenty murders were perpetrated in six days."[3]

Newspapers can be difficult to find or access but your local historical society, library, or county archive usually has a collection. Fortunately, there has been a long effort at the state and national level to catalog and preserve local newspapers, making the work of research so much more convenient. For example, the University of California, Riverside manages the California Newspaper Project and the California Digital Newspaper Collection. These projects cataloged more than fifteen thousand newspapers and microfilmed or digitized

1.5 million pages from 1846 in English, Spanish, Chinese, Armenian, and thirty-six other languages. It also created a searchable online database for title, date, place, subject, and date to access the digital scans more easily. Researchers can request microfilm copies from the California State Library through inter-library loan, and major California newspapers, such as the *Los Angeles Times*, *Sacramento Bee*, and *San Francisco Chronicle*, should be available from larger public libraries. The National Endowment for the Humanities funded projects in every state from 1982 to 2011 through its United States Newspaper Program (USNP), so you should be able to find similar resources in your region.

Nationally, the Library of Congress has created an online searchable database of U.S. newspapers in its "Chronicling America" website. It provides descriptive information and select digitization of more than 20 million historic pages between 1690 and 1963 (although most are from the late nineteenth and early twentieth centuries) searchable by state, newspaper, date, word, or phrase. This rich digital resource is permanently maintained at the Library of Congress and continues to grow and add new features, such as the ability to search for photos.

The report of the "desperate state of affairs" in California at Christmas time is a good reminder to use diverse sources to confirm the facts. Sources in historical research act like the legs on a stool, and ideally, you are seated on a firm and stable chair with more than one leg. Chapter 3 in *Nearby History* provides a terrific overview of the benefits and pitfalls of sources, including the admonition that we should "ask who has created this information and why."[4] If one newspaper is the only source, it provides a view limited by the political or social perspective of the journalist or publisher. For example, the *Alta California* provided this cheerier description of Christmas in 1851 compared to the *Glasgow Weekly Times*:

In California, despite the plunging rains and the dull, leaden, dreariness of the skies, Christmas day will not be without its cheer, its pleasures and merry makings suitable to the occasion, as celebrated in modern times and enlightened countries. The little folk will have listened with gaping wonder to the story of Santa Claus, and gathered the bounteous morning gifts of the good childrens' Saint. Religious ceremonies will be performed in the churches, and the usual profusion of hearty cheer will load tables and side-boards of our citizens. After Christmas dinners, will come Christmas balls and parties, several of which are on the tapis [*sic*], and will doubtless be well attended.[5]

No mention of robberies or murders—it is a holiday not much different from events in New England. But let's go a bit deeper. Although the *Alta California* claims to describe Christmas in the entire state, this newspaper was published in San Francisco and thus represents an urban perspective from the Bay Area (and boy, those regional differences still resonate today). Second, the newspaper primarily serves readers who read English (in other words, American immigrants) and meets their needs and interests to sell subscriptions and advertising. While this newspaper article provides us a good start on our understanding of Christmas in California, it is missing the details that allow us to tell a more complete story.

To add some more "legs" to support your research, there are four sources—the U.S. Census, travel narratives, photographs, and postcards—that will help you tell a richer story about Christmas in your community. There are others, but these are often overlooked even though they are usually easily available.

B. Census

The U.S. Census is the logical source to research a place but as *Nearby History* reveals, it is "readily accessible up to a point."[6] The U.S. Census Bureau website is complex and historical data at the city and county levels is difficult to find. For most decennial censuses, the bureau publishes a "compendium," which provides statistics by state, county, and major cities, often including comparison data to the earlier records. While population numbers will not reveal anything about Christmas, you may uncover ideas through ethnicity and foreign-born status. In 1920, for example, the largest foreign population in San Francisco was Italian and in Los Angeles it was Mexican—how might they have celebrated Christmas? What traditions did they carry? How might they have been adopted by the community? El Dorado, Nevada, and Sacramento Counties had large communities of Asians in 1860—how might their presence broaden your interpretation of winter holidays? How could they help you tell a more complete story about your community?

C. Memoirs and Travel Narratives

If your state was a popular destination for explorers or visitors in the nineteenth century, memoirs and travel narratives may be a valuable resource for gathering descriptions of Christmas traditions. In California, these publications span a wide range, from captivating stories of distant lands to analyses of potential business opportunities, and from published private letters and journals to depictions of cozy homes providing respite from winter and urban pollution. Given their enduring popularity, these resources may be readily available in your local library or easily found in reprints at nearby bookstores.

Access to memoirs and travel narratives is increasingly online. In 1997, the Library of Congress completed, "California as I Saw It: First-Person Narratives of California's Early Years, 1849–1900"—its first major digitization project—making available more than 180 books consisting of 40,000 pages and 3,000 illustrations. Researchers can search for words (such as "Christmas") and narrow the results by date, location, contributor, and subject (such as "women" and "ethnic groups"). In this collection I found chaplain and journalist Walter Colton's terrific description of a community gathering at the Cathedral of San Carlos Borromeo in Monterey in Mexican California at midnight on Christmas Eve, 1846 (see figure 2.1):

> While the bonfires still blazed high, the crowd moved toward the church; the ample nave was soon filled. Before the high altar bent the Virgin Mother, in wonder and love, over her new-born babe; a company of shepherds entered in flowing robes, with high wands garnished with silken streamers, in which floated all the colors of the rainbow, and surmounted with coronals of flowers. In their wake followed a hermit, with his long white beard, tarred missal, and his sin-chastising lash. Near him figured a wild hunter, in the

skins of the forest, bearing a huge truncheon, surmounted by an iron rim, from which hung in jingling chime fragments of all sonorous metals. Then came, last of all, the Evil One, with horned frontlet, disguised hoof, and robe of crimson flame. The shepherds were led on by the angel Gabriel, in purple wings and garments of light. They approached the manger, and, kneeling, hymned their wonder and worship in a sweet chant, which was sustained by the rich tones of exulting harps.[7]

So far, I have never encountered a description of *Los Pastores* (The Shepherd's Play) in a nineteenth-century newspaper, demonstrating the value of diversifying sources. Although "California as I Saw It" focuses on California, travelers passed through other regions (such as Nevada, Arizona, and Oregon), so this database may provide descriptions of your state or city. Furthermore, the Library of Congress now has hundreds of digital collections available online, including "American Notes: Travels in America, 1750–1920" and "Pioneering the Upper Midwest," which may be more useful for other regions. Do read the essays that accompany each collection—they provide insights into their strengths and weaknesses and point to other resources.

D. Photographs

Photographs provide a level of documentation that is particularly helpful for historic sites and house museums because they allow you to identify objects and study interiors in incredible detail. For example, after you have seen a dozen photos of Christmas trees from a hundred years ago, you will notice clear patterns in the branching of the tree and amount and type of decoration. Today's trees are much denser and often ornamented like a cake with a thick layer of frosting. They also can confirm when certain traditions change in your region, such as when trees increase in size or where stockings are placed.

While photographs are often assumed to accurately reflect reality, they can also be misleading. Magazines specializing in architecture and interior design, such as *Sunset, House and Garden, Arts and Decoration,* and *Architectural Digest,* often provide prescriptive advice and images. These suggest fashionable trends or potential home improvements, rather than portraying the actual living conditions of the average American. Moreover, photographers frequently enhance images, adjusting furniture and decor. Have you ever seen a historic photograph of used dishes left on a dining table or an unmade bed?

For this reason, *Nearby History* not only provides a useful introduction to the process of researching photographs and other visual documents but also their interpretation so you can get the most value out of them (and avoid misreading them). If you cannot find an image of Christmas for your historic site, adopt Waldo Tobler's First Law of Geography: "everything is related to everything else, but near things are more related than distant things." In other words, look for photographs from your neighborhood, then expand your search to include demographically similar places, such as households with similar incomes, ethnicities, or ages. The Christmas tree of silent film star Harold Lloyd in his forty-four-room Beverly Hills mansion would be fun to re-create, but for most house museums, it is quite unrelated to the typical decorations of homes in the 1930s (see figure 2.2).

Photographs are increasingly being cataloged and digitized, making research much easier. Interior photographs, especially before 1900, are rare but you may find them in your collection or in a nearby historical society, archive, or library. In the early twentieth century, outdoor Christmas celebrations were often photographed, especially if they were lit electrically. Search at the state and national levels as well because images of Christmas are popular and often preserved. Most research institutions hold photographs in various collections, often according to format, function, or source, so ask about scrapbooks, photo albums, postcards, greeting cards, and newspaper "morgues." Social media sites that emphasize imagery such as Pinterest and Flickr may reveal unexplored collections, especially private ones.

Figure 2.1.   For Christmas mass in the 1840s, the community gathered to watch the Shepherd's Play in the Cathedral of San Carlos Borromeo, Monterey, California. Photo by Carol M. Highsmith, LC-DIG-highsm-21091, courtesy of the Jon B. Lovelace Collection of California Photographs, Prints and Photographs Division, Library of Congress.

Figure 2.2.   An extravagant Christmas tree in the home of silent film star Harold Lloyd in Beverly Hills, California, in the 1930s. Photo by Sumner Spalding, courtesy of the Historic American Buildings Survey CA-2192, Library of Congress.

E. Postcards

Postcards fall within the larger category of visual sources but deserve special mention for Christmas research because they contain rich sources about communities and the holidays. As a hybrid of a photograph and a letter, postcards can offer a package of information: image, caption, message, location, date, and symbols. Rather than assume these mass-produced, ephemeral documents offer little value, look more closely and you will find new insights about Christmas in your town or state.

Starting in 1861, the federal government increasingly allowed the use of cards in the mail with a message or image on the front and the address on the back. It allowed Americans to easily, cheaply, and quickly send a message to friends and family, including holiday greetings. In 1907, the postmaster general allowed messages on the left half of the card's back, which introduced "divided back" and "real photo" postcards. While photo enthusiasts could produce their own photo postcards using a Kodak "postcard camera," many local photo studios would produce small quantities of postcards as a side business. Some grew into major businesses, such as the Frasher Studio in Pomona, California, who had sold over 3 million "Frasher Fotos" postcards nationwide in the first half of the twentieth century.

As a result of their popularity, postcards can be found in the collections of most museums, libraries, and archives but are rarely studied or even cataloged. They are often consolidated into a single postcard collection organized by location or subject, but they can also

"Christmas Day in the Open"—The "Kiddies" of Pomona don't have their Christmas trees indoors, with the furnace fighting the frost and cold. Instead, its ginghams and sunshine!

Figure 2.3. Some Christmas cards from California emphasized the absence of snow and cold, such as this 1912 postcard featuring a decorated tree outside with students in "ginghams and sunshine." Collection of Max A. van Balgooy.

be found in scrapbooks, combined with the photograph collection, or held within a larger family or corporate collection, which can make research more challenging.

Fortunately, there are efforts to make postcards more accessible to researchers. The Pomona Public Library, for example, received the Frasher Studio collection in the 1960s, but it was only with grant funding in 2002 that they were able to organize, catalog, scan, and make available online five thousand representative images of the Southwest from the 1910s to 1950s in its Frasher Foto Postcard Collection. Featured are "Main Street" views of small towns, imposing landscapes, and county fairs—and a dozen images of Christmas in California and Arizona.

Do look beyond research collections to find postcards in antiques shops, social media, and online auction sites. The website eBay is surprisingly effective because individual items are categorized and described so buyers can search by category and keyword. As a result, I found this terrific postcard of a kindergarten class in Pomona at Christmas (see figure 2.3).

The caption, symbology, and message is as important as the image. Gather a dozen post-cards from your community or state for a specific era and you'll notice patterns. For example, in Christmas postcards from California before 1925, poinsettias, roses, oranges, palm trees, and Spanish missions are frequently incorporated—rarely is there snow, holly leaves, pine branches, or Santa Claus.

F. Other Sources

Newspapers, census records, memoirs, travel narratives, photographs, and postcards are among the most useful sources for researching Christmas in California. Other useful sources include diaries, journals, oral histories, artifacts, buildings, and landscapes which are described in detail in *Nearby History* and in the bibliography at the end of this book. Often there is too much reliance on Google, Wikipedia, or a popular book of Christmas, leading to the assumption that if your state or city isn't mentioned, there is no information. Instead, look at the notes in each of the chapters of this book and you'll discover an incredible diversity of sources that the authors collected to tell their stories. Be curious and creative in your research.

Connecting

Individual people, events, places, and ideas alone don't weave a narrative unless they're connected and arranged in a meaningful way. Establishing these links is one of the most creative and rewarding aspects of research because they can show how a local community fits into state or national history, highlight the importance of specific events or individuals, and draw the past nearer to the present. It is exploration that uncovers unexpected connections between events, individuals, locations, and concepts, offering fresh insights into the past and sparking those "a-ha" moments that make history both thrilling and engaging.

If you have pages of notes, stacks of note cards, and a box full of articles about Christmas trees, plum pudding, church festivals, greeting cards, glass ornaments, and gifts, making those connections can be overwhelming. As science historian James Burke noted, "[W]e live surrounded by end products of thousands of connections. And in every moment that goes by, more connections are made."[8] Where do you start? How do you manage this scattered pile of information?

In many house museums and historic sites, the interpretation often remains at a basic level: defining terms, identifying objects, naming people, and describing events. However, a more engaging approach would move to the next level by making connections to organize facts, compare different viewpoints, debate choices, evaluate decisions, predict consequences, imagine solutions, and tell stories.[9]

Think of it like completing a thousand-piece jigsaw puzzle. Usually, you'd sort pieces by color and shape to create the picture on the box. But in historical research, there's no preset image to guide you. The process can be filled with dead ends and may feel pointless at times—until you start making connections and the seemingly random pieces begin to form a coherent picture.

Tackle this phase of research in two steps: grouping and connecting. Veteran writer Lee Child calls it the Rising Island method:

> Picture a mountain range stretching for many miles, but all of it underwater. Now the mountains start to rise. A few peaks start breaking the surface, appearing as isolated islands. Time passes and more islands break the surface, and they start to link together until finally the entire mountain range is visible. The mountain range is my novel.[10]

To create small islands of connected facts, fortunately there are only five ways to organize information: by location, in alphabetical order, by time, by category, and by hierarchy, often remembered by the acronym LATCH.[11] For historical research, the most useful are location, category, and time:

- *Location.* Organizing information geographically. This is commonly used in maps or floor plans. For example, what happened in the parlor or kitchen; in the house or in town; or in the Italian or Jewish community? This can reveal how activities may be segregated by sex, age, religion, ethnicity, or social status as well as where those boundaries are blurred. For house museums, it can help prioritize topics for interpretation in each space to reduce repetition and avoid mere room descriptions.
- *Category.* Organizing information based on types, groups, or classifications. This method groups similar items or concepts together under a shared characteristic or theme. For example, for Christmas, activities might be categorized based on their purpose (decoration, meals, gifts) or appearance (green, red, old, new).
- *Time.* Organizing information chronologically. This method is often used in time-lines, schedules, or story. The typical mega-timeline of major events showing several decades provides a useful big-picture overview, but a micro-timeline of a specific event or activity can provide insights as well. For example, outlining the steps for obtaining and decorating a Christmas tree can reveal when they occurred and who was involved.

To build bridges to connect these islands, look in four directions: Where did this idea come from? Where does it lead? What ideas/topics are similar? What ideas/topics are opposite?[12] If you're interpreting a historic house, consider the origins of the family's traditions. How did they evolve over time? Were elements of their celebrations (like gift-giving or special meals) also present at other family events? Were there similar traditions within the community? Who in the community didn't celebrate Christmas, or chose not to have a tree or exchange gifts? The answers can provide a richer understanding of the historical context and cultural diversity of the time rather than just a dry recitation of facts, names, and dates.

Linking these "islands" chronologically can reveal a fascinating chain of events, one leading intriguingly to the next. If you add location to the mix, comparing different places at the same time, you could unearth parallel narratives. For instance, consider the deaths of Thomas Jefferson in Virginia and John Adams in Massachusetts, which occurred on the same day—July 4, 1826—the fiftieth anniversary of the adoption of the Declaration of Independence. Can you see the web of connections forming in multiple directions? Can you imagine the intriguing narrative twist this could introduce in a tour?

As an example of the power of connections, consider this example. From a memoir by William Henry Brewer, a scientist working in California during the 1860s, I collected this passage:

The laurel, the madroño, the manzanita, the toyon, are rich in their dense green foliage; roses bloom abundantly in the gardens, the yards are gaudy with geraniums, callas, asters, violets, and other flowers; and there is no snow visible, even on the distant mountains.

Christmas here, to me represents a *date*, a *festival*, but not a season. It is not the Christmas of my childhood, not the Christmas of Santa Claus with "his tiny reindeer," the Christmas around which clings some of the richest poetry and prose of the English language. I cannot divest my mind and memory of the association of this season with snowy landscapes, and tinkling sleigh bells, and leafless forests, and more than all, the bright and cheerful winter fireside, the warmth within contrasting with the cold without.[13]

This note is packed with concepts and connections. In answering "What ideas/topics are similar?," I noticed links to my other notes. Many nineteenth-century visitors were captivated by the abundance of flowers, particularly roses, during Christmas. Furthermore, roses are featured on Christmas cards published in California (see figure 2.4). Thus, I'm bringing these observations together in a "roses" category.

Picking up another question from the compass: Where did roses come from? Its history stretches back thousands of years leading to dozens of potential paths to China, Persia, India, Greece, Anatolia, Egypt, and Rome, resulting in several irrelevant meanderings. Instead, I'll focus on the most relevant time period for interpretation: the nineteenth and twentieth centuries when modern Christmas traditions developed.

That pointed me to the 1880s, when roses had become so popular in California that there were several rose festivals, nurseries offered hundreds of varieties, the *California Florist*

Figure 2.4. The exotic nature of California in winter inspired Christmas cards such as this example from 1919 featuring palm trees, roses, and Old Baldy (Mt. San Antonio). On the back, the sender included a message, "I can see these mountains from our windows, they are covered with snow now while it is lovely and warm here—and the roses are blooming." Collection of Max A. van Balgooy.

and Gardener had begun publication, and San Francisco became the headquarters of the new State Floral Society.[14]

Finally, where does it lead? Roses disappeared from Christmas cards by the mid-twentieth century, but intriguing links point to Pasadena's renowned Rose Parade on New Year's Day. Established by the Valley Hunt Club in 1890, the parade requires that every float be entirely adorned with flowers (such as roses) or other natural materials (such as leaves, seeds, or bark). Although the connection is uncertain, it provides a path for future research and interpretation. After all, this world-famous parade offers an instant link to the present.

Choosing

Let's be candid. After the extensive research you have conducted, the temptation to include everything is high. You grasp the unfolding events, the involved parties, and the locations better than anyone else. However, to craft an effective argument, avoid distractions, and explain history accurately, you must prioritize and make choices. This may mean omitting much of your research to focus on creating a distinct experience, not impressing with a plethora of facts.[15] This is the process of choosing or interpretation—assembling facts to provide the most cogent explanation.

Historians and scientists debate among themselves routinely to determine the best explanation and understanding, and so should you. Interpretation rests on a foundation of facts, and those facts should be available for scrutiny. While interpretation can be based on conjecture and opinion, it is not a solid foundation and can lead to false or misleading conclusions. Even if everything in your interpretation is factual, it may not be helpful. Consider your facts like a piano with eighty-eight keys—you do not play all of them to create a melody.

Music is an apt metaphor for the process of choosing. Topics or subjects are like individual notes. By themselves, they go nowhere. But combine these nouns with well-chosen verbs and you can create a sentence with a point of view or a memorable melody. For example, the topics of Christmas, immigrants, or women could result in themes such as these:

- Christmas was not widely celebrated in the United States until the 1800s. Influenced by immigrants, traditions evolved, becoming a federal holiday in 1870.
- In the mid-nineteenth century, New England women who sought the abolition of slavery were instrumental in shaping the Christmas traditions we know and celebrate today.
- The modern restaurant-centered *réveillon* in New Orleans is part of a continuum of French holiday practices. While today's special meals—marketed to tourists and locals alike—are divorced from the private family customs that once nurtured the *réveillon*, this culinary tourism endeavor resuscitated local historical knowledge of the term.
- The continued practice of Japanese traditions during World War II, especially at Christmas, allowed Japanese Americans to maintain a small but important piece of their identity and cultural legacy while interred in government camps.

Much like unforgettable melodies in music, certain themes captivate us, offering vivid insights into historical eras, individuals, or events. They also have a point of view, are debatable, and strike chords with bigger universal ideas. Writers routinely climb the "ladder of abstraction" linking concrete events (for example, an 1848 Christmas celebration at Lindenwald) to abstract ideas (such as family bonds, cultural identity, or enslavement). Exceptional interpretation is not just a well-told story; it is a purposeful narrative that positively transforms hearts and minds.[16]

Contributing

If you have developed a terrific story about Christmas about your community or historic site, it is time to share it. Start with a traditional research report bolstered by footnotes and a bibliography. Aim for a succinct 750 to 1,250 words or three to five pages double-spaced. It is a length that provides sufficient information to understand the theme and identify key sources, plus it is more likely to be read by others and can be easily converted for other purposes, such as a newsletter, volunteer training handout, social media post, news release, or exhibition script.

Do not let perfection hold you back. Everything you write is a draft—it will never be definitive, comprehensive, or complete (including every chapter in this book!). Consider it as your contribution to the larger work of interpreting the holidays, one more step forward in a longer journey. Scholars on President Lincoln know this all too well because there seems to be a new book published about him every week, and yet each brings a different perspective and insight. If we all waited until things were perfect, we would never get anything done.

Armed with my research on Christmas in California, the Homestead Museum revised its guided tours during December to include the history of Christmas from 1840 to 1930; produced three articles for our newsletter; and created "A Southern California Christmas," a festival that included tours, craft demonstrations, performances of *Los Pastores*, holiday foods, music, local artists, and Santa Claus. For more than twenty years, it was hailed as one of the best holiday events for the region.

If you are challenged by holiday events that have lost their luster, dig into the history of your community and historic site. You will discover that Christmas did not just happen every year but continually evolved and always adapted in a unique and special way.

Notes

1. If you are unfamiliar with these applications, demonstrations and reviews can be found on YouTube.
2. David Kyvig, Myron Marty, and Larry Cebula, *Nearby History: Exploring the Past around You, Fourth Edition* (Lanham, MD: AltaMira Press, 2019), 49.
3. "Later from California," *Glasgow [Missouri] Weekly Times*, February 22, 1849, p. 2.
4. Kyvig, Marty, and Cebula, *Nearby History*, 40.

5. "Christmas Day," *Daily Alta California* 2, no. 378 (December 25, 1851), 2.
6. Kyvig, Marty, and Cebula, *Nearby History*, 85.
7. Walter Colton, *Three Years in California* (1850; reprint New York: Arno Press, 1976): 129–30. The play has its origins in medieval Europe and is part of a series that includes *Las Posadas* and *Los Tres Reyes*. It is described in "The Shepherds' Play of the Prodigal Son" by George Baker in *Folklore Studies* (Berkeley: University of California Press, 1953) and a script for a version performed in California in the 1810s is available in *Los Pastores: An Old California Christmas Play Reproduced from the Original Manuscript in the Bancroft Library* by Maria López de Lowther and Don Louis Perceval (Hollywood, CA: Homer Boelter Lithography, 1940?). An early twentieth-century unpublished typescript, "Miracle Plays in Old California" by Mary M. Bowman can be found in the Vertical Files of the Los Angeles Public Library. In the twentieth century, Los Pastores was largely forgotten and replaced by Las Posadas and Los Tres Reyes.
8. James Burke, *Connections* (New York: Simon and Schuster Paperbacks, 2007), Kindle location 185.
9. In *Creating Significant Learning Experiences an Integrated Approach to Designing College Courses* (San Francisco: Jossey-Bass, 2013), L. Dee Fink describes the dimensions of learning: knowledge, application, integration, human dimension, caring, learning how to learn.
10. Lee Child and Laurie R. King, eds., *How to Write a Mystery* (New York: Scribner, 2021), Kindle location 2374.
11. Richard Saul Wurman, *Information Anxiety 2* (Indianapolis: Que, 2001), 40–45.
12. This is based on Vicky Zhao's "Compass Points" model. She describes this analysis framework in "How to Take Smart Notes" (February 24, 2022) on YouTube.
13. William Henry Brewer, *Up and Down California in 1860–1864* (New Haven: Yale University Press, 1930), 360.
14. I. C. Winton, "Roses in California," *Overland Monthly and Out West Magazine* 8, no. 32 (August 1885): 191; W. A. T. Stratton, *California Roses* (San Francisco: E. C. Hughes, 1889), [3].
15. Other chapters in this book provide examples of excellent holiday programs.
16. The process of developing meaningful interpretation and achieving impact are best explained in *Interpretation: Making a Difference on Purpose* by Sam Ham and *Intentional Practice for Museums* by Randi Korn.

Resources

Euchner, Charles. *Writing about Place: The Complete Guide for Architects and Planners*. Milwaukee, WI: New American Press, 2018.

Ham, Sam. *Interpretation: Making a Difference on Purpose*. Golden, CO: Fulcrum, 2013.

Korn, Randi. *Intentional Practice for Museums*. Lanham, MD: Rowman & Littlefield, 2019.

Kyvig, David, Myron Marty, and Larry Cebula. *Nearby History: Exploring the Past around You, Fourth Edition*. Lanham, MD: AltaMira Press, 2019.

Rampolla, Mary Lynn. *A Pocket Guide to Writing in History, Tenth Edition*. New York: Bedford/St. Martin's, 2021.

CHAPTER 3

Unwrapping the History of Christmas

The Women Who Redefined a Holiday

Mary A. van Balgooy

IN 1834, a daring group of Bostonians shook things up with a controversial Christmas season fundraiser. They were committed to the abolition of slavery and took significant risks to support their cause. The success of the event spurred them on, and they continued their efforts in the ensuing decades. Along the way, they transformed Christmas from a boisterous adult celebration into a family-oriented holiday filled with gifts, decorations, and Christmas trees. What might surprise you is that this audacious group was made up entirely of women.

In the traditional narrative of Christmas, women's roles are often overlooked or downplayed. However, these women were instrumental in shaping the Christmas traditions we know and celebrate today. Delving into the history of Christmas unravels a thrilling opportunity to uncover hidden stories about women's roles during the holidays at your historic site or house museum, revealing a past that is been waiting to be discovered.

So, how did it all begin?

In the Early American Republic (c. 1780–1830) in certain regions, Christmas was a raucous holiday for adults, filled with role reversals, drunkenness, and street revelry. Attempts by community leaders to reform Christmas were unsuccessful until women stepped in.[1]

These women, defying societal norms between public and private spheres, began forming associations outside their church groups with broader benevolent aims such as abolition, peace, temperance, and moral reform. People accepted most of these new voluntary associations except for one—abolition. Here women transgressed gender and racial norms by speaking in public to mixed audiences (men and women; black and white), presenting petitions to politicians, organizing conventions, and joining antislavery societies.[2] And one of the most influential abolitionist societies in the Northeast was the New England Anti-Slavery Society (NEASS).

In 1831, William Lloyd Garrison organized the NEASS with *The Liberator* as its official publication. Women were allowed to become members, but they could not hold leadership positions or chair various committees, so they formed their own female association. Boston women—white and black—created the Boston Female Anti-Slavery Society (BFASS) to support Garrison's Society in October 1833.[3]

To support and encourage women to join, BFASS held sewing circles. It was not a new idea for rural and urban women to hold sewing circles in each other's homes. It gave them an opportunity to come together to socialize and make articles such as pieced quilts, crocheted blankets, and embroidered aprons; pin cushions and needle books; and costumes for children's dolls to sell at charity fairs.[4] But the idea of holding a fundraising bazaar for abolition during the Christmas season or any part of the year was unheard of.

First, antislavery was unpopular not only in the South but also the North. The North depended on the South for commerce and trade. Many white men in the North also worried freed blacks would take away jobs from them. Consequently, mobs routinely broke up abolitionist meetings, destroyed property, threatened its leaders, and harassed men and women advocating for an end to slavery.[5]

The fear of vandalism was so strong the organizers could not find a public space to hold the fair. Town leaders barred the BFASS women from renting any of the city's many halls. As a result, they were forced to hold the bazaar at the NEASS "Office over Baker & Alexander's Book Auction, Washington-St., just below the Post Office" that was next to the Old State House.[6]

Second, women planned to sell homemade articles and food, and donated goods from merchants in a public space—a man's space. They risked being ostracized by their community.

Third, BFASS faced the prospect their fair would be regarded as frivolous. Even Garrison's *The Liberator* publicly voiced objection to the women's charitable fairs in 1831: "We entertain very decided objections to these trumpery exhibitions. Their origin, we fear, may be oftener found in love of display, than in a philanthropic spirit; and their tendency is unquestionably pernicious."[7]

The fair organizers were undeterred. Louisa Loring and Lydia Maria Child, an influential author of women's and children's books as well as pamphlets on antislavery, were ready to risk their reputations.[8] They invited women to form sewing circles to make articles with antislavery messages on them to donate for sale (see figure 3.1); asked members of Boston's abolitionist community for goods and services; and solicited for volunteers to decorate the office with greenery for the fair in order to make it attractive to buyers. In 1834, the office decorations included an evergreen shrub.[9] According to one historian, "if any of the articles for sale at the 1834 fair were actually attached to this evergreen shrub (or placed around it) then *it* would have the honor of being the first public Christmas tree displayed in the United

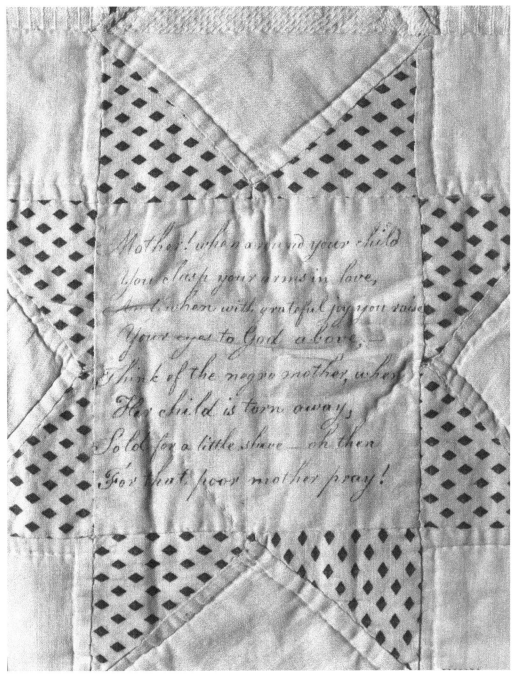

Figure 3.1.   Detail of a hand-inked antislavery poem in the center of a cradle quilt made by Lydia Maria Child. Courtesy of Historic New England.

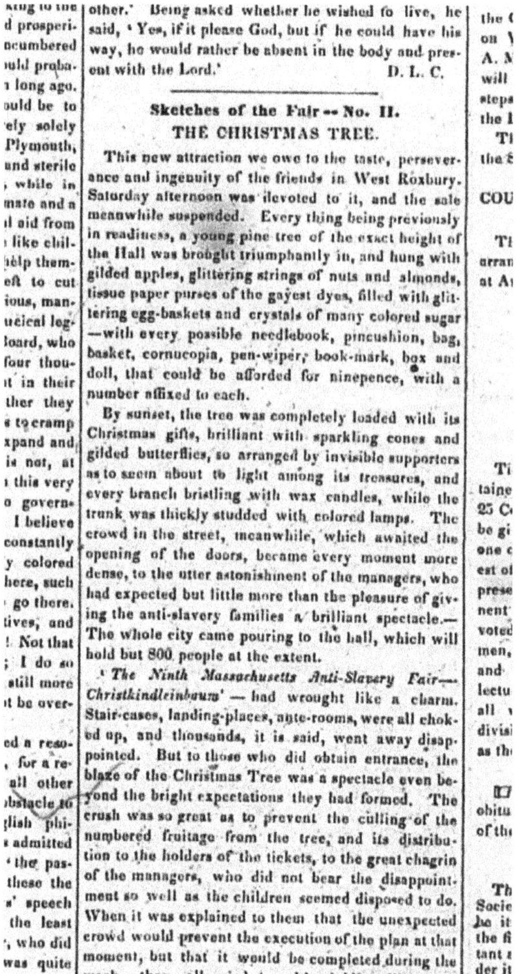

other.' Being asked whether he wished to live, he said, 'Yes, if it please God, but if he could have his way, he would rather be absent in the body and present with the Lord.' D. L. C.

Sketches of the Fair -- No. II.

THE CHRISTMAS TREE.

This new attraction we owe to the taste, perseverance and ingenuity of the friends in West Roxbury. Saturday afternoon was devoted to it, and the sale meanwhile suspended. Every thing being previously in readiness, a young pine tree of the exact height of the Hall was brought triumphantly in, and hung with gilded apples, glittering strings of nuts and almonds, tissue paper purses of the gayest dyes, filled with glittering egg-baskets and crystals of many colored sugar —with every possible needlebook, pincushion, bag, basket, cornucopia, pen-wiper, book-mark, box and doll, that could be afforded for ninepence, with a number affixed to each.

By sunset, the tree was completely loaded with its Christmas gifts, brilliant with sparkling cones and gilded butterflies, so arranged by invisible supporters as to seem about to light among its treasures, and every branch bristling with wax candles, while the trunk was thickly studded with colored lamps. The crowd in the street, meanwhile, which awaited the opening of the doors, became every moment more dense, to the utter astonishment of the managers, who had expected but little more than the pleasure of giving the anti-slavery families a brilliant spectacle.—The whole city came pouring to the hall, which will hold but 800 people at the extent.

'*The Ninth Massachusetts Anti-Slavery Fair—Christkindleinbaum*' — had wrought like a charm. Stair-cases, landing-places, ante-rooms, were all choked up, and thousands, it is said, went away disappointed. But to those who did obtain entrance, the blaze of the Christmas Tree was a spectacle even beyond the bright expectations they had formed. The crush was so great as to prevent the culling of the numbered fruitage from the tree, and its distribution to the holders of the tickets, to the great chagrin of the managers, who did not bear the disappointment so well as the children seemed disposed to do. When it was explained to them that the unexpected crowd would prevent the execution of the plan at that moment, but that it would be completed during the week, they all cried 'good,' yielding like good children to the necessity which could not be overcome, and came on Monday morning in successive crowds to receive their prizes.

Keep next Christmas season in mind, young friends; for we will, for the sake of the anti-slavery cause, be completely prepared for a crowd then! It is very fatiguing to make such preparations, but they keep the sufferings and the wrongs of the little slave-children before the public eye—they help to arouse the public conscience: and therefore the Christmas tree, next year, shall flame like a new constellation in the moral firmament.—M. W. C.

Correction.

Mr. Editor—There are several typographical er-

Figure 3.2. The Christmas tree at the 1842 fair as described in *The Liberator*, January 27, 1843.

States."[10] Advertisements for the fair described the sale as modest, featuring "generally useful" articles exhibited "without frivolity" to demonstrate the respectability of the fundraiser and the seriousness of the cause.[11]

Despite the unpopularity of abolition, the threat of vandalism, and objections from the community, the fair was a resounding success, raising over $300—over $10,000 in today's currency. Reporting on its success, *The Liberator* noted, "[T]he colored ladies of Salem particularly deserve thanks for the interest they took in the Fair and the articles they sent."[12] Apparently, Garrison had changed his mind about women's fairs.

Emboldened by their success, the society decided to continue to hold a fundraising fair every year with Maria Weston Chapman at the helm. Chapman, who married abolitionist Henry Grafton Chapman in 1830, became devoted to the cause. An upper-class woman of well-connected family and friends, she joined BFASS at its formation. The society could not have had a better fair manager—she was a genius at promotion and publicity.[13]

Chapman managed the fair from 1835 through 1858.[14] Under her direction the fair grew more elaborate each year. She solicited contributions from rural and urban women across Massachusetts and other states creating a network of women to work for the cause. Items "ranged from 'useful' and inexpensive objects crafted by 'ladies' sewing circles to 'fancy' items like crystal and china that were imported from around the world."[15] In 1839, she published, *The Liberty Bell*, an ornate giftbook for women containing poems, essays, and other pieces about antislavery she prepared and issued for the bazaar each year.[16]

By the 1840s, the fundraising fair flourished with abolitionists as well as non-abolitionists coming to the bazaar to shop for gifts and enjoy the decorations. And in December 1842 the women outdid themselves.

In that year, along with the usual decorative foliage and evergreens, volunteers installed a Christmas tree as tall as the hall itself with everything imaginable—"gilded apples, glittering strings of nuts and almonds, tissue paper purses of the gayest dyes, filled with glittering egg-baskets and crystals of many colored sugar." The tree was not only laden with Christmas presents but also "waxed candles" and "colored lamps at the trunk."[17] The community responded en masse. According to *The Liberator*, the Amory Hall in Boston could hold eight hundred people, and they had to turn "thousands" away. Those with tickets for that first day had to come back to receive "prizes" (gifts) for their children after the BFASS rearranged the hall in the following days (see figure 3.2).[18] The idea of Christmas with a tree and presents for children was now a tradition.

However, the Bostonian women were not the only ones using Christmas in the name of abolition. The idea spread across the Northeast, Mid-Atlantic, and the West.

In 1835, the Female Anti-Slavery Society in Philadelphia founded by leaders Sarah L. Forten, a black woman, and Quaker Lucretia Mott, debated whether to hold a fair because members questioned its propriety just like Garrison had done in 1831.[19] After a debate, they decided to hold a bazaar. The next year, Forten wrote a letter to a friend about how she spent the last four months preparing for the antislavery fair:

We hired the Fire Mens Hall in North St—below Arch—and decorated it with evergreens—and flowers—and had it brilliantly lighted. There was six tables—including a refreshment Table—on which most of the eatables were presented—three large Pound Cakes—Oranges—and Grapes.[20]

Forten wrote that the proceeds amounted to more than $300. By the mid-1840s, the Philadelphia society made the fair its focus and they coordinated with other antislavery women throughout southwestern Pennsylvania in rural areas and New Jersey to establish other fairs.[21]

By 1858, Chapman made a significant decision to replace the annual Christmas fair with direct cash subscriptions because few women contributed their homemade items to the fair and the best-selling gifts were manufactured or imports. She felt the fairs had become more about shopping for the season than advancing the cause of abolition. The subscriptions it turned out were just as successful as the fairs.[22]

Nevertheless, as antislavery fairs wound down, Chapman and her fellow female abolitionists played a pivotal role in shaping modern Christmas traditions. The fascinating question to consider is how households, predominantly managed by women, incorporated new Christmas traditions, given the regional variations. To complicate matters, these households could also consist of female servants, enslaved individuals, and extended family members, each bringing their unique viewpoints and anticipations to the holiday table. How did these diverse Christmas interests find common ground?

I suggest a handful of possibilities to get you started:

1. Begin your research with the historical era your site interprets. For each woman from this period, create an individual file. At the onset, this file might only contain basic information such as a name or even a first name and her relationship to the site living, working, or visiting—mother-in-law, daughter, niece, servant and/or enslaved.[23] As your research progresses, you can add more details about her life, role, contributions, and experiences. This detailed, individual-focused approach will allow you to construct a comprehensive and nuanced narrative about each woman's life, her impact on the site's history, and her influence on the era's societal norms and traditions.

2. Use the information you gather to create a visual diagram illustrating the relationships among the women and their interactions during Christmas. This will map out their roles in preparing for the holiday, the traditions they followed, their relationships with other household members, and their influence on the holiday's celebration. A visual representation can help you better understand complex relationship dynamics, household hierarchies, and the social fabric of the household during the festive season.

3. Construct a timeline, bearing in mind that it might deviate when it comes to holidays. A timeline can help contextualize the evolution of Christmas traditions over time, the role of women in shaping these traditions, and the broader societal changes reflected in these shifts. It can also highlight the diversity of experiences and traditions across different households and regions. For example, the French celebrated *réveillon* in Louisiana and the Spanish/Mexicans celebrated *Los Pastores* in California.

4. Identify objects and documents related to Christmas in your collection. This could include receipts for gift purchases or food during the Christmas season, dinnerware, cookbooks, household management books, and magazines. These items provide tangible evidence of the material culture of Christmas and the roles women played in holiday preparations. They can reveal details about the expectations of the holiday, culinary traditions, household dynamics, and the influence of women in shaping these practices.

5. Examine the spaces and objects of the house from a woman's perspective.[24] Consider how women would have used these spaces and objects in their daily lives and during special occasions like Christmas. Preparing food for the family during Christmas, a servant may view it in a different light than the woman of the household because she may not be able to give her own family a bountiful feast and even her time to the holiday. What did she see as she cleaned the house with a Christmas tree full of presents and stockings on the hearth that her family may not have been able to afford? The woman of the household may also be overwhelmed whether she has help or not. Decorating, shopping for presents, relatives visiting right after Thanksgiving—exhausting. This approach can provide insights into women's lived experiences, their roles and responsibilities, and their influence on the domestic environment. It can also shed light on the gender dynamics, power relations, and social norms within the household.

6. Expand your research beyond your site to include the surrounding community. Local newspapers, family histories, and records of women's involvement in organizations can all provide valuable insights.[25] This broader research can reveal how women's experiences at your site were connected to larger social, cultural, and historical trends. It can also provide a comparative perspective, highlighting similarities and differences across households and communities.

7. Finally, build upon the research. Many women were involved in organizations through their church, clubs, or other associations. Make a list of newspapers, pamphlets, and books published by organizations at the local, state, and national levels. Many of these organizations published their accomplishments and may mention what they did for their community at Christmas.

By unwrapping the history of Christmas through women's eyes, a richer story comes into play. It shows a whole new aspect of women's roles and responsibilities as active agents: how they lived up to expectations as the holiday became more elaborate; various perspectives from the wife, husband, servant, enslaved, children, and extended family; and how they participated in Christmas events in their community outside. It bridges the past to the present on how we celebrate Christmas today that continues to evolve with women at the helm.

Notes

1. Stephen Nissenbaum, *The Battle for Christmas* (New York: Vintage Books, 1997), 90–131.
2. Nancy Woloch, *Women and the American Experience, Vol. 1* (New York: McGraw-Hill, 1994), 170–90.
3. Kerri K. Greenidge, *The Grimkes: The Legacy of Slavery in an American Family* (New York: Liveright Publishing Corporation, 2023), 55–56; Woloch, *Women and the American Experience, Vol. 1*, 185–90.
4. Naomi Gardner, "Embroidering Emancipation: Female Abolitionists and Material Culture in Britain and the USA, c. 1780–1865" (PhD diss., University of London, 2016), 111–26. In the appendix on figures, Gardner located over sixty-five surviving objects in historic houses and museums with antislavery motifs.
5. Greenidge, *The Grimkes*, 3–6. For example, in 1834 in Philadelphia, a white mob destroyed over thirty black homes and two black churches over four days. Many black residents fled for their lives never to return.
6. *The Liberator*, December 13, 1834. Washington Street intersected with Cornhill Street where William Garrison published his newspaper; Alice Taylor, "Selling Abolition: The Commercial, Material and Social World of the Boston Antislavery Fair, 1834–1858," monograph (PhD diss., University of Western Ontario, 2007), 63.
7. *The Liberator*, April 16, 1831.
8. Debra Gold Hansen, "The Boston Female Anti-Slavery Society and the Limits of Gender Politics," in *The Abolitionist Sisterhood: Women's Political Culture in Antebellum America*, eds. Jean Fagan Yellin and John C. Van Horne (Ithaca: Cornell University Press, 1994), 48–49; Taylor, "Selling Abolition," 63.
9. *The Liberator*, December 20, 1834.
10. Nissenbaum, *The Battle for Christmas*, 187.
11. *The Liberator*, December 20, 1834.
12. *The Liberator*, December 20, 1834.
13. Lee Chambers-Schiller, "A Good Work among the People," in *The Abolitionist Sisterhood: Women's Political Culture in Antebellum America*, eds. Jean Fagan Yellin and John C. Van Horne (Ithaca: Cornell University Press, 1994), 252–56.
14. By 1839, the BFASS had dissolved into two factions. Chapman and her supporters created the Massachusetts Anti-Slavery Society. Debra Gold Hansen, "The Boston Female Anti-Slavery Society and the Limits of Gender Politics," 45–65.
15. Taylor, "Selling Abolition," 22; *The Liberator*, December 23, 1842.
16. Taylor, "Selling Abolition, 57; Chambers-Schiller, "A Good Work among the People," 258–59.
17. *The Liberator*, January 27, 1843.
18. *The Liberator*, January 27, 1843.
19. Jean R. Soderlund, "Priorities and Power: The Philadelphia Female Anti-Slavery Society," in *The Abolitionist Sisterhood: Women's Political Culture in Antebellum America*, eds. Jean Fagan Yellin and John C. Van Horne (Ithaca: Cornell University Press, 1994), 80–81.
20. Dorothy Sterling, ed., *We Are Your Sisters: Black Women in the Nineteenth Century* (New York: W. W. Norton & Company, 1984), 123–24.
21. Soderlund, "Priorities and Power," 81.
22. *The Liberator*, July 2, 1858; Chambers-Schiller, "A Good Work among the People," 269–73.

23. The U.S. Census manuscript can help you find people and is available through National Archives and Records Administration (NARA) and ancestry.com. For immigrants, you may need to research Ellis Island or San Francisco records online.

24. *Great Tours: Thematic Tours and Guide Training for Historic Sites* by Barbara Levy, Sandra Mackenzie Lloyd, and Susan Schreiber (Lanham, MD: AltaMira Press, 2001) includes a section on interpreting multiple perspectives with worksheets and activities.

25. Many local and major newspapers are online thanks to the National Endowment for Humanities digitizing project and easily searchable. Newspapers can be a great resource reporting on happenings or events. Often this includes who was coming to visit, names the roles of the women, men, and groups involved in Christmas events, and monies raised for the community and why. Newspaper articles also can convey the evolution of Christmas through the years. If your local newspaper has not been digitized, visit your local library, historical society, or state archive for assistance. Also, these local, county, and state resources may be able to help identify other records such as family histories regarding Christmas (e.g., diaries, letters, cards) to give insight to women's involvement with one another and their community.

Resources

Gordon, Beverly. *Bazaars and Fair Ladies: The History of the American Fundraising Fair*. Knoxville: University of Tennessee Press, 1998.

Welts Kaufman, Polly, and Katherine T. Corbett (eds.). *Her Past around Us: Interpreting Sites for Women's History*. Malabar, FL: Kreiger Publishing, 2003. Although this book is not about Christmas, it is an excellent guide on how to research and uncover women's stories.

CHAPTER 4

The Spirit of Christmas Past

A Hampton NHS Holiday Experience

Gregory R. Weidman

HAMPTON NATIONAL HISTORIC SITE (NHS) is a rich historical and educational resource for the people of Maryland and the nation. A National Park Service (NPS) property established in 1948 for its architectural merit, the sixty-two-acre park is one of the region's best-preserved estates. The site preserves the core of a once-vast plantation which represents a microcosm of life in the Chesapeake region, reflecting two hundred years of American social, historical, and economic development. Hampton is primarily the story of its people, as the estate evolved through the actions of seven generations of the Ridgely family, enslaved African Americans, European indentured servants, and paid laborers within a nation struggling to define its own concept of freedom.

At the height of the Ridgely family's wealth in the early nineteenth century, their land holdings in Maryland comprised over twenty-four thousand acres, where nearly 350 enslaved individuals labored at iron furnaces, in agriculture, and in domestic service. Hampton NHS now preserves Hampton Mansion (possibly the largest private house in the United States when completed in 1790), many outbuildings, a farm site with overseer's house, elaborate dairy, stables, and standing slave quarters, formal terraced gardens, and other landscape features. Ten of the mansion's principal rooms are currently furnished to interpret varying historic periods of occupancy from 1790 to 1910. Hampton's diverse museum collections include forty-five thousand objects, most original to the site, and vast archival collections which document all aspects of life on the estate from the mid-eighteenth to the mid-twentieth centuries. As highlighted below, these documents can be crucial to the accurate interpretation of holiday events.

Hampton NHS's NPS interpretive staff and volunteer guides seek to tell the stories of all the people who lived and labored there, providing visitors with an honest view of the difficult stories of the past and strive to ensure a more robust understanding of history. The interpreters are empowered to more consistently integrate information about the practice of slavery and the experiences of enslaved people into a visitor experience that feels respectful. The goal is to use challenging stories about the experiences of enslaved African American people to enrich Hampton NHS visitors' experiences.

Presenting Historically Accurate Holiday Exhibits

Recognizing that the popularity with the public of traditional holiday displays and events, Hampton NHS like many museums and historic sites uses these as an important way to achieve the goal of attracting visitors. However, we also recognize the importance for our institution to stay true to our mission. Like many sites, we maintain an obligation to do more than just entertain the public, to merely show them a house festively decorated. Therefore, Hampton NHS staff recognizes four key responsibilities in creating and presenting holiday events:

- Historical accuracy
- Authenticity to our particular site, its inhabitants, and its locale
- Educational, informative, and interesting presentations that engage the public
- Telling diverse stories related to all who lived and labored at Hampton in the historic era

The holiday installations at Hampton NHS provide many specific examples to illuminate these points for historic houses that focus on historical accuracy. As noted above, Hampton's vast museum and archival collections provide rich primary sources of information, which are supplemented by additional troves of original, site-related manuscript material at other institutions such as the Maryland Center for History and Culture and the Maryland State Archives. These sources, enhanced by materials from primary and secondary sources of related interest, can provide a wealth of information on which to base both accurate and interesting displays during the holidays. Since Hampton Mansion's period rooms reflect different eras of occupancy, the holiday room setting for each is varied to show the evolution of different traditions. The curatorial staff plans these settings for each room to accurately reflect the customs of the time to which the room is furnished and the functions of that room. Objects are selected for seasonal display, which can help tell the interpretive stories.

The primary event during the Christmas season at Hampton NHS is "Holidays at Hampton," an open house tour of the mansion with related activities in other locations on-site. Because of the increased volume of visitation for the event, the normal pattern of guided tours for small groups of the mansion's rooms led by interpretation staff or trained volunteers is not feasible. Instead, we offer an open house tour format where visitors walk through the mansion at their own pace. Interpreters are stationed in each room to provide information and answer questions. Interpretive summaries for each period room have been written and distributed to interpreters in advance to provide both general and holiday-specific information. There are security barriers in every room, so the public can access only the entrance areas of each space.

The Parlour

The room at Hampton Mansion interpreting the earliest period of occupancy (1790–1810) is the Parlour, one of four large rooms located immediately next to the spacious Great Hall on the first floor. Given that the traditional holiday display with Christmas tree would be inappropriate at this early date, settings more appropriate for the period have been chosen for exhibition. Two fashionable Federal-era social events, an evening tea party, and a late supper after a Twelfth Night ball, are occasions when friends might gather at Yuletide. These settings are usually displayed in the Parlour on alternate years in order to provide variety for the visiting public. The tea party in particular was selected because the mistress of the plantation, Priscilla Dorsey Ridgely, was an ardent Methodist, known for her piety and plain dress, thus a less "spirited" type of gathering is shown. Tea parties were festive evening events attended by both sexes at this period, almost the equivalent to a modern-day cocktail party (but with less alcohol).

There is a formally set tea table from which Mrs. Ridgely would have used her magnificent Philadelphia silver tea set to serve her guests. They sip their tea from one of the several surviving sets of imported porcelain tea services owned by the Ridgelys, either Worcester or Davenport from England or Haley from Paris. For the gentlemen in a more celebratory mood, there is also a table near the fireplace with traditional eggnog (a beverage dating back to at least the seventeenth century), wine, and other refreshments. The foods served would have principally been desserts such as cakes and cookies. The party at Hampton features traditional fruitcake, a "pyramid" of dried fruits, candied violets, and a whimsically decorated "hedgehog cake" that was popular in the eighteenth and nineteenth centuries. Though some recipes were based on almond marzipan, another one ("tipsy hedgehog") calls for sponge cake soaked with brandy, iced and decorated with almonds for the spines, and served with *crème anglaise*. Period recipes for these can be found on the internet to inform interpretation or to share with visitors.

In alternate years, the Parlour is set for a Midnight Supper, ca. 1805. The supper setting more reflects the interests and habits of the estate's owner, governor Charles Carnan Ridgely, a prominent figure in Maryland history known for his lavish lifestyle and entertaining. It would also reflect his Anglican heritage and regional traditions of the South, which differed from the more severe protestant traditions prevalent in New England. In the Western Christian calendar, Twelfth Night (January 6) was the last day of the twelve days of Christmas. It marks the Feast of the Epiphany, which celebrated the visit of the three wise men to the Holy Family in Bethlehem. This occasion had been a favorite time for merriment and festive holiday gatherings since before the Middle Ages, and the holiday also had roots in pagan traditions.

The Parlour setting features appropriate faux foods served to accompany the festivities of a Twelfth Night Ball held in the Great Hall at Hampton that evening. The ball itself likely would not have started until 9 p.m. or even later, thus a light meal would have been offered the guests several hours later to refresh them from dancing. A focal point of the celebratory feasting was often an elaborately decorated Twelfth Night cake, particularly popular in the late eighteenth and early nineteenth centuries in both England and America. Other foods served at Hampton's midnight supper included meats, cheeses, breads, and fruits, plus desserts such as pies, cakes, and cookies.

To be fully accurate and inclusive, the interpretive information used at Hampton also highlights the roles of the many enslaved servants in the Federal era. For an event such as the midnight supper, long hours of labor by many enslaved house servants would have been necessary to create such a festive occasion for the Ridgelys and their guests. Housemaids cleaned the room and all its furnishings. Laundry workers washed and ironed the linens. Marketmen brought out special foodstuffs from town, such as oysters. Cooks baked the cakes, cookies, and pies. Waiters polished silver, trimmed candles, set up tables, placed the food and drink, and then served the guests as they arrived. When the party was over, they, the housemaids, and the kitchen staff did the cleanup and dishwashing, put away the valuable silver, china, and glass, and returned the room to its daytime configuration. With a big occasion such as the ball and supper, guests would not have left till the early hours of the morning, meaning the enslaved house servants would have been working virtually around the clock. There would have also been house guests to cook, clean, and care for both before and after the party, so there was little or no rest for the weary.

For the holiday decorations in the Federal Parlour, the locally abundant holly (only faux at Hampton NHS) is used, though sparingly, as would suit both the time and the mistress's preference for simplicity. Holly is probably the most frequently depicted evergreen in the pictorial sources from this era and well into the nineteenth century. Traditionally, it was used in vases and containers of all kinds, often on mantels, and to deck picture frames and looking glasses. Using holly in the English tradition is very old: a sixteenth-century poem advises, "Get Iuye [ivy] and hull [holly], woman deck up thyne house."[1] The green plant materials used for display should be appropriate both to the region as well as the time period. Thus, for example, we try to avoid variegated holly in early settings like the Parlour, and do not use greenery that could not be found locally (e.g., *Magnolia grandiflora* in Maine).

Dining Room

Hampton's Dining Room displays a Christmas dinner party for ten, circa 1820, with the three-part dining table extended and set for dinner, including appropriate faux foods (see figure 4.1). At this period, dinner was usually held in the mid-afternoon and would have lasted several hours (a dinner invitation sent to Governor Ridgely in the 1810s by his adult son states the time for 3 p.m.). The Hampton dining table is laid with all the plates and service dishes in an orderly, symmetrical pattern, a display based on diagrams shown in housekeeping guides and cookbooks of the period. These sources provide a wealth of other details. For example, the soup and fish dishes (always at the head and foot) were important

Figure 4.1.   The Dining Room at Hampton set for a dinner party during the holidays (ca. 1820) with historically accurate faux food. Photo courtesy of Hampton National Historic Site, National Park Service.

parts of the first course and after they were served, those dishes were taken away and replaced with two new dishes called "removes." Even though Hampton's first course shows thirteen individual dishes, a second course of equal size would also have been served. All the dishes, cutlery, decanters plus the top tablecloth would have been removed (we display a second cloth underneath the first) then the second course would have been placed on the table. When this was consumed, the entire table would have been cleared (including the cloth) and the dessert course would have been placed on the table.

On the Hampton dinner table, the central dish, a faux roasted wild turkey, is elevated on a rare piece of Ridgely family silver, a "dish cross" that has a small burner in the center to keep the food warm. Another special addition to the dinner table that causes much comment from visitors are the pair of Anglo-Irish cut-glass "celery vases," circa 1825, with Hampton provenance. Although known since ancient times, celery was a fall/winter vegetable enjoying a revival of popularity in the early nineteenth century. It was considered a luxury, so elegant specialized vases were designed for its presentation on the table. Displaying this fashionable fare in expensive containers symbolized the status of the Ridgelys. Another statement of the Ridgelys' wealth is the porcelain dinner service, made in Paris by the Feuillet manufactory circa 1825 and custom decorated with the Ridgely family coat of arms.

The sideboard was an important focal point of any early nineteenth-century dining room and was used to feature an elegant display of the family's silver and glassware, plus desserts. In *The House Servant's Directory* (1827), Robert Roberts states,

> In setting out your sideboard, you must study neatness, convenience and taste; as you must think that ladies and gentlemen that have splendid and costly articles, wish to have them seen and set out to best advantage. . . . The grapes which are to go on with dessert, etc. with all the spare glasses that are for dinner, must go on the sideboard. . . . Your glasses should form a crescent, or half circle, as this looks most sublime.[2]

At Hampton, we follow Roberts's suggestions in the overall appearance plus the display of additional glassware. In addition to the fruit and nuts in the epergne on the sideboard, the rest of the desserts are on a side table, along with the extra dessert plates and eating utensils. On the front of the dessert table displayed as a centerpiece is a silver salver holding small, fluted glasses of "syllabub," a frothy combination of cream, sweet wine, citrus juice, and sugar. Hampton's syllabub cups are elegant Anglo-Irish cut glass, circa 1810, and original to the site.

Similar to the description of the numbers of workers involved for the Parlour supper setting, many enslaved house servants would have been needed to put on a large holiday dinner party. Certain key individuals were the leaders of the team, however: the waiters. Many enslaved men served as "waiters" (butlers) during Governor Ridgely's time, both at his townhouse on Gay Street in the center of Baltimore and at Hampton. Although the name of the head waiter during Governor Ridgely's era is not known, a few years later that individual was Mark Posey (1815–living 1880). As head waiter, Mark set up the Dining Room and served at table. Since head waiter was an important role in the household, Mark was regularly seen by the Ridgelys' guests, so he received special clothing to wear ("livery"), including jackets with custom-made buttons with the stag's head crest from the Ridgely coat of arms. Research undertaken during the Hampton NHS ethnographic study enables interpreters to also share information on Mark's personal life, family, and experience post-Emancipation. One notable story is of his daughter Becky (1837–living 1865) who, despite her father's high status in the household, sought her freedom in 1852. Becky is recorded on the Christmas Gifts list as "gone" that year (see figure 4.2). By the 1860s she was living in Baltimore City.

Drawing Room

The Drawing Room (1840–1860), Hampton Mansion's most formal and elaborate space, is the room where the park interprets the pre–Civil War era. It is important to focus on the estate's many enslaved individuals in this location. Fortunately, many plantation-related documents in Hampton NHS's and other archival collections noted above allow the site to bring this story fully to life in holiday settings. In Hampton's collection in particular, a remarkable document related to holiday traditions and the enslaved survives. Eliza "Didy" Ridgely (1828–1894), the teenage daughter of Hampton's owners in the mid-nineteenth century, recorded "CHRISTMAS GIFTS of the Colored Children of Hampton, Given by E. Ridgely," a lengthy list enumerating the names of over fifty enslaved children and the specific gifts they were given each year from 1841 to 1854 (see figure 4.2).[3] The gift list (a scanned copy of which is on view in the room) records items such as dolls, doll furniture, toy animals, musical instruments, and toy soldiers, which the staff uses as a guide in displaying both antique and reproduction toys. In her journal from this period, Didy wrote that on Christmas Eve she "fixed some of the servants Christmas gifts" (the Ridgelys always referred to their enslaved workers with the euphemistic term "servants").[4] The next day, after giving gifts to the enslaved adults, "then we fixed the room and a whole troop of little servants came in. When they had received their presents, we sent them away and then went down into the yard to shoot firing crackers."

Thanks to Hampton NHS's recently completed Ethnographic Overview and Assessment, the later histories and families of many of the enslaved children listed to receive Christmas gifts are now known and can enhance interpretation.[5] Examples include farm worker Jim Pratt (1832–1902), a son of Charlotte and brother of Joe and Caroline Pratt. Jim continued to work as a farm laborer at Hampton long after he was emancipated in 1864. He and his wife Laura lived in the Towson area and are said to have had twenty-two children. Jim was still living at Hampton at the time of his death in 1902. A circa 1897 snapshot of him survives in Hampton's collection. Another large family on the gift list are the Davis siblings (Anne, Bill, Caroline, Ellen, Harriet, Lewis, Lloyd, Susan, and Tilghman), the children of Bill and Susan Davis. The whole family had been purchased in the spring of 1841 from the estate of James Hawkins of Frederick County. Several of the siblings, including Lewis, Anne, and Caroline, continued to work at Hampton after Emancipation in 1864, but others moved away. Tilghman (1847–1905) became a coachman and moved to Baltimore City. Ellen (1831–1911) married head Hampton coachman Nathan Harris in the late 1840s and had eleven children. The family lived south of Govans by the 1870s, where Nathan had a livery stable. The Harris family had many descendants, many of whom still live in the Towson area.

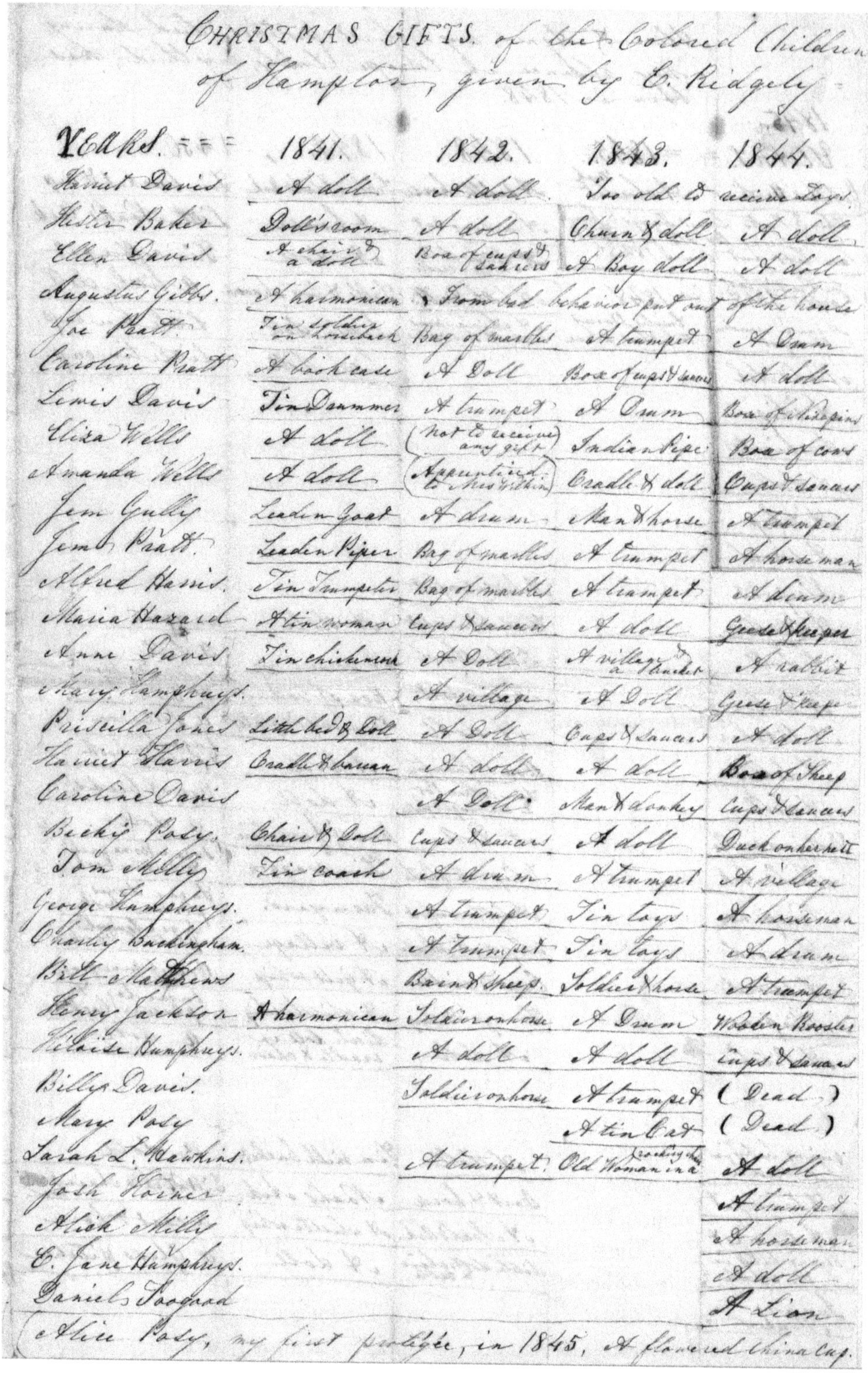

CHRISTMAS GIFTS of the Colored Children of Hampton, given by E. Ridgely

YEARS ===	1841.	1842.	1843.	1844.
Harriet Davis	A doll	A doll	Too old to receive toys
Hester Baker	Doll's room	A doll	Churn & doll	A doll
Ellen Davis	A chair & a doll	Box of cups & saucers	A Boy doll	A doll
Augustus Gibbs	A harmonica	From bad behavior put out of the house		
Joe Pratt	Tin soldiers on horseback	Bag of marbles	A trumpet	A Gun
Caroline Pratt	A book case	A Doll	Box of cups & saucers	A doll
Lewis Davis	Tin Drummer	A trumpet	A Drum	Box of ninepins
Eliza Wells	A doll	(not to receive any gift)	Indian rice	Box of cows
Amanda Wells	A doll	Apprenticed to Mrs. Gittin	Cradle & doll	Cups & saucers
Jem Gully	Leaden goat	A drum	Man & horse	A trumpet
Jem Pratt	Leaden Piper	Bag of marbles	A trumpet	A horse man
Alfred Harris	Tin Trumpets	Bag of marbles	A trumpet	A drum
Maria Hazard	A tin woman	Cups & saucers	A doll	Geese & keeper
Anne Davis	Tin chickens	A Doll	A village & a garden	A rabbit
Mary Humphreys		A village	A Doll	Geese & keeper
Priscilla Jones	Little bed & doll	A Doll	Cups & saucers	A doll
Harriet Harris	Cradle & bureau	A doll	A doll	Box of sheep
Caroline Davis		A Doll	Man & donkey	Cups & saucers
Becky Posy	Chair & doll	Cups & saucers	A doll	Duck on her nest
Tom Milly	Tin coach	A drum	A trumpet	A village
George Humphreys		A trumpet	Tin toys	A horseman
Charly Buckingham		A Trumpet	Tin toys	A drum
Bill Matthews		Bird & sheep	Soldier & horse	A trumpet
Henry Jackson	A harmonica	Soldier on horse	A Drum	Weather cock
Louise Humphreys		A doll	A doll	Cups & saucers
Billy Davis		Soldier on horse	A trumpet	(Dead)
Mary Posy			A tin cat	(Dead)
Sarah L. Hawkins		A trumpet	Old Woman in a rocking chair	A doll
Josh Posier				A trumpet
Alick Milly				A horse man
E. Jane Humphreys				A doll
Daniel Soogood				A Lion

Alice Posy, my first protégée, in 1845, A flowered china cup.

Figure 4.2. "CHRISTMAS GIFTS of the Colored Children of Hampton, Given by E. Ridgely." Original manuscript of Eliza "Didy" Ridgely White, 1841–1854, Catalog # HAMP 14733. Photo courtesy of Hampton National Historic Site, National Park Service.

It is important to note that the Hampton Christmas Gift List records information that shows this practice was certainly not entirely altruistic but could also be used as a way of control and punishment. In 1842, Eliza Wells (age nine) was "not to receive any gift" because she had supposedly killed Didy Ridgely's pet squirrel. According to Didy's journal, Eliza had disliked the very unpleasant task of cleaning the "disagreeable" animal's cage. Even more disturbing, a child named "little Ann" is noted as receiving a doll in 1852, "nothing" in 1853, and "sent away" in 1854.

Regarding certain details of the display in Hampton's Drawing Room, holiday greens include a plant that would not be accurate for most other mid-nineteenth-century American houses. Eliza Eichelberger Ridgely (1803–1867), wife of the third owner of Hampton, was a noted horticulturist who often introduced unusual and exotic plants to the estate's gardens and greenhouses. Eliza's account book in Hampton's archives records her purchase of "Eurphorbia Poinsettia" on December 15, 1848. The plant had only been introduced from Mexico to the United States just twenty years earlier by U.S. diplomat Joel Roberts Poinsett. It was not in widespread use as a holiday decoration until the twentieth century. Besides the faux poinsettias on display, roses are often featured in an arrangement on the center table, permissible in December since there was a "Rose House" among Hampton's nineteenth-century greenhouses.

Music Room

The period room in Hampton mansion that features the most traditional type of holiday display is the Music Room (1870–1890). Oral history from family members has informed the placement of the tree in the southwest corner of this room. This same source notes that in the twentieth century, the family typically used a native red cedar, but the artificial examples of this species of tree are unavailable. Christmas trees were introduced to the United States by German immigrants, probably in the early nineteenth century, and their widely publicized use by Queen Victoria at midcentury helped to increase knowledge of this tradition. Although decorated trees did not become commonplace in American homes until after the Civil War, it is known from a diary kept by Helen Stewart Ridgely's (1854–1929) grandmother and now in the Hampton archives that her family had a tree in their Baltimore townhouse as early as 1861. Though no historic house museum should light real candles, they can either be displayed unlit with a directed light source elsewhere in the room or with clip-on LED candles. The ornaments on the tree would likely have featured dolls, toys, musical instruments, flags, cornucopias, greeting cards, and baskets of treats in addition to a few glass ornaments. For Christmas settings in the 1850–1900 period, rather than using a tall tree standing on the floor, consider putting a smaller tree on a table, as shown in many illustrations of the time.

In the Music Room, in addition to toys placed around and nearby the tree, there are only a few wrapped gifts. In the historic era, toys for the children would usually have been unwrapped, and those that were would have been in plain brown paper or tissue perhaps tied with fabric ribbon. Holiday gift wrapping paper as we know it today was not invented until the World War I era. The toys might be under or near the tree, but many illustrations show them set up near the fireplace where the stockings are hung.

The display at Hampton also features a variety of books the Ridgely children regularly received for Christmas, many of which have survived in the collection. This reflects the very popular nineteenth-century custom of books published specifically to be holiday gifts. Eliza "Didy" Ridgely's 1842 journal notes that on Christmas Eve, she and her visiting friends "read the new Christmas gift books." On and near the center table in the Music Room are a selection of books specifically published to be holiday gifts such as *The Bird's XMAS Carol* (ca. 1890), *May to Christmas at Thorne Hill* (1882), and *Holly Berries* (1881), a book of holiday-themed poems for children open to the poem titled "Christmas Morning." Illustrated children's books sometimes feature Christmas trees with candles or other holiday scenes on their covers and inside, contributing useful visual documentation. These illustrations are prominently displayed to be visible to visitors to show the sources of our settings. For example, near a display of dolls and girls' toys is an illustrated book of short stories, *We Young Folks* (1886), which features a Christmas tree with candles on the cover. Finally, copies of a pamphlet of nineteenth-century Christmas carols from Baltimore's Grace Church is on display for later use by family and friends, accompanied by piano and harp.

By this later nineteenth-century period, the holiday greenery in American homes had become much more profuse, with rooms literally swathed in garlands and swags. Ivy was one of the most popular plants of the era and was frequently used for room decoration both at the holidays and year-round. At Hampton, garlands of faux ivy are entwined around light fixtures, over mantels, and across tabletops in the Music Room.

Given the 1870–1890 date of the Music Room exhibits, the interpretive emphasis highlights the post–Civil War lives of Hampton's formerly enslaved workers. Following Emancipation in 1864, several formerly enslaved workers continued to work at Hampton for Margaretta Howard Ridgely in the 1870s and 1880s. (Most of those freed from Hampton, however, sought new lives and livelihoods in Baltimore City or the Towson area.) Those remaining at Hampton included several members of the Davis family including nurse Anne Davis Williams, Louis and Nancy Brown Davis, and Caroline Davis Brown and her son Lewis/Louis Davis (named for his uncle). Caroline was the Hampton dairy maid during the late nineteenth century and was renowned for the quality of the butter she churned in the dairy. Her son Lewis worked at Hampton as a farm hand in the 1870s–1880s but eventually became the farm manager. Caroline's husband Tom Brown, a first cousin of Nancy Davis, succeeded Mark Posey as longtime head waiter at Hampton from the 1870s to circa 1910. House servants such as Anne and Nancy continued to receive Christmas gifts from the family, with the Ridgely family daughters responsible for continuing this tradition. These gifts were usually small personal items such as kerchiefs.

Children's Bedchamber

Ridgely family children's bedroom on Christmas morning, circa 1845. Eliza "Didy" Ridgely mentions in her journal that on Christmas Day "[w]e were up early, looked at the stocking and the good things it contains." At this time, those good things were usually limited to fresh fruit, candies, and other sweet treats. Later in the day, Didy and her school friends enjoyed Christmas presents: "Mary read and Lizzy and I had a play with the paper dolls."

On the trunk at the foot of the bed, we display reproduction paper dolls based on plates in *Godey's Ladies' Book*, along with a book of children's verses *Little Tales, with Lots of Pretty Pictures, for Little Folks* (ca. 1850), which is original to the Ridgely family. It is open to a poem called "Santa Claus' Silver Crown," which says that Santa brings presents on New Year's Eve, rather than Christmas! The other colorfully illustrated book on the chest is not so much fun, as it is filled with stories and poems about children learning their lessons—the hard way. *Evil Deeds and Evil Consequences* (ca. 1850) was given to Charles Ridgely Jr. (1853–1873) in 1857 by his great-great-uncle Otho Eichelberger, who perhaps felt the four-year-old needed some firm admonition. Less forbidding is the beautifully illustrated book on a nearby desk, *Birds of the Bible*, given to little Charles by his doting grandmother Eliza Ridgely (1803–1867) in 1854. A dolls' tea party is also set up in the room on a table to the left of the bed, featuring an Old Paris porcelain dolls' tea service (ca. 1835) given to Didy Ridgely by her mother Eliza and the child's silver tea set with repoussé decoration, made in Baltimore by Samuel Kirk, circa 1850.

On the bed is a "night dress" made in the early 1850s for a child of the Ridgely family. Despite its appearance, this garment was made for a boy, specifically John and Eliza Ridgely's eldest grandson, Henry White (1850–1927). Henry, who spent much of his childhood at Hampton, grew up to be an internationally renowned diplomat. As children's portraits and photographs from the nineteenth century document, little boys were often dressed in clothing today thought to be suitable for girls.

Hampton NHS is fortunate to have a wealth of both primary and secondary source information on which to base its period room installations during the holidays. Site-specific documentation gives interpreters the ability to share the stories of all those who lived and labored on the Hampton estate.

Notes

1. Mary Miley Theobald, "With Boughs of Holly," *Colonial Williamsburg Journal* (Autumn 2008).
2. Robert Roberts, *The House Servant's Directory* (Boston, 1827; Waltham, MA: The Gore Place Society, 1977), 49.
3. "Christmas Gifts of the Colored Children of Hampton given by E. Ridgely," HAMP 14733; Ridgely Family Papers, MS. 1001, Hampton National Historic Site, National Park Service.
4. *Journal of Eliza Ridgely of Hampton, Maryland, 1841–2,* HAMP 3911; Ridgely Family Papers, MS. 1001, Hampton National Historic Site, National Park Service.
5. Cheryl Janifer LaRoche, "Tracing Lives in Slavery, Reclaiming Lives in Freedom: An Ethnographic Solution to a Historical Problem" [Ethnographic Overview and Assessment for Hampton National Historic Site] (Washington, DC: Northeast Region Anthropology Program, National Park Service, 2020).

Resources

A Taste of History by Joyce White, ATasteofHistory.net
Afroculinaria by Michael W. Twitty, Afroculinaria.com

Part II

DIFFERENT TRADITIONS AT DIFFERENT TIMES AND PLACES

CHAPTER 5

Réveillon

A New Orleans Holiday Tradition

Karen Trahan Leathem

O N CHRISTMAS DAY in 1892, a short story by French Creole author Marie Louise Points appeared in the *New Orleans Daily Picayune*. A classic example of the "local color" genre then in vogue, "Clopin-Clopant: A Christmas Fragment of Early Creole Days" is a tale of colonial times, relying on nostalgic recollections with a smattering of French phrases and local dialect. "[A]ll day long music and laughter echoed from the old brick buildings, and . . . the belles demoiselles loitered among the roses and jasmines of the courtyards, twining bouquets and planning for the 'reveillon' which every Creole home from that day to this holds on Christmas eve," Points wrote. But the action quickly moves to the streets with young men blowing horns, shouting, lighting fireworks, and shooting pistols, resulting in the "merry, maddening Christmas eve of New Orleans." The group spends the rest of the story plotting a réveillon celebration at a corner café in the French Quarter.[1]

Réveillon, still celebrated in France and various former French colonies, carries several meanings. It is the festive meal following Midnight Mass on Christmas and then reprised for New Year's Eve.[2] According to *Larousse Gastronomique*, *réveillon* derives from "*réveiller*, meaning to begin a new watch (*veillée*) after Midnight Mass. The length of the . . . mass . . . and the time taken to walk to church and back used to justify a substantial meal eaten in the early hours of Christmas morning."[3] In the nineteenth century, a public réveillon developed, similar to that celebrated by the lively crowd in "Clopin-Clopant" intent on gathering in a café.

The winter feast paired with a boisterous celebration has deep roots. Scottish food writer Nichola Fletcher points to the "desperate overeating and drinking when nights are long and cold," setting the tone for the midwinter festivals, which "banish darkness and cold . . . and reawaken life" with "fire, dance, noise, greenery, warming food and drink."[4] Historian Bruce David Forbes explains that during the ancient Roman Saturnalia, taking place over the course of a week in December, "Friends visited each other from home to home and also joined in boisterous street processions."[5]

Christians first began to observe Christmas in the fourth century. The holiday arrived in France fairly early, by 496. It became enmeshed in a series of celebrations that began with the feast day of St. Nicholas on December 6, when children received candy and other small gifts, to Epiphany on January 6. One of the many customs that became a part of French Christmas celebrations is *réveillon*. But réveillon is not just a festive meal to mark the holiday; it also breaks a fast, which most Catholics observed on Christmas Eve. While réveillon is technically after midnight, it shares characteristics with Christmas Eve meals earlier in the evening in which fish is featured, such as carp in Germany, Austria, and Poland and eel in Italy.[6]

When did the term *réveillon* come into use? In circulation by the early eighteenth century, it was not necessarily connected to Christmas. A 1712 French-German dictionary defines réveillon as a meal eaten in the middle of the night, after a social gathering or a dance.[7] By the 1800s, réveillon was associated with Christmas and New Year's celebrations. In Emile Littré's authoritative 1869 French dictionary, it was defined as "a special meal eaten in the middle of the night, particularly on Christmas night." French historians Michelle Perrot and Anne Martin-Fugier look at the typical post–Midnight Mass meal, which included two traditional dishes, vanilla porridge served with waffles and grilled sausage. Cold dishes, such as truffled turkey, were common, as were a variety of pastries.[8]

The private practice of réveillon was one thing, but the public réveillon was another, and this practice picked up steam in the second half of the nineteenth century. In the 1860s, the Parisian working class observed réveillon in cafés.[9] In 1897 one British observer noted, "Christmas Eve is a fete in Paris." "Late in the evening," he wrote,

> the cafés become crowded, and the café-restaurants that are to keep open all night for the Christmas "réveillon" begin to arrange their tables. . . . The "réveillon," or Christmas Eve supper at midnight, is more important to the Frenchman than the Christmas dinner, and the indulgence in it may somewhat account for the general atmosphere of almost gloomy abstinence that seems to hang over Paris on Christmas Day. Oysters represent the favorite first course, and any one interested in statistics may like to know that half a million dozen oysters were sold . . . on Christmas Eve in 1896, and of écrevisse, that appetizing crawfish, sixty-thousand represents the number consumed during the "réveillon." Impecunious clerks and reckless Latin Quarter students go dinnerless . . . the week beforehand, and . . . often a month afterwards, that they may partake of a proper "réveillon.". . . The thoroughly up-to-date Parisian divides his Christmas supper into many courses, taking each one at a different place.[10]

In this public observance, réveillon became unmoored from its Catholic origins, instead merging with secular holiday traditions.[11]

Today, réveillon remains beloved in France. In the late fall, food magazines feature numerous réveillon articles with seasonal recipes. The traditional feast often consists of many courses. Roast turkey—with or without truffles—persists, and Parisians treasure a first course of oysters on the half shell. Regional favorites include daube (a stew of braised meat) and goose in southwest France, sauerkraut and foie gras in Alsace, and omelets with escargots in the Alps. In Provence, salt cod dishes and the "thirteen desserts," which represent Jesus and the twelve apostles, are common.[12]

In North America, réveillon took root wherever French or French-descended people settled, most notably in Canada (Québec and the Maritime provinces) and Louisiana, but also in such places as New England, Michigan's Mackinac Island, and Ste. Genevieve, Missouri. In the late nineteenth century, Elizabeth Baird recalled the copious spread of food for réveillons during her childhood in the 1810s and 1820s, which included roast pig, roast goose, boeuf à la mode, headcheese, and small cakes. "This affair was considered the high feast of the season," she noted.[13]

Christmas in New Orleans

New Orleans's embrace of réveillon originates in its French heritage. Founded in 1718, the city was part of the colony of Louisiana, which France ruled from 1699, when Pierre Le Moyne, sieur d'Iberville, established the first European settlement, until 1762. In that year, weary of the unprofitable colony and embroiled in war with Great Britain, France turned Louisiana over to Spain in the secret Treaty of Fontainebleau, an action made public with the Peace of Paris in 1763. Spain was slow to take control, though. The first governor did not arrive until 1766, and he was driven away by a revolt of French Louisianians. Even after Spanish officials reasserted control in 1769, French culture and language dominated. Vernacular religious practices remained virtually the same, as Spain, like France, mandated Catholicism as the official religion. In New Orleans, as in France, secular Christmas celebrations blended with those established by the church. Midnight Mass was important, but for many, so was rowdy singing, noisemaking, and revelry on the streets.[14] Such carousing was similar to the mumming that had been practiced all over Europe since the 1500s, with disguised men roaming in groups, often demanding drinks from the wealthy, from mid-December until past Christmas Day.[15]

When New Orleans and Louisiana became a part of the United States in 1803 with the Louisiana Purchase, many local Christmas traditions more closely resembled Yuletide customs in the Mid-Atlantic and the South, in contrast to New England, where Christmas was eyed with suspicion. From the Carolinas and Virginia to Pennsylvania and New York, Christmas revelers shot guns into the air and visited neighbors in disguise, begging for food and drink.[16]

Beginning in the late 1830s, Christmas was transformed from this disorderly merry-making to a much tamer family event. This tension between family-centered and unruly Christmas continued, however, an opposition that played out in New Orleans. Réveillon, focused on Midnight Mass and family meals, made up one part of this equation. Fireworks and frivolity on the street made up the other.

In 1838 Louisiana became the first state to make Christmas a legal holiday. More than a dozen states followed suit before 1860, including Arkansas, Maine, New York, Virginia, Minnesota, and California. It is unclear why Louisiana led the charge, but New Orleans's importance as a banking and commercial center could be the reason. Most of the declarations of Christmas as a holiday during this period were part of legislative acts dealing with commercial regulation and bill payment. The Louisiana act, intended to "regulate the damages on protested bills of exchange," designated December 25, along with January 1, January 8 (the anniversary of the Battle of New Orleans), February 22 (George Washington's birthday), Good Friday, and July 4, along with Sundays, as "public days of rest," giving debtors an extra "day of grace" in determining when promissory notes and bills of exchange were due. Like the Louisiana law, many of these legislative acts did not specify "Christmas" in the language of the bill, merely listing the date, "twenty fifth December."[17]

The state's focus on commerce, booming due to the lucrative slave economy, however, did not preclude a growing sentimentality concerning Christmas. The *New Orleans Daily Picayune*, which had nothing to say about the new "day of grace" in 1838, praised the "glorious times of mirth, good humor and enjoyment" that came with the day, and opined that "there is a continued love in the heart for the gaities [*sic*] of Christmas." The paper's 1839 summation of the day painted a picture of a "bright, beautiful, sunny, social Christmas," with children playing with their new toys and parents looking on with "joy" and "delight."[18]

Despite such scenes, among francophone New Orleanians, like much of western Europe, December 25 was not the primary day for exchanging gifts. Instead, they opened presents on New Year's Day, known as *le jour de l'an*. As the French and Creole population became more Americanized, they began to follow Anglo customs and adopted the evolving American Christmas, which featured Christmas trees, Santa Claus, and elaborate gifts.[19] However, older French-rooted traditions continued west of New Orleans, with New Year's gift-giving, called *étrennes*, as in France.[20]

In the 1930s, Works Progress Administration (WPA) writers noted that réveillon became popular in Louisiana in the latter half of the nineteenth century, duplicating the custom's evolution in France.[21] Perhaps the first appearance of the word in New Orleans newspapers came in 1861 in a serialized English translation of Henri Murger's famous novel *Scènes de la vie de bohème* (1847–1849), on which Puccini based his opera *La Bohème*. As their Paris neighborhood celebrates *réveillon*, Rodolphe and Marcel stare longingly at a truffled turkey in a vendor's window display. The impoverished men end up settling for bread and wine.[22] Apart from that French import, *réveillon* rarely appeared in the New Orleans press, showing up in the French *L'Abeille* by 1880, but not in reference to local customs in English-language newspapers until 1891.[23]

In 1899 *Harper's Weekly* documented Christmas in New Orleans with an illustration of a scene similar to what is now considered normal for New Year's Eve—the sidewalk is jammed with people in evening garb, and more than a few carry large noisemakers. There are fireworks everywhere. One observer around this time noted that "there are people in New Orleans who may dispense with roast turkey stuffed with truffles, but nobody can do without fireworks."[24] This pyrotechnic holiday had long been the norm. As the *Daily*

Picayune remarked in 1869, "Christmas has been celebrated with the festivity and frolic usually attending it. . . . The sound of exploding fireworks, the merry shout and laughing jest . . . attested the widespread joy and general enthusiasm."[25] In the 1890s, on Christmas Eve "a continuous noise of firecrackers, trumpets, horns, shouts, . . . and music permeated the air," resulting in an "atmosphere . . . reddened with the glare of fire-works and other Kaleidoscopic lights."[26]

Clearly, New Orleans had a public Christmas celebration in addition to private rituals in the home, strongly resembling Parisian Christmas Eve during the same period. In the mid-twentieth century, Roger Baudier, a historian of Catholic New Orleans, recalled the rowdy Christmases of years past, with the "bursting of firecrackers, and much singing." In keeping with New Orleans's reputation as a tipsy town, people indulged in orgeat, anisette, and brandy as they passed the time before Midnight Mass.[27]

Indeed, fireworks on Christmas Eve were popular throughout the South, and observers in the late nineteenth and early twentieth centuries railed against this practice, which began to be regulated with restrictions imposed by fire chiefs in the 1910s. During that decade, police chiefs, fire departments, and public safety advocates promoted a "Safe and Sane" Christmas campaign, urging people to take care with fireworks. In New Orleans, the sale and consumer use of large fireworks was prohibited.[28]

The Menu

What did nineteenth-century New Orleanians eat at their réveillons? Writing in the 1950s, New Orleans journalist Harnett Kane gave a detailed description:

> By Creole food standards, the meal was a comparatively small one, but its ingredients were rich: eggs in one or two styles, several different kinds of wines; sweet breads, raisin breads, and platters of the long crisp loaves. . . . And always there was a Creole *spécialité* of *spécialités,* the imaginatively flavored *daube glacé* . . . with bay leaf, pepper cloves, and other ingredients transforming the dish into a dark delight. There were seldom leftovers of *daube glacé,* and nobody in New Orleans has been known to refuse the offer of a second or even a third slice.
>
> The meal ended with a cake filled with jelly, dripping with wine or rum, and topped with a hill of whipped cream, or a molded dessert from one of the several noted confectioners who flourished in the French Quarter.[29]

Files from the Louisiana Works Progress Administration reveal a similar menu. The meal was a cold one, often featuring a "galantine"—which meant a jellied, pressed, cold meat, so in essence, *daube glacée.* Completing the menu were "a salad or two, slices of bread and butter, fruit cake, fruit and . . . 'café brûlot.' Wines were served with supper and Champagne frappe with the cake. Toasts were drunk for happiness and health of all." The festivities lasted until daybreak. And as in France, Christmas Day was a mere afterthought.[30]

While turkeys are more frequently mentioned in connection with Christmas Day meals rather than réveillon, its status as a ubiquitous holiday food make it worthy of inclusion here

Figure 5.1. Aimee Becnel Schexnayder with a live turkey in her son's photography studio, Edgard, Louisiana. Photo by Olidé P. Schexnayder, ca. 1890s, 1998.01.16.038. Courtesy of the Louisiana State Museum.

(see figure 5.1). In the early twentieth century, Eliza Ripley recalled the holiday turkeys sold in New Orleans in the 1840s:

> If it is near Christmas time … we might meet a flock of turkeys marching up Camp Street, guided by a man and boys with long poles. In those days fowls were not offered for sale ready dressed or plucked, but sold "on the hoof," as we say of cattle. … No roast turkey gobbler, or … boiled turkey hen with oyster dressing, tastes now like the ones mother had on her table when I was a child.[31]

Turkey purchasing rituals continued, as evidenced by an 1885 illustration showing a woman selecting her Christmas turkey from the streetside vendor.[32] Nearly a century later, cookbook author and raconteur Leon E. Soniat Jr. related how his family would go about buying the holiday turkey in the late 1920s and early 1930s:

> At the French Market, we would go from cage to cage until we found a likely prospect for dinner. Then the poultry man was requested to remove the bird from the cage for inspection. Memere and Mamete [his grandmother and mother] would both have to agree before the turkey was finally chosen. The bird was examined from beak to toenail. It was felt all over to determine its plumpness or lack thereof[,] … and after due deliberation the bird was bought and carted off for home. At home he was immediately put in a cage to be fattened even further.[33]

The holiday turkey—unlike daube glacée—is a standard holiday dish that New Orleans shares with the rest of the United States (see figure 5.2). The 1901 edition of the *Picayune's Creole Cook Book* featured turkey on the regular menu for Christmas, the "More Economical Christmas Menu," and even the "Old-fashioned Creole Suggestion for Holiday Menus," where it received the extra flourish of a still-beloved New Orleans accompaniment, oyster stuffing, also known as oyster dressing.[34]

Other dishes found on nineteenth-century Christmas menus include ham roast with champagne sauce, stewed venison, cream of celery soup, and bonbons à la Créole. Oysters usually made up the first course, truffled turkeys, gumbo, and turtle soup (both mock and real) were popular, and at the end of the meal, cheeses, pies, and cakes were served.[35]

Revival of a Tradition

Most New Orleanians today know the réveillon as a multicourse, prix fixe restaurant meal. While it has become popular among locals, it originated as a tourist promotion. In 1985, Sandra Dartus, the executive director of the French Quarter Festival (FQF), a nonprofit festival first held in 1984 to bring New Orleanians back to the city's historic center after a lengthy round of street and sidewalk work, began discussions about ways to boost the tourist economy around Christmas.[36] The consulting firm of Jeskin and Linge produced a guiding report, "Noel New Orleans—A French Quarter Holiday!" Along with Louisiana-themed decorations, Papa Noël ("Father Christmas" for French Louisiana) processions, and

Figure 5.2.   Aimee Becnel Schexnayder with a turkey ready for stuffing in her kitchen, Edgard, Louisiana. Photo by Olidé P. Schexnayder, ca. 1890s, 1998.01.16.027. Courtesy of the Louisiana State Museum.

a "March of the Toy Soldiers" in Jackson Square, the report recommended réveillon as part of a strategy for "adapting historic Christmas customs."

Jill Jeskin and Gordon Linge, principals of the firm, briefly described nineteenth-century Creole family réveillons and advised that "restaurants could sumptuously revive this festive tradition (at an earlier evening hour)." They envisioned period music and costumed waiters, so that patrons would be "whisked back in time." This historical dining experience was a serious matter, which would be staged with "careful documentation provided by the Gallier House," a historic house museum in the French Quarter.[37]

To put réveillon into action, Dartus did in fact start with Gallier House, enlisting its executive director, Ann Masson, along with two key players in the restaurant industry who had a strong interest in New Orleans food traditions, Ralph Brennan from the Brennan family, which operated Commander's Palace and Mr. B's Bistro, and Richard Stewart, owner of the Gumbo Shop. After conducting archival research on nineteenth-century New Orleans menus, the group circulated sample menus and recruited restaurants to participate.[38]

While the cynical might view the restaurant réveillon adaptation as a mere marketing ploy, there was much substance behind it, from historical research to the vetting committee (initially Masson, Brennan, and Stewart), which reviewed proposed menus and nixed anything that would not have been served in the 1800s, such as blackened dishes, then at the height of popularity due to chef Paul Prudhomme's blackened redfish.[39]

The committee remained in place until recently. For many years, the two main criteria for the menus were foods that would have been served in the nineteenth century and regional foods. In 2012, to reflect current dining trends, French Quarter Festivals added a new menu category—contemporary réveillon. Thus, while restaurants offering traditional menus adhere to such standards as gumbo, turtle soup, and panéed oysters, the contemporary menus reflect global influences and fusion cuisine, such as boudin arancini and Trinidadian doubles. In 2014, French Quarter Festivals added Réveillon on the Rocks, consisting of seasonal craft cocktails. B'réveillon, a brunch réveillon, and the "petite réveillon," offering small plates, were new options beginning in 2018.[40]

How successful has the réveillon promotion been? In the late 1980s and early 1990s, usually only a dozen or so restaurants participated.[41] In 2019, sixty restaurants offered official réveillon menus. Due to the COVID-19 pandemic, the 2020 program dwindled to about twenty restaurants, but began rebuilding with thirty establishments signing up in 2021.[42]

The modern restaurant-centered réveillon is part of a continuum of New Orleans holiday practices. While today's special meals—marketed to tourists and locals alike—are divorced from the private family customs that once nurtured the réveillon, this culinary tourism endeavor resuscitated local historical knowledge of the term. One might even argue that the Holidays New Orleans Style réveillon has in fact reawakened the public réveillon feasting associated with both Christmas and New Year's Eve in the late 1800s and early 1900s. Moreover, while some might view the broadening of the program to include contemporary foods as sacrilege, nineteenth-century réveillons were not frozen in time. As with all Christmas customs, réveillon is a malleable institution, adapting to new ideas.

Historic houses and museums can also follow the example of the Felix Valle State Historic Site in Ste. Genevieve, Missouri, which presents a candlelit réveillon that draws not only on the specific French heritage of the region, which was part of French Illinois Country in the eighteenth century, but also turns out a pan-French spread, with such dishes as gâteau de sirop (a Louisiana cane syrup cake), tourtière (the French Canadian meat pie essential for réveillon), and Provence's thirteen desserts.[43] From New Orleans to Missouri to French Canada, regional foodways—French or otherwise—provide an entrée to Christmas past. Historic sites can serve as essential guides in reviving dormant or fading food traditions that carried deep meaning for generations.

Notes

1. Marie Louise Points, "Clopin-Clopant: A Christmas Fragment of Early Creole Days," *New Orleans Daily Picayune*, December 25, 1892.
2. William D. Crump, *The Christmas Encyclopedia, Third Edition* (Jefferson, NC: McFarland, 2013), 54.
3. "Christmas," in *Larousse Gastronomique*, rev. ed. (New York: Clarkson Potter, 2001), 298.
4. Nichola Fletcher, *Charlemagne's Tablecloth: A Piquant History of Feasting* (New York: St. Martin's Press, 2004), 205.
5. Bruce David Forbes, *Christmas: A Candid History* (Berkeley: University of California Press, 2007), 8.
6. Forbes, *Christmas*, 9; Crump, *Christmas Encyclopedia*, 25, 157, 159, 193; William Kaufman, *The Catholic Cookbook: Traditional Feast and Fast Day Recipes* (New York: Citadel Press, 1965), 13.
7. Matthias Cramer, *Le Vraiment parfait Dictionnaire Roial, Radical, Etimologique, Sinonimique, Phraseologique, et Sintactique, François-Allemand, pour l'une et l'autre Nation*, Vol. 4, R–Z (N.p.: n.p., 1712), s.v. "Reveillon—faire le reveillon."
8. Michelle Perrot and Anne Martin-Fugier, "The Actors—Bourgeois Rituals," in *A History of Private Life, Vol. 4: From the Fires of Revolution to the Great War*, ed. Michelle Perrot, trans. Arthur Goldhammer (Cambridge: Belknap Press of Harvard University Press, 1990), 291.
9. T. W. R., "Christmas and New Year's Day in Paris," *London Society* 5 (January 1864): 9.
10. William Shepard Walsh, *Curiosities of Popular Customs and of Rites, Ceremonies, Observances, and Miscellaneous Antiquities* (New York: Lippincott, 1897), 235.
11. Perrot and Martin-Fugier, "The Actors—Bourgeois Rituals," 290.
12. Crump, *Christmas Encyclopedia*, 187; *Larousse Gastronomique*, 298.
13. Elizabeth T. Baird and State Historical Society of Wisconsin, *Reminiscences of Early Days on Mackinac Island* (Madison: Democrat Printing Company, State Printers, 1898), https://www.loc.gov/item/28012392/; "Pass the Tourtiere, c'est Le Reveillon!, https://www.newengland historicalsociety.com/pass-the-tourtiere-cest-le-reveillon/; Gerard J. Brault, *The French-Canadian Heritage in New England* (Hanover, NH: University Press of New England, 1986), 18, 153.
14. Peggy Scott Laborde and John Magill, *Christmas in New Orleans* (Gretna, LA: Pelican Publishing, 2009), 45–51.
15. Penne L. Restad, *Christmas in America: A History* (New York: Oxford University Press, 1995), 10; Stephen Nissenbaum, *The Battle for Christmas* (New York: Alfred A. Knopf, 1996), 5–8.
16. Restad, *Christmas in America*, 8–15, 38–40.
17. *Acts Passed at the Second Session of the Thirteenth Legislature of the State of Louisiana*, 1838, Act No. 52, 44–45; Robert E. May, *Yuletide in Dixie: Slavery, Christmas, and Southern Memory* (Charlottesville: University of Virginia Press, 2019), 23. Many secondary sources present

Alabama as the first, in 1836, but without a specific citation, and scholars who have researched the matter have failed to turn up evidence. See Restad, *Christmas in America*, 96, 194, n12; Kelly Kazek, *Christmas Tales of Alabama* (Charleston, SC: History Press, 2011). For a list of dates when Christmas was declared a legal holiday (which includes the incorrect Alabama date), see Crump, *Christmas Encyclopedia*, 424–25.

18. *Daily Picayune*, December 25, 1838; December 26, 1839.
19. Harnett Kane, *The Southern Christmas Book—The Full Story from Earliest Times to Present: People, Customs, Conviviality, Carols, Cooking* (New York: Bonanza Books, 1958), 235; Laborde and Magill, *Christmas in New Orleans*, 65–66.
20. Barry Jean Ancelet, Jay Edwards, and Glen Pitre, *Cajun Country* (Jackson: University Press of Mississippi, 1991), 84; Marcelle Bienvenu, Carl A. Brasseaux, and Ryan A. Brasseaux, *Stir the Pot: The History of Cajun Cuisine* (New York: Hippocrene Books, 2005), 100; Perrot and Martin-Fugier, "The Actors—Bourgeois Rituals," 291.
21. Lyle Saxon, et al., comp., *Gumbo Ya-Ya* (1945; reprint, Gretna, LA: Pelican Publishing, 1987), 165.
22. *Daily Picayune*, May 26, 1861.
23. *L'Abeille de la Nouvelle-Orléans*, December 25, 1880; "The Golden Hours," *Daily Picayune*, December 25, 1891.
24. W. A. Rogers, illus., "Christmas Eve in New Orleans—Merrymakers on Canal Street," *Harper's Weekly* (December 30, 1899); Julia Truitt Bishop, "Where Christmas Is Like the Fourth of July," *Ladies' Home Journal* (July 1898), 4.
25. *Daily Picayune*, December 26, 1869.
26. *New Orleans Daily States*, December 25, 1892. See also Laborde and Magill, *Christmas in New Orleans*, 38, 71–74.
27. Roger Baudier, "Creole Lenten Customs," *New Orleans Item*, March 2, 1952.
28. May, *Yuletide in Dixie*, 23–24; "A 'Safe and Sane' Christmas Spent," *New Orleans Daily Picayune*, December 26, 1913; *New Orleans Times-Picayune*, December 13, 1920; *Annual Report of the American Scenic and Historic Preservation Society to the Legislature of the State of New York* New York (N.p.: n.p., 1913), 254.
29. Kane, *Southern Christmas Book*, 228.
30. Louisiana Works Progress Administration, "Christmas Eve—New Year's Day," 1-2, State Library of Louisiana; "Galantine," in *The Oxford Companion to Food*, ed. Alan Davidson (Oxford: Oxford University Press, 1999), 328. For more on daube glacée, see Susan Tucker, "Daube Glacée," in *New Orleans Cuisine: Fourteen Signature Dishes and Their Histories*, edited by Susan Tucker (Jackson: University Press of Mississippi, 2009), 73–86.
31. Eliza Ripley, *Social Life in Old New Orleans; Being Recollections of My Girlhood* (New York: Appleton, 1912), 161.
32. *Frank Leslie's Illustrated Newspaper*, December 12, 1885, 260.
33. Leon E. Soniat Jr., *La Bouche Creole* (Gretna, LA: Pelican Publishing, 1981), 167.
34. *The Picayune's Creole Cook Book* (New Orleans: Picayune, 1901), 434; Andrew F. Smith, *The Turkey: An American Story* (Chicago and Urbana: University of Illinois Press, 2006), 65–66.
35. St. Charles Hotel menu, December 25, 1872, Williams Research Center, Historic New Orleans Collection; *New Orleans Daily Crescent*, December 24, 1857; *The Picayune's Creole Cook Book*, 372–73. "As Viewed by a Woman," *Daily Picayune*, December 25, 1895; "For Women's Eyes," *Daily Picayune*, December 24, 1896; Bishop, "Where Christmas Is Like the Fourth of July"; Eva C. Pasteur, "Women's World," *New Orleans Item*, December 24, 1901.

36. John Pope, "Festival to Celebrate Street Work in Quarter," *Times-Picayune*, November 9, 1983. The French Quarter Festival, under city auspices, expanded its reach in subsequent years under the name French Quarter Festivals. In addition to the original French Quarter Festival, now one of the city's major annual tourist events, the nonprofit sponsors Holidays New-Orleans Style and Satchmo SummerFest, a music festival honoring jazz great Louis Armstrong.

37. Jeskin and Linge, "Noel New Orleans—A French Quarter Holiday: A Conceptual Guideline for Developing Holiday Ambience in the Vieux Carré," June 1985, 11–12, French Quarter Festivals archives.

38. Dartus, personal communication, December 2008; Ann Masson, personal communication, December 2008.

39. Bienvenu, Brasseaux, and Brasseaux, *Stir the Pot*, 47–48.

40. In 2008, French Quarter Festivals granted access to their files as I began researching New Orleans réveillon. I gave my first public presentation on the subject at the Louisiana State Museum on December 18, 2008. In 2012, the organization asked me to serve on the réveillon review committee, and for a decade I served as a historical adviser to the program. Due to staffing changes at the French Quarter Festival and the pandemic, the committee has not met since 2018. On changes in the program, see Susan Langenhennig, "Reveillon Dinners Blend New and Old Traditions," *New Orleans Times-Picayune*, December 11, 2012; Ian McNulty, "Revving Up Reveillon," *New Orleans Advocate*, December 3, 2014, and "Rethinking Reveillon," *New Orleans Advocate*, November 25, 2018.

41. Harsha E. Chacko and Jeffrey D. Schaffer, "The Evolution of a Festival: Creole Christmas in New Orleans," *Tourism Management* (December 1993): 480.

42. Ian McNulty, "A Smaller Réveillon Returns," *New Orleans Advocate*, November 29, 2021.

43. Ste. Genevieve Journal, "Le Reveillon: Customs for an Early French Christmas," December 20, 2019, https://stegenevievejournal.blogspot.com/2019/12/le-reveillon-customs-and-recipes-for.html.

Resources

Laborde, Peggy Scott, and John Magill. *Christmas in New Orleans*. Gretna, LA: Pelican Publishing, 2009.

May, Robert E. *Yuletide in Dixie: Slavery, Christmas, and Southern Memory*. Charlottesville: University of Virginia Press, 2019.

Moon, Michelle. *Interpreting Food at Museums and Historic Sites*. Lanham, MD: Rowman & Littlefield, 2016.

CHAPTER 6

"Presented Me as a Christmas Gift"

Presenting Slavery and Christmas at Southern Historic Sites

Emmanuel Dabney

IN NOVEMBER 1844, twelve-year-old Louis Hughes was sold in Richmond, Virginia, the epicenter of the interstate slave trade in the upper South. Already sold three times before, this time he was alone. Louis was purchased by Edward McGee, a resident of Pontotoc, Mississippi, for $380.

Louis reached the McGee plantation on Christmas Eve 1844 when "Boss took me into the house and into the sitting room, where all the family were assembled, and presented me as a Christmas gift to the madam, his wife."[1] He slept on the dining room floor that night and awakened the next morning to the McGee family and relatives ready for eggnog before breakfast. Louis served them and "helped myself, after the service was finished, and I was delighted, for I had never tasted anything so fine before." Having been in smaller slaveholding households in Virginia, he was shocked by the number of enslaved people on the McGee plantation. He remembered the dinner for the white household and the Christmas rations given to the farm laborers who received "a pint of flour of which they made biscuit, which were called Billy Seldom, because biscuits were very rare with them" and "a piece of bacon or fat meat, from which they got the shortening for their biscuit." The field laborers got a four-day Christmas rest, which some people did extra work to net "fifty cents a day for chopping."[2]

The break was not because McGee was being benevolent, but rather to have all the field hands present for the labor that went into the cotton plantation immediately after Christmas.

Louis Hughes's first Christmas in Mississippi is contrasted throughout his narrative published thirty-two years after his emancipation with the horrors of slavery. Many recollections from those formerly enslaved have memories of Christmas, but, as Robert E. May commands us, Americans need "to divest themselves of all romantic illusions about Christmas in slave times."[3] Numerous studies in plantation tourism have called out disturbing and ahistorical tours that focus on the predominately white, slaveholding families in surviving "big houses" that visitors often pay to access. These tours often do not integrate the story of slavery and the people who were in bondage well and sometimes not at all. Routinely, historic sites "have staged their seasonal events as sensory delights of sight, sound, taste, and ubiquitous 'holiday cheer' centered on decorative touches and master-class dining, musical, and gifting customs."[4] It is what I call "the cider and cookies program." These almost always feature hot apple (nonalcoholic) cider, cookies, fresh garlands dripping with fruit ala Colonial Williamsburg's Colonial Revival decorations, and tours or other gatherings of visitors and staff in discussion about how the elite family celebrated Christmas with alcohol and food, out of town guests, and church services.

Interpreting Christmas at Southern historic sites that have connections with slavery can go, and too often has gone, down a destructive path. This essay centers on how historic sites can improve on interpreting Christmas for white and black Southerners. I hope that the advice offered here will provide more than just a candle's glow on how to handle your site's holiday programming.

Step 1: Stop

It may surprise readers that my first bit of advice is to stop doing what you have been doing. Decorating with pineapples, apples, oranges, and lemons? Putting up a Christmas tree at your eighteenth-century site? You may now be scratching your head and asking, "Why are we doing this?" This would be the time to pause your holiday programming.

Humans struggle with letting go of traditions and it is even more difficult for holidays. Dr. Sean Brotherson wrote, "A key benefit of family traditions is predictability."[5] Predictability is a reason for some historic sites to keep doing what they have done because it may drive repeat visitation from some of your most dedicated visitors. However, predictability can also pose a problem for historic sites. Traditionally, the experiences of black people have been downplayed, silenced, or ridiculed at plantation sites. This has created levels of distrust among some visitors and low visitation numbers by black people and often by other nonwhite people. Therefore, doing the same Christmas program that has been done for the past several years or decades may continue to alienate an increasingly diverse America from your site.

At this point, ask yourself and the staff the following:

1. What is the mission of the historic site? How does Christmas-themed programming help advance the mission?

2. Does this programming only appeal to the traditional and/or repeat visitor to the site?

3. Am I and/or my staff/volunteers prepared to handle discussions about slavery and racism in America's past? Am I and/or the staff/volunteers prepared for visitors to draw connections to today? Can we reasonably decide when to have a meaningful discussion over visitor concerns or agree to disagree and respectfully disengage for our and others' health and safety?

4. How do we engage with interpreting slavery beyond December?

5. Do we know the historical information well enough to put on a meaningful program?

Answers to these questions will vary based on the site in question. The questions, however, really should not vary from whether you are incorporating Christmas into a guided tour routinely given, a special program, or virtual interpretation.

Step 2: Research

Research should be firmly based on facts obtained through a thorough examination of primary and secondary sources. It is common for long-term employees or volunteers to perpetuate site lore, often shared orally or occasionally found in staff/volunteer books. However, best practice encourages an exploration of what can be accurately understood about the specific location being interpreted.

If they are available, the documents of the plantation-owning family serve as an excellent starting point for primary source research. Many historic sites have these papers. Despite often being fragmented, they can provide valuable insights into historical Christmas activities. Staff at Thomas Jefferson's Monticello near Charlottesville, Virginia, have created a digital encyclopedia page titled "Christmas" (see figure 6.1). This page documents not only Jefferson but his family's correspondence and that of overseers. Within these documents there is a revelation of the frivolity the Jefferson family enjoyed, but also business expenses that needed to be handled as the year closed. This research compilation also shares the desires of the enslaved community to be with family disconnected on parts of Jefferson's lands, to drink, and their position within America's slave society to be used as hired laborers for others.[6]

A lesser-known site is Melrose, John T. McMurran's presentation house in Natchez, Mississippi, now stewarded by the National Park Service. In Melrose's historic furnishings report, the author documents Christmas activities from the 1840s to the late 1860s that come from the McMurran family papers housed at Louisiana State University. This included the McMurrans' use of Christmas trees in the antebellum years to the doling out of clothing and accessories as well as upgraded food supplies to the enslaved community.[7] George Washington's Mount Vernon admits that its documentation on aspects of Christmas for the Washingtons and the enslaved community is not as plentiful as other aspects of life there. Yet, the employees there have taken what is available and use it to interpret the site to visitors.[8] Not every site is fortunate enough to have this level of documentation. In these cases, primary source evidence can be supplemented with local, regional, and colonial or state contextual information to provide a more complete picture.

Christmas

As it is for many people today, Christmas was for Thomas Jefferson a time for family and friends and for celebrations, or in Jefferson's word, "merriment." In 1762, he described Christmas as "the day of greatest mirth and jollity." [1] Although no documents exist to tell us how, or if, Jefferson decorated Monticello for the holidays, Jefferson noted the festive scene created by his grandchildren. On Christmas Day 1809, he said of eight-year-old grandson Francis Wayles Eppes (shown at right): "he is at this moment running about with his cousins bawling out 'a merry christmas' 'a christmas gift' Etc." [2]

During Jefferson's time, holiday celebrations were much more modest than those we know today. Socializing and special

Figure 6.1. Thomas Jefferson's Monticello has a digital encyclopedia page titled "Christmas," which documents not only Jefferson but his family's correspondence and that of overseers.

Kenmore, located in Fredericksburg, Virginia, is most notably recognized for its exquisite plaster ceilings. Originally the residence of Betty Washington Lewis, George Washington's sister, and her husband, Fielding Lewis, the interpretive period of this house is rooted in the Revolutionary War era. This aligns with the timeline of the Lewises moving into their home in 1775, situating it within the historical context of Fredericksburg and Spotsylvania County. Sadly, there is no trove of Lewis family papers. Most of the work Meghan Budinger, curator for the George Washington Fredericksburg Foundation, and other staff do on slavery comes from Fielding's 1781 probate inventory, a "Divvy List" written by his widow in 1782, a public auction list, and a final disposition list both completed in 1798.[9] Still, the documents provide names of the men, women, and children Fielding and Betty enslaved. They do not directly reference Christmas, but it gives the interpretive staff names to identify who was around and doing work within the surviving house but also elsewhere.

Colonial contextual work completed by former employee Joseph Ziarko used royal Governor John Murry, 4th Earl of Dunmore's emancipation proclamation, which had been printed in November 1775, just one month before the Lewises celebrated Christmas in their newly finished house. Lord Dunmore declared within the document "all indentured Servants, Negroes, or others, (appertaining to Rebels,) free that are able and willing to bear Arms."[10]

Though it is unknown if any of those enslaved by the Lewises fled to Norfolk that autumn, Ziarko notes slaveholders were furious at this idea. They would have known that one white indentured servant escaped from the Lewises' estate.[11] Meghan Budinger's research continues to mine fragmentary evidence of the people enslaved by the Lewises. In a 1794 letter, Betty wrote to her famous brother that two enslaved men had left the estate a few days before Christmas of 1793. The *Virginia Gazette* advertisement she placed for Stephen and Guile found that the men left on December 20, 1793. Budinger's research taps into the labor differences between field hands, domestic servants, and those hired out. She makes a good case that the two men likely were field hands who took advantage of a short Christmas break to make their escape.[12]

Numerous enslaved people used the Christmas season to escape. A famous Christmas-time flight includes Harriet Tubman's December 24, 1854, return to Maryland to rescue her brothers from slavery. Another was William and Ellen Craft, when Ellen disguised herself as a white man (she being sufficiently light skinned to pass) while her husband William portrayed her personal servant as they traveled north to freedom.[13] Two factors contributed to why people chose to escape during this time of year. First, enslaved individuals typically had some discretionary time. Second, the longer nights provided more hours of darkness, facilitating their flight. For example, Samuel took his leave on Christmas Day from Charles Yancey in North Carolina. Yancey believed Samuel was headed to Philadelphia or New York.[14] Newspaper advertisements serve as a crucial research instrument. Even if your historical site lacks direct documentation of enslaved people seeking freedom during December, references to neighboring and regional locations in these ads may imply that the enslaved individuals at your site might have been aiding others in their pursuit of liberty.

Consider interpreting the experiences of enslaved individuals who were hired from others or hired out from your property. Slave hiring often commenced around New Year's Day. This practice served as an additional income source for those who hired out the enslaved, further profiting from their labor. In some cases, those who were hired could negotiate their own terms or arrange for direct payment for extra work. Typically, these hiring contracts concluded around Christmas Eve. Interpreters can then delve into the contrasting emotions experienced during this period—the joy of reuniting with family and friends during Christmas, juxtaposed with the pain of New Year's Day.

Use slave narratives as a part of your research. The earliest of these were published prior to the Civil War and are people who escaped from bondage. Others were published after the Civil War, when more formerly enslaved people gained literacy. The University of North Carolina's "North American Slave Narratives" project is a free resource with hundreds of narratives covering the South.[15] The Library of Congress has digitally published "Born in Slavery: Slave Narratives from the Federal Writers' Project, 1936 to 1938" (see figure 6.2). This website includes the interviews, and their recollections can be useful for understanding children in bondage and traditions passed down from older people about life within slavery. There are people, however, who remember Christmas while enslaved.[16]

These narratives have some weaknesses because most interviewees were children before emancipation or were recalling some seven decades in their pasts. Additional limitations exist in whether the interviewer was white or black. Formerly enslaved interviewees may have feared telling the truth could rupture their income and housing.[17] Still, the narratives can provide context or some insight into what may have been happening at specific times and with regional or cash crop variations.

Time off was a critical part of the enslaved community's thoughts for Christmastime. How much time off depended primarily upon the slaveholder. Generally, as Robert May has

Figure 6.2. The Library of Congress website, "Born in Slavery: Slave Narratives from the Federal Writers' Project, 1936 to 1938" includes the interviews with people who remember Christmas while enslaved.

found, the time off was "two-and-a-half days to four days." There are no plantation records, journals, or diaries referencing burning Yule Logs to govern when enslaved people returned to work.[18] On Louisiana's sugar plantations, work sometimes continued at Christmas so as to not lose the cane juice.[19]

Enslaved people often used the break for weddings, since otherwise enslaved agricultural laborers only had Sundays off. Domestic servants and those tending animals worked seven days a week. Nevertheless, Christmas became an important time when many gathered. Enslaved people resisted, acquiesced, and persisted in marriages, and interpreting this brings their humanity into focus and shows slaveholders did not legally recognize slave marriages but socially recognized them.

Do not fear the Civil War and its aftermath. Your site may have a particularly powerful story surrounding Christmas during the Civil War or after the war. If your best examples of Christmas are not from the colonial or antebellum periods, there is no sense in trying to make your square peg fit into a round hole.

Step 3: Setting the Stage

Gregory Weidman's essay in this book provides recommendations for decoration. Consider other ways to create a mood by interpreting the spaces of the enslaved. At the John Marshall House in Richmond, Virginia, for example, visitors can peer into a small room under the stairs to learn about Robin Spurlock, Marshall's enslaved butler. This room was appropriately arranged as a work room with a reproduction broom, period table, fireplace tools, a pitcher, soap, and other small household items. This was a workspace and not intended for show with faux pine garlands, holly, and boxwood.

In North Carolina, scene setting at Stagville and Somerset Place includes representing Jonkonnu. This unique North Carolina and Caribbean islands' tradition of performance and dance has been documented in the Bahamas as early as 1801.[20] At Stagville there are individuals who perform this activity in a special event in front of the original slave quarters. Stagville social media posts note that the site has a documented history of Jonkonnu.[21]

At Somerset Place, a reconstructed slave quarter interprets a married couple, Lewis and Judy, in 1843. On an interior wall hangs a set of horns, a nod to Jonkonnu, where enslaved people donned costumes using animal parts for their performance in front of the slaveholding family. This is not a true decoration, but its presence pays homage to a historic account from 1850.[22] Historians do not have a full understanding of how Jonkonnu ended up being present in North Carolina but absent largely elsewhere in the mainland United States. Yet historic sites in North Carolina with connections with slavery have an opportunity to discuss it and make Caribbean connections.

Food is and was an important part of Christmas. Start with the surviving records of the issuing of rations among the enslaved community at your site. Ask what can be known or discovered about gardens that the enslaved community created. Use of contemporary journals can help shed some insight. For example, *De Bow's Review* has the plantation rules of South Carolina rice planter P. C. Weston.[23] Weston stated that the Christmas rations he doled out "[t]o each person doing any work, and each superannuated person" was three pounds of fresh meat, three pounds of salted meat, one quart of molasses, four quarts of short grain rice, and a half bushel of salt. Nonworking children were each given one and a half pounds of fresh meat, one and a half pounds of salt, one pint of molasses, and two quarts of short grain rice.[24] Some slaveholders allowed enslaved people to drink alcohol, particularly whiskey, during the holiday season.[25]

If you are fortunate to have slave quarters on site, you can represent the meals of enslaved people through faux foods. Representing food in the "big house" is also important. It seems many sites have easily incorporated faux foods in dining rooms but consider representing preparation and cleanup in kitchens and dining rooms. Foodways and the opposing diets and labor of the enslaved community versus those who owned the land is an easy way to highlight the stark realities of slavery.

Step 4: Do Not Abandon Your Principal Themes

A crucial consideration for any special event is to maintain focus on your primary themes. By sharing my experiences from two historical sites, I aim to illustrate how you can effectively weave your primary themes into your Christmas-themed tours.

Holiday programming cannot upend the site's important stories. When sociologist Jennifer L. Eichstedt and historian Stephen Small visited the John Marshall House in Richmond, Virginia, more than twenty years ago, they rated the tour as engaging in "symbolic annihilation."[26] Eichstedt and Small defined symbolic annihilation as the complete erasure of the lives and experiences of enslaved people or the effort to minimize the experiences of those once enslaved.[27] Two decades after the publication of their book, visitors today should find the site attempting to move toward Eichstedt and Small's version of "relative incorporation/in between."

The authors describe relative incorporation as a site that presents guests information about slavery at the site, details about the enslaved people at the site, the subjugation of black people and the socioeconomic power of those who enslaved black people; and slaveholders are complicated beyond romantic, hospitable, and political persons.[28] When I recently visited in December, the guide at the Marshall House welcomed us and noted where historic outbuildings once stood—including a kitchen, where Henry prepared the Marshall family's food. The guide included that Christmas would have been an especially busy time for enslaved domestic servants as guests came often.

The tour took us into the interior where we saw the principal rooms befitting an elite family. We exited back into the hall where we rotated about to see the workspace of Robin Spurlock, Marshall's enslaved butler and personal servant. The guide noted this was a busy space in the house for Robin and other enslaved domestic servants. Here we were told that Robin was gifted when John Marshall married Mary "Polly" Ambler on January 3, 1783. Though the guide did not mention it, in the 1780s, many elite Americans continued to celebrate Christmas until January 6. The Marshalls' lives changed that year and so too did Robin Spurlock's. Robin's work in polishing silver, trimming candle wicks, and other chores were highlighted as taking place here.

We learned Robin's wife was Mary and they had two sons, Jack and Robin Jr., and a daughter, Agnes. Spurlock lived in a house in what is now Jackson Ward, though it was not something he owned in his own name. A visitor asked about his surname and received a truthful answer that it was not known how Robin got his last name, but it predated John Marshall's wedding. In Marshall's will, Spurlock was offered two versions of emancipation or one of enslavement.

Our guide explained that the compensated emancipation Marshall offered was $100 if Spurlock moved to Liberia or $50 if he remained in Virginia. If he declined these offers, he would have to select one of the Marshall children to remain enslaved by. Robin chose to remain with one of Marshall's daughters and her husband so as not to be separated from family.

As I revisited Somerset Place, the staff continues to use a combination of recorded oral histories of enslaved people, documentary records from the Collins family, local and regional information from nearby plantations and towns, and archaeology to tell the stories of the enslaved and free people who lived and labored on the estate. Much of this work is due to Dorothy Spruill Redford, a descendant of enslaved people at Somerset Place. Redford spent a decade researching her family's genealogical connection with Somerset Place, organized a reunion with over two thousand descendants of Somerset's enslaved community in 1986 and served as the site's director in 1990 until 2008.

My guide was determined to not let the Christmas decorations distract from the multitude of voices and experiences at the site. We discussed the late eighteenth-century history of the site being transformed by eighty Africans, stolen by Josiah Collins and his business partners from West Africa and brought to North Carolina. The Africans worked with American-born enslaved people and white overseers digging a canal to connect Lake Phelps and the Scuppernong River. This forced labor benefited the absentee owners and caused much physical and mental anguish to the enslaved people there.

It was Josiah Collins III who became a resident-owner and had the surviving house at the site constructed for him and his family. Visitors spend considerable time exploring the grounds outside the fence where the Collins family placed themselves with a view of the lake, and as was evident once a visitor is inside, with multiple points of observation of the enslaved community and the hired white overseers. Various reconstructed buildings help give visitors an understanding of how most Somerset Place's residents were living. Few overt references to Christmas were made, though one story is haunting.

Rebecca Hathaway (later Drew), born about 1825, was fifteen when she was brought to Somerset Place to work as a field hand. That year at Christmas, she left the estate to go see her mother in Edenton. The temperatures were well below freezing and she got caught. The overseer put her in the stocks located in front of his house. Her feet were so badly frozen that her lower legs had to be amputated; but she survived, married, and had children. She died in 1901. Today, visitors can see a re-creation of the stocks and a reconstruction of the overseer's house at the site. Having previously visited in the summer, I found that Somerset has not dramatically altered its usual tour for the holiday.

In the case of Somerset Place, their dedication includes their social media pages. Their staff on the site's Instagram account posted daily about Christmas from December 20 to December 27, 2021. These posts highlighted the celebratory and religious events of the Collins family, who attended church, ate sumptuous meals; and two of Josiah Collins III and his wife Mary's sons were married during the Christmas season. They also examined the experiences of the enslaved community such as Rebecca Hathaway's marriage to Virgil Drew during the Christmas holiday in 1855. Another post detailed the enslaved community's participation in Jonkonnu.[29]

I believe in sharing the truth about the past that is the totality of events that occurred before a singular moment, whether we acknowledge them or not. It is our responsibility as stewards of these sites of enslavement to tell it like it was. I agree with Rex Ellis that we cannot avoid this subject matter "if we are to understand America's past, grapple with America's present, and realistically plot America's future."[30] In short, clove-decorated oranges are a fragrant stench often used to mask black people's resilience, joy, and sufferings throughout their years in bondage and what freedom truly meant to them. Historic sites that fail to integrate the truth of slavery and the holidays are giving their guests a rotten representation of the past.

Notes

1. Louis Hughes, *Thirty Years a Slave: From Bondage to Freedom* (Milwaukee: South Side Printing Company, 1897), 13, https://docsouth.unc.edu/fpn/hughes/hughes.html.
2. Hughes, *Thirty Years a Slave*, 16.
3. Robert E. May, *Yuletide in Dixie: Slavery, Christmas, and Southern Memory* (Charlottesville: University of Virginia Press, 2019), 11.
4. May, *Yuletide in Dixie*, 244.
5. Sean Brotherson, "Differing Family Traditions at the Holiday Season," *North Dakota State University*, https://www.ag.ndsu.edu/cff/posts/differing-family-traditions-at-the-holiday-season (accessed January 11, 2021).
6. Mindy Keyes Black, Elizabeth Chew, and Dianne Swann-Wright, "Christmas," Monticello, https://www.monticello.org/site/research-and-collections/christmas (accessed January 12, 2022).
7. Carol Petravage, *Melrose Historic Furnishings Report* (Washington, DC: National Park Service, 2004), 23–24, 62, 68, 71, 102, 119, 128.
8. Mary V. Thompson, "Christmas at Mount Vernon," https://www.mountvernon.org/library/digitalhistory/digital-encyclopedia/article/christmas-at-mount-vernon/ (accessed January 12, 2022).
9. Meghan Budinger, "Abraham and the Ropewalkers: Finding Large Stories in Small Details," *Lives and Legacies*, https://livesandlegaciesblog.org/2019/11/06/abraham-and-the-ropewalkers-finding-large-stories-in-small-details/ (accessed January 12, 2022).
10. Joseph Ziarko, "A Christmas of Uncertainty, December 1775," *Lives and Legacies*, https://livesandlegaciesblog.org/2015/12/16/a-christmas-of-uncertainty-december-1775/.
11. Ziarko, "A Christmas of Uncertainty."
12. Meghan Budinger, "The Christmastime Escape of Stephen and Guile," *Lives and Legacies*, https://livesandlegaciesblog.org/2020/12/20/the-christmastime-escape-of-stephen-and-guile/.
13. Kate Clifford Larson, *Bound for the Promised Land: Harriet Tubman, Portrait of an American Hero* (New York: Ballantine Books, 2003), 110–19; William Craft, *Running a Thousand Miles for Freedom; or, the Escape of William and Ellen Craft from Slavery* (London: William Tweedle, 1860), https://docsouth.unc.edu/neh/craft/craft.html (accessed April 25, 2022).
14. Charles Yancey, "30 Dollars Reward," *Raleigh Register and North Carolina Weekly Advertiser*, January 9, 1829, https://dlas.uncg.edu/notices/notice/678 (accessed April 27, 2022).
15. Documenting the American South, "North American Slave Narratives," https://docsouth.unc.edu/neh/ (accessed January 12, 2022).
16. Library of Congress, "Born in Slavery: Slave Narratives from the Federal Writers' Project, 1936 to 1938," https://www.loc.gov/collections/slave-narratives-from-the-federal-writers-project-1936-to-1938/ (accessed January 12, 2022).
17. Library of Congress, "The Limitations of the Slave Narrative Collection," https://www.loc.gov/collections/slave-narratives-from-the-federal-writers-project-1936-to-1938/articles-and-essays/introduction-to-the-wpa-slave-narratives/limitations-of-the-slave-narrative-collection/ (accessed April 24, 2022).
18. Library of Congress, "The Limitations," 37–43.
19. May, *Yuletide in Dixie*, 37–38.

20. For more on Jonkonnu, see Elijah Gaddis, "Jonkonnu: Black Performance in White Spaces," https://docsouth.unc.edu/commland/features/essays/johnkonnu-2/ (accessed January 11, 2022).

21. Historic Stagville (@historicstagville), "Celebrate Jonkonnu, A Remarkable African American Holiday Tradition," https://www.instagram.com/p/CW_N4fuuX2O/ (accessed April 20, 2022).

22. Somerset Place State Historic Site (@somersetplaceshs), "Although Jonkonnu Illustrates How Enslaved People," December 24, 2021, https://www.instagram.com/p/CX415C2KjZ2/ (accessed April 20, 2022).

23. Available through *Making of America* at https://quod.lib.umich.edu/m/moagrp/index.html.

24. P. C. Weston, "Management of a South Plantation," *De Bow's Review* (New Orleans, 1857), 22, ser. 3: 38, available online at https://babel.hathitrust.org/cgi/pt?id=iau.31858033648282 (accessed April 19, 2022).

25. For an example, see Foby, "Management of Servants," *Southern Cultivator* (Augusta, GA: 1853), 11, 8: 228, available online https://books.google.com/books?id=xGxNAAAAYAAJ &newbks=1&newbks_redir=0&printsec=frontcover#v=onepage&q&f=false (accessed April 19, 2022).

26. Jennifer L. Eichstedt and Stephen Small, *Representations of Slavery* (Washington, DC: Smithsonian Institution Press, 2002), 274.

27. Eichstedt and Small, *Representations of Slavery*, 107.

28. Eichstedt and Small, *Representations of Slavery*, 203–4.

29. Somerset Place State Historic Site (@somersetplaceshs). "How We Celebrate Christmas in the 21st Century," Instagram, December 20, 2021, https://www.instagram.com/p/CXuitt 1Ikqt/; Somerset Place State Historic Site, "As an Elite Southern Family" December 21, 2021, https://www.instagram.com/p/CXxApDuBnLh/; Somerset Place State Historic Site, "Although the Christmas Season Was Short," December 22, 2021, https://www.instagram .com/p/CXzlYExt467/; Somerset Place State Historic Site, "Many of the Traditions We Associate," December 23, 2021, https://www.instagram.com/p/CX2KInpPyof/; Somerset Place State Historic Site, "Although Jonkonnu Illustrates How Enslaved People," December 24, 2021, https://www.instagram.com/p/CX415C2KjZ2/; Somerset Place State Historic Site, "The Collins Family Were Devout Episcopalians," December 26, 2021, https://www.insta gram.com/p/CX9xvncpMrn/; Somerset Place State Historic Site, "Ultimately, in Granting a Christmas Holiday," December 27, 2021, https://www.instagram.com/p/CYAdYhftpAx/.

30. Rex M. Ellis, "Foreword," in *Interpreting Slavery at Museums and Historic Sites*, edited by Kristin Gallas and James DeWolf Perry (Lanham, MD: Rowman & Littlefield, 2015).

Resources

Eichstedt, Jennifer L. and Stephen Small. *Representations of Slavery: Race and Ideology in Southern Plantation Museums*. Washington, DC: Smithsonian Institution Press, 2002.

Gallas, Kristin L. and James DeWolf Perry, eds. *Interpreting Slavery at Museums and Historic Sites*. Lanham, MD: Rowman & Littlefield, 2015.

Hunter, Tera W. *Bound in Wedlock: Slave and Free Black Marriage in the Nineteenth Century*. Cambridge, MA: Belknap Press, 2019.

Kaye, Anthony E. *Joining Places: Slave Neighborhoods in the Old South.* Chapel Hill: University of North Carolina Press, 2009.

Martin, Jonathan D. *Divided Mastery: Slave Hiring in the American South.* Cambridge, MA: Harvard University Press, 2009.

May, Robert E. *Yuletide in Dixie: Slavery, Christmas, and Southern Memory.* Charlottesville: University of Virginia Press, 2019.

Parry, Tyler D. *Jumping the Broom: The Surprising Multicultural Origins of a Black Wedding Ritual.* Chapel Hill: University of North Carolina Press, 2020.

Zaborney, John J. *Slaves for Hire: Renting Enslaved Laborers in Antebellum Virginia.* Baton Rouge: Louisiana State University Press, 2012.

CHAPTER 7

We're Getting a Rocket for Christmas!

Gift Giving and the Space Race

Erik Greenberg

A N EXAMINATION of the meaning of Christmas gifts at a particular moment in American history, while it makes no explicit reference to museum work (at least not until its conclusion), points to ways in which museums might focus more time and resources on exhibitions about Christmas gift giving. Indeed, one of our fearless editors suggested it may serve as an exhibition script—an idea that I like very much. This chapter offers my colleagues future food for thought about how one might study Christmas gifts of the past (or at least their advertising) as a tool toward understanding, explaining, and exhibiting various cultural histories of American Christmas. This example is a study of the Space Race of the 1950s and its attendant "Military Industrial Christmases."[1]

The Launch of Sputnik and American Cold War Anxiety

In October of 1957, the Soviet Union launched a small, basketball-sized satellite into orbit around the Earth, thus opening a new chapter in the Cold War. They named their metallic projectile "Sputnik," Russian for companion. As the historian Walter Hixson has observed, the technologically crude "*Sputnik* carried little strategic significance, yet the launch stunned the American public and excited fears that the nation was in danger of losing its advantage in missile and space technology." People spoke of a "Paradox of Plenty," an existential fear that the prosperity of the postwar years had rendered Americans soft, lazy, hedonistic, and devoid of national purpose.[2]

Over the next three years (1957–1959) American scientists proved unable to surpass their Soviet counterparts' achievements, and the nation's concerns grew. Prominent Cold War figures like John F. Kennedy and Lyndon Baines Johnson called on Americans to develop greater knowledge of and facility with Space Age technology and the country took notice. Early in 1958, for example, directors of the University of California's extension program were taken by surprise when a class on space technology originally scheduled for 400 students enrolled 2,900 people statewide. Amateur astronomy clubs sprouted up throughout the country from Westchester County, New York, to Wichita, Kansas, and beyond.[3]

Many of the want ads of the period articulated a significant link between surpassing Russia's achievements in space and an individual's economic prosperity. And some Americans, like Douglas aerospace engineer R. L. Johnson, feared the worst, claiming, for example, that our moon would someday serve as a battleground for World War III, as Russia and the United States "engaged in a struggle to obtain overwhelming retaliatory advantage of lunar missile bases for protection of earth nations."[4]

I suspect that the story of how the launch of Sputnik frightened the American public and the consequent Space Race that ensued is not particularly surprising to those who are familiar with twentieth-century American history. Within four years of the launch, the recently elected president John F. Kennedy called on the nation to focus their technological efforts toward landing a man on the moon by the close of the 1960s, which it did. What may prove surprising was the way in which American fears over the USSR's success in space resulted in a notable change in the way advertisers framed the purchase and consumption of goods.

As this chapter argues, the close of the 1950s witnessed a unique approach to advertising that linked the most domestic and mundane of goods with the lofty goals and objectives of the Space Race. These tactics proved visible and significant during the nation's Christmas celebrations. After all, as historians of American Christmas have observed, by the late nineteenth century, Christmas gift giving became a significant—if not the most significant—aspect of American Christmas celebrations. The centrality of Christmas presents would become even more clear in the twentieth century as the nation shifted from a producer to consumer society—by which I mean a societal system built around the idea that the purchase and consumption of goods are the defining characteristic of our economy, political discourse, and policy, as well as our broader culture and personal identities.[5]

I have termed this connection between Space Age technology and American Christmas advertising as the Military Industrial Christmas, and as I will argue below, this phenomenon was more than a bald-faced ploy to sell goods, though I suspect old-fashioned hucksterism played a part. Still, the context of the moment and the advertising that ensued revealed a great deal about the nation's hopes and fears. As America proved unable to surpass Soviet achievements in space, advertisers increasingly stressed the connection between consumer goods and the Space Race, a phenomenon that reached its apotheosis during the Christmas season. This was true of advertisements for boys' toys (after all, gender disparities in education, employment, and other elements of society were even greater at the close of the 1950s than they are today); but we can find similar examples in advertising for other goods as well.

The Military Industrial Christmas: Boys' Toys

Christmas advertising for boys' toys occurred within a larger societal debate about the efficacy of American education. In the wake of Sputnik's launch, prominent Americans argued that a U.S. victory in the nascent Space Race required improvements in math and science education and that training students in these subjects had become a critical component of the national security strategy.[6] While many obsessed over the quality of math and science education in the nation's schools, others claimed that such learning should begin at home. Several commentators promoted an experiential approach to learning science, recounting in various articles how prominent scientists educated their own children at home. These pieces frequently suggested that the entire world was a classroom, but they also promoted science-based toys as an important component of a child's education.

Press reports of the age make clear that manufacturers of the period responded to Americans' demands for science-based toys. Commenting on the wide array of science toys, for example, the *New York Times* noted that children interested in learning math and science would find as much fun in "proper equipment . . . as little tykes do in blocks and balls."[7] A *Times* headline from 1957 proclaimed "TOYS GO OUT OF THIS WORLD." On the other side of the country, one *Los Angeles Times* story noted that "[i]f toy manufacturers and shops about town have their way this Christmas science education will begin in the nursery." A 1959 *New York Times* headline on the International Toy Fair offered, perhaps, a more ominous observation when that headline proclaimed that science education "Cloaked in the Guise of New Toys Invades the World of Children."[8]

The military industrial promotion of "educational" boys' toys took several forms. While some ads merely included simple phrases like "educational," "Terrific Toy for Science-Minded boys," or "greatest scientific toy achievement in a decade," other advertisers advanced their message by linking such playthings with aerospace professionals and educators. One advertisement for the *Thrills in Space* model kit proudly announced that it was designed by no less an authority than science writer and rocketry expert Willy Ley. Virtually every advertisement for the *Alpha I Ballistic Missile* model, a frequently advertised toy throughout 1958–1960, included the phrases "designed by real missile engineers" and "educator approved."

Christmas ads for the Revell Model Company's *Rocket to the Moon* proclaimed it was "scientist designed." The same technique was used in ads for the Galaxy Model Company's *Aerobee Hi* rocket, which asserted that its product bore the "Seal of Approval of the National Association of Rocketry."

By connecting Space Age toys to technical and educational professionals, these Christmas ads reinforced existing links between science education and future employment in the military industrial complex. Indeed, one piece for the Gilbert Toy Company prominently

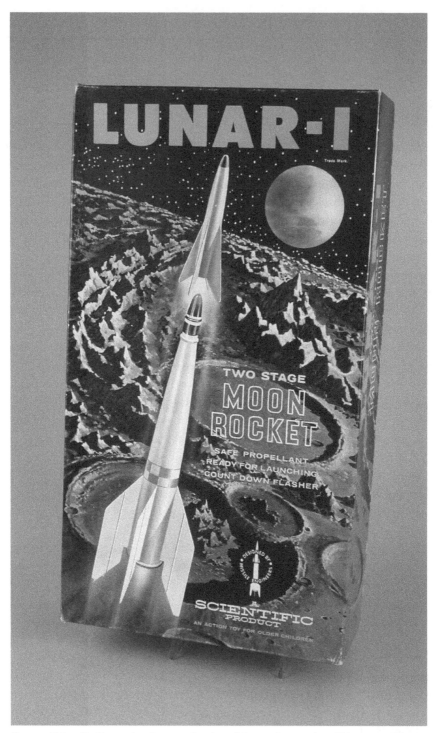

Figure 7.1.   Both packaging and advertising of popular Chistmas gifts in the 1950s and 1960s reinforced links between science education and future employment in the military industrial complex. The Lunar-1 Two Stage Moon Rocket (1960) proclaimed that it was designed by missile engineers and was a "Scientific Product." Courtesy of The Strong, Rochester, New York.

displayed several science- and engineering-based gifts under the heading of "Career Build-ing Toys (see figure 7.1)."[9]

While the Gilbert Company may have advertised its children's gifts as "toys," other military industrial ads avoided the term, insisting instead that their gifts were educational tools. A prominent full-page advertisement for the Young Readers of America series offer-ing a free telescope and microscope with every purchase, reminded readers that such items were not toys.

The 1958 advertisement for the *Aerobee Hi* rocket model was even more forceful, assert-ing in bold print that it was "Not a Toy—But a Scientific Model." A 1958 *Los Angeles Times* advertisement for a scale model of Cape Canaveral referred to the item not as a toy, but as a "Rocket Research Center for the Boy Who Loves the Future." Yet another 1958 ad, for Monogram Models' Complete Missile Collection, noted that though their "identical scale models" were "for fun," they were also "for study," a useful tool for understanding the "news from Cape Canaveral." And a 1960 piece for the Ideal Company's *Astro Base* lunar rocket promoted the model as a "space ship." Such advertisements reinforced the societal belief in the importance of bringing scientific education into the home.[10]

Military Industrial Christmas ads often reinforced a toy's realism by linking it directly to branches of the military or active military projects. Advertisements of the period often asserted that the missile or rocket in question was "just like the Army's" or "Navy's." The Ideal Toy Company's advertising strategy exemplified this technique. Throughout 1958–1960, the company offered a wide array of "authentic" military and aerospace toys. A 1958 advertisement for its *Countdown* missile base, for example, proclaimed, "An electronic mis-sile launching base just like the Army's." Other Ideal ads touted exact replicas of the Army's atomic cannon and "Honest John" missile.[11]

Nor was Ideal the only company to stress the realism or authenticity of its playthings. Other toy model companies made known the connection between their models and ongoing military and aerospace projects. Hawk Models advertised scale replicas of the army's Jupiter C and Atlas rockets and the air force's mid-range Martin Matador Missile, complete with launching pad. In one 1958 full-page ad, the Revell Hobby Kits Company featured models for six separate military industrial projects including Douglas Aerospace's Nike Hercules rocket, Martin's Lacrosse missile launcher, and Corvair's Terrier missiles. Also in 1958, the Monogram Model Company advertised an entire U.S. missile arsenal, which included most of America's aerospace projects.[12]

Whether by promoting a toy's educational qualities or stressing the similarities between their playthings and ongoing military industrial projects, companies like Gilbert, Ideal, Revell, Monogram, and others positioned their products as opportunities to participate in the national quest for space travel and aerospace dominance (see figure 7.2). These ads reveal much about America's Cold War fears over the launch of *Sputnik* as well as a sense of urgency that, in some sense, demanded the participation of all (or at least most) citizens in this national quest linking science and consumerism. While little girls were largely excluded from this pursuit, other Americans were not. Indeed, both men and women, in varying degrees, were also encouraged to develop a proper relationship with Space Age technology through the purchase of consumer goods.

For Grown Ups

Unlike promotional material for boys' toys, Military Industrial Christmas ads geared toward men and women rarely promoted an item's educational qualities, nor did they highlight explicit links between consumer goods and ongoing projects in the military industrial complex. Such narrative strains were unnecessary. Thanks to the news stories and want ads of the period, most adults were already well aware of the material and security benefits of participating in the Space Race and of purchasing Military Industrial Christmas gifts. The military industrial themes one does find in the era's Christmas ads followed several important narrative strains.

One of the most pervasive forms of military industrial advertising was the use of Space Age names for products that had nothing to do with outer space. Radios and televisions proved one of the most common examples of this phenomenon. The Packard Bell Corporation, itself a significant player in the military industrial economy, ran a host of Christmas ads throughout the 1959 shopping season for their Astronaut 88 television. Nor was Packard Bell the only company to create military industrial televisions. The Magnavox company advertised a *Constellation* TV, and during Christmas of 1958, the RCA company released a "sleek, tapered," seventeen-inch portable *Flightline* TV. Similarly, the Zenith Corporation introduced a wireless remote-control device, which it called *Space Command*. Camera and radio companies also named their products so as to identify them in the public mind with the Space Age. During the 1960 Christmas shopping season, the Sears Roebuck Company advertised an Astronaut movie projector. The profusion of such ads makes clear the importance retailers placed on associating their products with America's mission in space.[13]

By far the most explicit Christmas advertising copy linking technical excellence, Space Age technology, and consumer goods was for the Bulova watch company's Accutron wristwatch. Nearly every day during the 1960 Christmas shopping season, Bulova ran full-page ads touting their product's technical brilliance and accuracy. According to the ads, the Bulova Company spent over eight years researching and developing a watch that proved so accurate (they claimed a rate of 99.9977 percent) that it served as the key timing device in a U.S. satellite. By purchasing this watch, consumers could literally own a piece of a satellite, a technologically advanced item that directly linked Americans to the nation's conquest of space. And should consumers somehow miss the connection between Space Age communion and the purchase of an *Accutron* made so explicit in the text, the advertisement reinforced the link through a remarkable series of images equating the watch with an orbital satellite.[14]

It is important to note that Christmas advertisements were geared primarily toward men. Nevertheless, women were targeted by military industrial advertising, albeit generally depicted as the users rather than the purchasers of America's Space Age bounty. Still, women played a significant role in military industrial society. Indeed, according to feminist studies scholar Laura Scott Holliday, women entered into a kind of national contract, according to which, through their roles as raisers of the nation's children and supporters and maintainers of the nation's domestic spaces (white, middle- and upper-class) homemaking women would be recognized as central to American greatness. As such, they would be

Figure 7.2.   Even something as commonplace as a child's savings bank was not immune to the national quest for space travel and aerospace dominance as demonstrated by this bank commemorating the NASA project Mercury Space Capsule and US Astronaut Alan B. Shepard JR.'s suborbital space flight on Friday, May 5, 1961. Left: "Launch Security at Stoneham Savings Bank, Stoneham, Mass." Right (bottom of bank): "Sub-Orbital Trajectory Friday May 5, 1961." Photo by Robert A. Wilson, collection of Kenneth C. Turino.

supported by a whole range of institutions, from government departments to magazines to university and corporate research units.[15]

Undoubtedly, the zenith of military industrial support for women came as modern or Space Age kitchen appliances. Here some of the most important names in the military industrial complex, in particular General Electric (GE) and RCA, provided tools that eased household drudgery through American Cold War ingenuity and production—a significant theme in Vice President Nixon's famed 1959 kitchen debate with Soviet premier Nikita Khrushchev.

As Holliday and other scholars have noted, Space Age technologies promised women a significant reduction in housework. Several Christmas ads for General Electric's *Mobile Maid Dishwasher*, for example, promised women increased time with their families. Another advertisement promoting the installation of an entire GE kitchen offered families "better living all year round," allowing "her [the lady of the house] more time to spend with the family."

Though such ads were clearly geared toward "women's work," it is important to remember that men were expected to purchase these "big-ticket" gifts. A 1959 full-page Christmas advertisement for the Waste King Company clearly demonstrates this phenomenon. The advertisement hinted at the amorous rewards a husband would receive if he purchased a Waste King garbage disposal and dishwasher for his wife.

As if marital bliss were not a compelling enough reason for a husband to purchase Waste King products, the advertisement employed Space Age iconography to link the acquisition of such goods to the American mission in space. The bottom left-hand corner of the piece displayed several icons including a depiction of several orbital crafts encircling the earth, underneath which was the phrase "Technical Products for Military and Industry."[16]

Perhaps the Military Industrial Christmas advertisement that most closely linked Space Age technology with household goods came from the Corning Glass Works Company. During the 1958 Christmas shopping season Corning introduced its renowned line of freezer to stove casserole plates known as *Corningware*. The company touted its new line as a Space Age breakthrough in cooking technology. Indeed, according to a 1958 advertisement in *the Los Angeles Times*, Corningware was a "Miracle Discovery from the Space Age," employing "super ceramic Pyroceram first made ... for guided missiles," to create a miraculous temperature-resistant cooking surface. Like the ads for Bulova's Accutron wristwatch, Corningware advertisements offered consumers a concrete physical link between the purchase and reception of Christmas gifts and American Cold War technology.[17]

The above-cited texts illustrate the beliefs of producers and advertisers about the American Christmas marketplace in the late 1950s. As American news reports made note of the Soviet successes in space and the need for Americans to learn more about and engage more fully with Space Age technology, manufacturers and their advertisers did their best to fill the market with consumer goods that, in some small way, exhibited a connection to science education and advanced, Space Age technology.

It is reasonable to ask if the consumers themselves engaged in a Christmas tradition of the purchase of such goods. Naturally data on such a tradition is hard to come by. After all, the idea of the Military Industrial Christmas is one that I have imposed on my research to make sense of what I have found. To my knowledge, no one in the late 1950s claimed to be participants in such a celebration. Some data of the age indicates an American passion for the purchase of military industrial goods. During the 1958 Christmas shopping season, for example, sales jumped some 8 percent over the previous year. And the all-important sales of toys steadily increased throughout the late 1950s. At the 1959 International Toy Fair in New York City, toy manufacturers forecast a 6.4 percent increase in toy sales during the Christmas season, a prediction directly based on the significant increase in toy sales during the 1958 Christmas season. Though we cannot directly correlate such increases to my assertions, we do know for sure that the closing years of the 1950s witnessed a tremendous increase in the purchase of space-based toys, as well as a significant improvement in retail sales.[18]

Some Concluding Thoughts

For two decades, I have studied and discussed Christmas and the consumer society as critical elements in understanding cultural history, and I have found that most people take to these concepts easily. One of the prime reasons for this easy acceptance is the widespread embrace of Christmas as a festive occasion across the globe. In some sense, the American

Christmas celebration has become a worldwide phenomenon, and this universality lends itself to a broad social understanding of the concepts I have addressed in this chapter.

Indeed, while writing this piece, I was reminded of the concept of "social objects" from Nina Simon's 2010 work *The Participatory Museum* and how that phenomenon helps explain why a study/exhibit of Christmas gifts would likely appeal to a general audience. As the reader may recall, Simon tells us that social objects are the kinds of pieces that generate connection and engagement between visitors. One can easily identify the prime social objects in an exhibition because they are the artifacts that draw a crowd of people willing to talk to each other (either in person or virtually) about memories or meanings related to a particular piece or collection of objects.[19]

The "sociality" of such pieces might be scaffolded (i.e., designed) to generate social engagement, but still other objects may create human connection because of their relationship to the day-to-day lives of our visitors. For example, in my previous position at the Newport Restoration Foundation in Newport, Rhode Island, I have found that one of the most social sets of objects in Rough Point (the summer home of the famed twentieth-century heiress Doris Duke) is the items in her kitchen. One can routinely find people in the kitchen looking at the pots and pans and the old McCormick's spice bottles we have on the counter and talking to each other about the similarities and differences between their kitchens and the kitchen at Rough Point.

This seems completely understandable to me. After all, practically all of us live in homes with kitchens, and regardless of one's wealth or standing, most of us can relate to kitchen tools and appliances as part of our everyday lives. When, for example, we look at the oversized refrigerators at Rough Point, we might find ourselves comparing them to the size of our fridge, we might recall a story about our first refrigerator or the time that our refrigerator broke down just before a big party. In short, there is something universal about a kitchen and its appliances that seems to appeal to all kinds of people from all kinds of places and such objects can generate a social connection that, for example, a large-scale van Dyck portrait cannot.

The same universality and sociality surely applies to stories and objects related to the American Christmas celebration. After all, regardless of our religious or cultural background, Christmas is a central component of the American holiday calendar, and I suspect that very few Americans (or those interested in American culture) have never seen a Christmas tree or watched people unwrap Christmas presents. When combined with broader cultural concerns of a particular moment in history, such connection should prove both socially appealing and historically instructive to the average museum visitor.

What is more, there are a wide range of social objects that should be able to communicate the basic concept behind this chapter, namely, that the exchange of Christmas gifts can, at times, prove remarkably instructive about the social and cultural milieu of a particular moment in history. Consider, for example, what the Cabbage Patch Kid mania of the 1983 Christmas shopping season might tell us about the state of the American family. Readers may recall that parents and other adults behaved like wild animals on the hunt to acquire these odd-looking dolls, which their children then adopted as their own through the mock papers provided in each boxed set. No doubt, other Christmas consumer trends might easily appeal to museum visitors and critically illustrate other aspects of American culture at other moments in the past.

Perhaps the most significant (if limited) contributions this chapter can make to any future exhibition about Christmas gifts and their meaning is how I have documented the context in which the Military Industrial Christmas occurred and how one might employ advertising as a primary topic worth studying and exhibiting. Above all, I hope this piece has clarified that such texts are more than mere sales pitches. Advertising is one of the most viewed forms of communication in the world, and it would be very foolish indeed to dismiss such texts as mere commercial fluff. Indeed, as I hope I have demonstrated for the reader, very often they can direct us to some of the central concerns of American society.

Notes

1. Several sections of this piece are excerpted from my 2005 master's thesis, "The Military Industrial Christmas." To learn more about this work and how to obtain an online copy, please visit the California State University, Northridge's OneSearch search engine at https://csu-un.primo.exlibrisgroup.com/discovery/search. In preparation for this piece, I reached out to several museum professionals from various institutions across the country. I would like to particularly thank the following colleagues for their time and input: Carlene Bermann (graduate student in the Cooperstown Museum Studies Program), Jeff Saulsbery (site manager at the David Davis Mansion in Illinois), Susan Baker (collections manager at the House of Seven Gables in Massachusetts), and Julie Arrison-Bishop (former communications manager at House of Seven Gables).

2. Walter L. Hixson, *Parting the Curtain: Propaganda, Culture and the Cold War, 1945–1961* (New York: St. Martin's Press, 1998), 123. Robert H. Zieger, "The Paradox of Plenty: The Advertising Council and the Post-Sputnik Crisis," *Advertising & Society Review* 4, no. 1 (2003): http://muse.jhu.edu.libproxy.csun.edu:2048/journals/advertising_and_society_review/v004/4 .1zieger.html (accessed December 10, 2004).

3. For more on Lyndon Baines Johnson's reactions to Sputnik see, Lyndon Baines Johnson, *The Vantage Point: Perspectives of the Presidency, 1963–1969* (New York: Holt, Rinehart and Winston, 1971), 272. Also see Doris Kearns Goodwin, *Lyndon Johnson and the American Dream* (New York: Harper & Row, Publishers, 1976), 244–46. Mary Ann Callan "Skyward into the Unknown: The Space Race Fills UC Classes," *Los Angeles Times*, February 14, 1958; Donald G. Cooley, "Astronomical Number of Skywatchers," *New York Times*, January 26, 1958.

4. "Future War on Moon over Lunar Rocket Stations Seen," *Los Angeles Times*, October 7, 1959.

5. For histories of American Christmas, see Penne Restad, *Christmas in America: A History* (New York: Oxford University Press, 1995); Leigh Eric Schmidt, *Consumer Rites: The Buying and Selling of American Holidays* (Princeton: Princeton University Press, 1995); and William B. Waits, *The Modern Christmas in America: A Cultural History of Gift Giving* (New York: New York University Press, 1992). There is a vast historiography on the history of America's consumer society, including Thomas Hine, *Populuxe* (New York: Alfred A. Knopf, 1986); T. J. Jackson Lears, *Fables of Abundance: A Cultural History of Advertising* (New York: Basic Books, 1994); Gary Cross, *An All Consuming Century: Why Commercialism Won in Modern America*

(New York: Columbia University Press, 2000); Lizabeth Cohen, *A Consumer's Republic: The Politics of Mass Consumption in Postwar America* (New York: Alfred A. Knopf, 2003).

6. In December 1957, for example, President Eisenhower's secretary of health education and welfare, Marion Folsom, released a memo calling for a major expansion of math and science training. Education officials in California went to the state legislature seeking funds to begin science education in the first grade. In March 1958, 125 New York state educators convened in Great Neck, Long Island, for a two-day conference on how to provide advanced science education to gifted and talented students. That same month, families in Costa Mesa, California, gathered to discuss ways for the community to help support science in the schools. "Science in 1st and 2nd Grades," *Los Angeles Times*, February 19, 1958; "Teachers Favor Help for Gifted," *New York Times*, March 11, 1958; "Science Aid to be Studied," *Los Angeles Times*, March 19, 1958.

7. Dorothy Barclay, "Young Scientists—and How They Grow," *New York Times*, December 6, 1959; Marianne Besser, "How Scientists Teach," *Los Angeles Times*, June 15, 1958.

8. "Toys Go Out of This World," *New York Times*, November 10, 1957; "Toys? Out of This World," *Los Angeles Times*, November 18, 1959; "Science, Cloaked in the Guise of New Toys Invades the World of Children," *New York Times*, March 8, 1959.

9. "Park's Two Stage Rocket," *Los Angeles Times*, November 23, 1958; Viewmaster Vanguard Launch advertisement, *New York Times*, November 17, 1958; Owl Drugstore Toyland advertisement, *Los Angeles Times*, December 8, 1958; Monogram Toys advertisement, *Los Angeles Times*, November 22, 1959; Alpha I Ballistic Missile advertisement, *Los Angeles Times*, November 23, 1958; Aerobee Hi advertisement, *New York Times*, December 7, 1958; Gilbert Toys advertisement, *Los Angeles Times*, November 22, 1959; Revell Model Company advertisement, *Los Angeles Times*, November 23, 1958.

10. Ibid.

11. Toytown advertisement, *Los Angeles Times*, November 22, 1959; Lennie's of Reseda advertisement, *Los Angeles Times*, December 4, 1960.

12. Hawk Model advertisement, *Los Angeles Times*, November 23, 1958; Revell Model advertisement, *Los Angeles Times*, November 23, 1958; Monogram Models advertisement, *Los Angeles Times*, November 23, 1958.

13. Ads for the Packard Bell Company's Astronaut 88 television can be found in almost every issue of the *Los Angeles Times* during the 1959 Christmas season, such as December 2, 1959, December 13, 1959, and December 20, 1959. Constellation TV advertisement, *Los Angeles Times*, November 23, 1958. Flightline TV advertisement, *Los Angeles Times*, December 7, 1958. The Space Command remote control was a widely advertised device throughout the 1958 Christmas shopping season.

14. As noted above, ads for the Accutron were almost ubiquitous during the 1960 Christmas shopping season. For example, in the *New York Times* on November 20, 1960, and November 27, 1960, and in the *Los Angeles Times* on December 5, 1960, and December 18, 1960.

15. Laura Scott Holliday, "Kitchen Technologies: Promises and Alibis, 1944–1966," *Camera Obscura* 16, no. 2 (2001): 80.

16. For more information on women and gender during the Cold War, see Elaine Tyler May's, *Homeward Bound: American Families in the Cold War Era* (New York: Basic Books, 1988); General Electric Mobile Maid Dishwasher advertisement, *New York Times*, December 4, 1958; General Electric Kitchen Installation advertisement, *New York Times*, December 7, 1958; Waste King advertisement, *Los Angeles Times*, November 15, 1959.

17. Corningware advertisement, *Los Angeles Times*, November 30, 1958.
18. "Retail Upswing Due to Go Higher," *New York Times*, January 12, 1959; "U.S. Toy Makers Forecast Gains," *New York Times*, June 27, 1959.
19. Nina Simon, *The Participatory Museum* (Santa Cruz, CA: Santa Cruz Museum 2.0, 2010). The book is available online at http://www.participatorymuseum.org/read/ (accessed on January 10, 2022).

CHAPTER 8

Christmas behind Barbed Wire

Andrew R. Dunn

IKE MANY AMERICANS, the Tamura family enjoyed holidays. They looked forward to sitting around a large wooden table together and eating the food their family had enjoyed making for generations. These included ham and other familiar table items, but also the complicated and time-consuming mochi that represented a cultural staple for families of Japanese descent. This connection to Japan, though, would force the Tamura family to face terrible injustice during World War II.

Facing a painful dilemma between maintaining certain elements of their heritage and assimilating by adopting the cultural practices of a mistrustful nation, the Tamura family's experience represents thousands of other American families of Japanese descent. Continued practice of holiday traditions during the war, especially at Christmas, allowed Japanese Americans to maintain a small but important piece of their identity and cultural legacy. This is a story we must understand if we hope to grasp the full experience of holiday in the United States and prevent current injustices by recalling the struggles of previous generations.

Japan's attack at Pearl Harbor on December 7, 1941, is largely recognized as a catalyst for banding Americans together against a common foe. Widespread efforts to mobilize the battlefront brought a sense of patriotic fervor while production demands on the home fronts took the United States out of the Great Depression and placed it directly into a wartime economy. These movements centered on idealistic images of Americans "doing their part" for the greater war effort. America's "date which will live in infamy," though, also created division by leading to one of the largest government-sanctioned civil rights infractions in the nation's history.

Targeted by fear and blatant racism, those with Japanese heritage living in the United States became outlets upon which many white Americans projected their fear, frustrations, and hate. Blatantly racist Americans used the attack as a platform to sow distrust and hostility while U.S. military commanders blamed early naval losses on fictitious fifth-column activities (domestic espionage and sabotage).[1] Convinced that those with Japanese descent (Nikkei) posed a threat to national security, President Franklin Roosevelt issued Executive Order 9066 on February 19, 1942, creating a military exclusion zone along the mainland's Pacific Coast. Military commanders quickly initiated the forced removal and relocation of over 110,000 Japanese Americans. Two-thirds were U.S. citizens and many had few, if any, meaningful ties to Japan. Numbered tags replaced names as the military rounded up those who looked like the enemy. Torn from homes, friends, jobs, and businesses, Nikkei were placed on trains with blacked-out windows. They did not know where they were going or how long they would be there. Locked up behind barbed wire in one of ten incarceration camps scattered across the United States without due process, Nikkei faced nearly insurmountable hurdles. Despite a lack of any condemning evidence, innocent families spent the war years attempting to adapt and accept the loss of their previous lives.

Behind Barbed Wire

Located on undeveloped federal land tracts, a central goal for these centers included using the large labor force of relocated Japanese Americans to establish farming communities for future white farmers.[2] These goals proved successful, and eventually Nikkei transformed harsh landscapes into profitable properties. Staffed by white-appointed personnel from all over the country, the War Relocation Authority oversaw daily camp operations. The cost came high. As Nikkei strove to break through racial stereotypes and prove their patriotism by supporting the Allied war effort, they neglected their own food supplies and lost certain cultural practices of their own.

The Minidoka Relocation Center sprawled across thirty-three thousand acres on south-central Idaho's sagebrush desert. Occupied largely by former Portlanders, Seattleites, and Bainbridge Islanders, Minidoka became the new home for nearly thirteen thousand Japanese Americans during 1942–1945. The harsh desert climate proved a challenge for all residents but served as an especially demoralizing element to Nikkei. Hailing from the predominantly high-precipitation areas of the Pacific Northwest, the ever-present dust, heat, and lack of water became serious inhibitors to Nikkei health and happiness.

The center included four hundred residential barracks split up into thirty-six blocks, three miles long.[3] Each block consisted of twelve barrack buildings serving as living quarters, a mess hall, a laundry building that eventually included lavatory accommodations, and a recreation hall. The barrack buildings also served as administrative offices, churches, and classrooms. Each barrack provided only 114 square feet of living space per incarceree. Because of the need to quickly provide housing for arriving evacuees, the buildings received rudimentary construction consisting of tarpaper-covered wood frames void of any insulation.[4] The first Nikkei to arrive had to help finish constructing their own prison camp. Security included a guardhouse at the front entrance area manned by military police. Eight guard towers bordered the camp's perimeter and barbed-wire fencing enclosed the thirteen miles of camp buildings.[5] As the center's population quickly grew to nearly ten thousand, Minidoka became Idaho's seventh largest city at the time.[6]

During its operation, Minidoka's incarcerees faced constant demands to prove their loyalty by abandoning any Japanese customs and adopting mainstream American values. Although many Nikkei accepted these forced degradations and went to great lengths to show their willingness to contribute to the overall war effort, it is important to note that they did so largely because they were already Americans and genuinely wanted to help. Minidoka had the highest rate of volunteers from all the camps to fill labor shortages on nearby farms, which helped sustain domestic and military food supplies. In addition, once allowed to serve in the military, Minidoka had the largest percentage of any camp to enlist for military service.[7] Nikkei willingly made these contributions while their families underwent a stripping of their identities. Stories of these families, recorded through oral history projects, the camp-run newspaper *The Minidoka Irrigator*, and other primary sources show how keeping the holiday spirit alive helped families navigate life imprisoned behind barbed wire.

Holidays

Family dining practices represented one of the cultural elements that suffered most during incarceration. Mealtimes in the camps proved a stark contrast to what most Nikkei practiced pre-internment. Before their incarceration, family matriarchs usually prepared meals in Nikkei households. Many had a very personal relationship with their food, eating seasonal items they grew themselves.[8] Families took their meals together at a central table, and this served as a critical time for familial conversation and bonding.

Upon arrival to the camps, the simple task of eating together became a luxury few could partake in. Many families broke apart during the day to complete various tasks, and thus attended meals with their working companions when the meal bell rang. Even when families attended the mess halls together, the very nature of a cafeteria-style mess hall made gatherings noisy and chaotic. Children often ate with their friends away from parental supervision. Fujiko Tamura-Gardener, imprisoned at Minidoka as a child, recalled that her father felt such shame and depression over their wrongful incarceration that he and his wife took food back to their living quarters and refrained from communal mealtimes.[9] The inability to prepare their own food and dine with immediate family created a disruption in traditional consumption customs and caused a destabilization of Nikkei family structure. Many families never recovered.

Holidays served as an occasion where Nikkei attempted to balance pressure to assimilate with desires to maintain cultural practices and temporarily overlook adversity. As the first Thanksgiving at Minidoka approached in 1942, many wondered how incarceration would affect their holiday experience. Because such a large percentage of their available labor spent the harvest season caring for the nation's food supply on outside farms, their own had been neglected. Furthermore, their status as an undesired minority without access to reliable food supplies compounded their confusion, and they questioned their ability to partake in a favored holiday.[10]

News that the project steward ordered seven thousand pounds of turkey for Thanksgiving celebrations kicked off camp-wide efforts to make the event as festive as possible. Social events such as dances, or "Turkey Hops," provided exciting opportunities to get into the holiday spirit. Appointed personnel also provided cheerful—yet misguided and patronizing—messages that Nikkei fair treatment and freedom depended upon their willingness to adopt American customs.[11] These messages ignored, though, that many Nikkei already practiced American customs and holidays prior to Pearl Harbor.

Thanksgiving celebrations continued at Minidoka all three years the center remained in operation, but they steadily declined in fervor and optimism. Specifically, President Roosevelt's decree that incarcerees remain working on food production during holidays reduced much of the romanticized excitement many associated with Thanksgiving. Mealtimes also became more strictly regimented camp-wide in regard to when each block could report to their respective dining halls, limiting the social atmosphere of the holiday. The availability of food also decreased.

After the first Thanksgiving, turkey became unavailable to incarcerated Japanese Americans, forcing Nikkei to instead rely on eating chickens they raised themselves.[12] After their first year at Minidoka, Nikkei developed the camp farms and grew traditional Japanese foods such as daikon and nappa. Producing their own food gave them more control over what they cooked during the holidays and allowed them to regain some modicum of control. The Turkey Hops continued, but many Nikkei looked to Christmas as a better opportunity to eat more culturally appropriate foods while hoping their excitement for Christmas would help show their patriotism to mainstream Christian Americans.

The Christmas season enjoyed more consistent celebrations than Thanksgiving. Thirty-six Christmas committees worked to raise money, wrap gifts, purchase candy and decorations, organize entertainment, and decorate dining halls and trees in an effort for what camp personnel called "a grand Christmas celebration."[13] Motifs with phrases like "Santa Remembers Minidoka" became popular accessories and highlighted the hope many felt for the holiday.[14] Eager evacuees decorated dining halls to showcase their skill and ingenuity by making extravagant displays using only waste and scrap materials. These included Christmas wreaths made from sagebrush and wood, and ornaments crafted from saved egg shells, cupcake wrappers, and orange peelings.[15] Speaking about Christmas at Minidoka as a child, Nobu Suzuki stated that "it was cold and certainly different," but they made the best of it by gathering brush, melting wax, and putting a wick through it to make sagebrush candles.[16] Tsugo Ikeda recalled, "We didn't have much to give each other. We were all deprived of that, but . . . we also had the pleasure of socializing and using our creative ideas and motivation to decorate, so we loved that competitiveness. So Christmas was great."[17]

Themes chosen for decorations often lamented the absence of family members serving in the U.S. military and bygone days of freedom (see figure 8.1).[18] A high school student's Christmas wish in December 1943 highlights the patriotism and selflessness many Nikkei felt during the holidays:

Figure 8.1.   Minidoka residents made displays to beautify their space while celebrating a favorite holiday. Here, Uncle Sam and Santa Claus wish incarcerees a "Happy New Year" while reminding them of their "duty" to support the war effort. The letter "V" cutouts were part of the nationwide "V for Victory" campaign. These and other displays were made of waste materials. Courtesy of the National Archives and Records Administration.

Dear Santa:

The season has rolled around again when we think of you, and wonder what you will bring us. I hope you are in the best of health for I imagine you will be very busy this year. There are so many needy people all over the world who are praying for food, clothing, and shelter that I feel rather ashamed to ask you for anything when I am much better off than they are.

However, there is one Christmas present that I wish for this year. No doubt you have had many requests for it. If you would bring an armistice, it would make me very happy, for it would mean that my brother could come home. An armistice also would mean that everyone all over the world will be happy, too, because families would be together and would not have to worry or fear anything. Especially at this Yuletide season, which is a time of peace on earth, good will toward men, it seems that men should be helping each other and working together instead of fighting one another. Even if you can't deliver my present on Christmas day, please bring it as soon as you possibly can.

Sincerely yours,

y.m.[19]

Holiday efforts aimed heavily at the schools and classrooms, and they received promises for "nice" Christmas trees. The trees never materialized, however, and families improvised by using decorated clumps of sagebrush.[20] Unwilling to let their dreary surroundings ruin the holiday spirit, many children spent time singing American Christmas carols taught by their Caucasian teachers.[21] Efforts such as these by Minidoka's appointed personnel—although generally well-meaning—contributed overall to the whitewashing and forced assimilation of incarcerated Nikkei.

On Christmas day, each dining hall held a party for their associated blocks, complete with a visit from Santa Claus bearing gifts for the children (see figure 8.2).[22] Minidoka's large Buddhist population also took part in the Christmas celebrations. Fumiko Uyeda Groves noted that "being Buddhist, it wasn't a real big thing before we went to camp—but then when we were in camp Christmas became a big thing because we always had the competition between the blocks . . . and that's when you became real aware of Christmas."[23]

The holidays further represented a time of increased (yet temporary) acceptance and support from those outside the camps. Donations poured into Minidoka from churches and those employed at the camp, which they used to purchase three thousand pounds of candy and five hundred pounds of nuts.[24] When seventeen thousand gifts arrived for children from nearly every state, the *Irrigator* celebrated that "Christmas this year will not be a disappointment for Hunt's youngsters."[25]

Figure 8.2.   Santa visited children incarcerated at Minidoka and distributed presents sent by outside organizations and churches. In the background are a tree and a sagebrush, decorated for Christmas. Courtesy of the National Archives and Records Administration.

Businesses from nearby towns who catered to Nikkei customers also flooded the *Irrigator* with ads and well-wishes. During Christmas 1945, the *Irrigator* staff sent several five-pound food packages consisting of dehydrated soup, dried shrimp, nori, and rice to soldiers on the front in gratitude for the "Merry Christmas" ad paid for by members of the 232nd Engineers.[26] Christmas served a different purpose for different people. Some observed it for religious reasons while others used it, like many Americans, as a cultural event, and for those outside the camps it served as an opportunity to aid others.

In contrast to much of the Christmas hype and community support, the meals available over the holidays only partially fulfilled Nikkei desires. Although Christmas received the most promotion from camp personnel, the three-day Yuletide season around New Year's Day was the most traditionally important holiday to Japanese Americans. When incarcerees discovered only twenty-seven sacks of sweet-rice—which they used heavily in New Year's recipes—they lamented their inability to make traditional foods.[27] Teriyaki chicken proved another sacrificed staple because of the absence of sugar (needed to enrich the sauce) because of the nationwide rationing program.

To their credit, the camp steward division ordered mochi, an important holiday food that many enjoyed pre-incarceration. Part of this food's importance, though, resided in its preparation by multiple family members, an element lost at Minidoka. Tamura-Gardener related the bonding which took place during the synchronous art of making mochi, which entailed timing the process perfectly to dart hands in to flip the dough as others pounded it.[28] Many similar family acts of passing on cultural traditions were lost behind Minidoka's barbed wire.

As with Thanksgiving, Nikkei reflection on the loss of their former lives led to a counter-narrative promoted by white officials which increasingly pushed the concept of assimilation onto Nikkei. Although this emphasis by those in power led many Nikkei to favor assimilation as a means of demonstrating loyalty to obtain freedom, they simply desired to retain some of their cultural heritage by cooking their own meals, eating together as families, and eating foods they grew up with. Those hostile to Nikkei saw any Japanese practices as inherently threatening and failed to acknowledge that white Americans followed similar customs every year with their own family traditions.

Overall, holidays became significantly less promoted the longer the centers stayed open. A few reasons explain this trend. Government attempts to move Nikkei from the camps to eastern states became a higher priority than evacuee comfort as the war progressed. Military enlistment also dominated much of the focus both nationwide and in the camps as Nikkei were required to register for the draft and serve in the military while their families remained incarcerated. Simply put, the strain on Japanese American families became greater as the war dragged on.

America's Infamy

The World War II relocation of Japanese Americans is universally acknowledged as unjust. In 1988, Congress formally apologized and offered redress payments for the wrongful incarceration. Ensuing court cases challenging the constitutionality of the incarceration revealed a complete lack of evidence for the perceived Japanese threat on the mainland United States.

Box 8.1.   Heart Mountain

The Heart Mountain Interpretive Center in Wyoming stands on the site of the fourth largest of the Japanese American incarceration camps of World War II. In the summer, the site bustles with visitors on their way to and from Yellowstone National Park, which is less than an hour's drive away.

In the winter, when the gates of Yellowstone close, the center shifts its focus to outreach among local communities. Most prominent is the Holiday Open House, a free attendance day that draws visitors from as far as Billings (two hours' drive). The Holiday Open House features special activities based on holiday activities from the camp era. For example, visitors create Christmas cards using potato stamps to replicate the block printing done in the camp, and sample the rice cakes called *mochi*, which incarcerees would make from their collected sugar rations.

Holiday programs also allow the center to focus on topics and stories that are rarely covered in the center's day-to-day activities, which by necessity focus on the broader story of incarceration. A special winter display in 2019 highlighted winter activities from the camp's newspaper, as well as special notes of appreciation posted in the classified section from Wyoming and Montana businesses that hired Japanese Americans from the camps for labor.

Cally Steussy
Museum Manager
Heart Mountain Interpretive Center

Indeed, politicians and military commanders suppressed evidence during the incarceration to advance their own racist ideas and to shirk the blame for military failures.

Elderly, first-generation Japanese immigrants (Issei) felt the impact hardest. Mixed emotions over their home country fighting the nation they had chosen for their children, and the shame many felt for their powerless situation, caused lingering cases of depression. Many withdrew and refused to talk of their experience or pass along traditional Japanese culture to their children. Several of those who faced incarceration as children are just now trying to reconnect with their Japanese cultural roots.

Holidays served as a distraction to the monotony and degradation experienced in the camps. They provided a reminder for what was lost as they faced pressure from authorities to toe the line. Holidays behind the barbed wire at Minidoka emphasize the humanizing impact that holidays can have both in regular cultural traditions as well as in the face of adversity.

Moving Forward

Today, Minidoka National Historic Site (MNHS) is under the stewardship of the National Park Service (NPS), aided by their philanthropic partner Friends of Minidoka. The site closes for the winter months because of its remote location and harsh travel conditions. With no staff on-site during Christmas, NPS uses social media and other digital media platforms to interpret the Minidoka story during the holiday season. Park Ranger Kurt Ikeda—chief of interpretation at MNHS—relates that "Christmas connects with the average person" and the best way to do this is by focusing on the "children's experiences."[29] NPS engages with the public by highlighting quotes, poems, and other reflections of Minidoka's inhabitants; exposing their vast number of followers to the injustices of the incarceration through the lens of holiday experiences at Minidoka.

While the National Park Service and Friends of Minidoka are specifically responsible for MNHS, several other great agencies preserve and educate on the broader Japanese American wartime experience. A few of these include Densho, Japanese American National Museum, and Wing Luke Museum of the Asian Pacific American Experience. These groups are critical repositories of information and are the first place one should go for more information.

Incorporating sensitive subjects such as wartime incarceration of minorities into programming, namely, during the holidays, is an important but achievable task. Keeping terminology and tone appropriate to the subject are crucial first steps. Primary source accounts from camp personnel trying to improve morale, and other propaganda from agencies like the War Relocation Authority, often used upbeat and optimistic tones. While common at the time, this patronizing language would be extremely condescending to use today. Although they used holidays as an opportunity to temporarily improve their situation, the incarceration remained an injustice that was terribly detrimental to Americans of Japanese descent.

Understanding the human components behind broader stories like Minidoka helps us empathize while facilitating our ability to move forward appropriately. Remembering that most of those affected were American citizens helps put the injustices into perspective. Ranger Ikeda suggests engaging with primary sources and talking to their families and others with firsthand knowledge of the experiences.[30] Cultural competency refers to understanding those with different cultures and coming to terms with any inherent bias one may have. Those who did not undergo the stripping of their identity and civil liberties at sites like Minidoka will never fully understand the depth of this story. In addition, perpetuating stereotypes such as "model minority" and the "forever foreigner" prolongs the damages and suffering. Adopting and incorporating standards of cultural competency will allow us to better understand this history and allow us to engage with the material in productive, rather than destructive, ways.

Notes

1. Roger Daniels, *Prisoners without Trial: Japanese Americans in World War II* (New York: Hill & Wang, 1993), 24.
2. Arthur Kleinkopf, "Relocation Center Diary" (1942–1945), Twin Falls Public Library and "Bob Sims Collection," Special Collections, Boise State University, 26.
3. Kleinkopf, "Relocation Center Diary."
4. Friends of Minidoka, "Minidoka NHS Walking Tour App," Mia Russell (2016), http://www .minidoka.org (accessed January 1, 2018).
5. Kleinkopf, "Relocation Center Diary."
6. Bessie M. Shrontz-Wright, ed., "Evacuees Arrive: The War Relocation Authority," *Hunt for Idaho* (self-published, 1994); available upon request from Minidoka National Historic Site.

7. Kleinkopf, "Relocation Center Diary," 26.

8. Fujiko Tamura-Gardener, interview by Andrew Dunn at Lakewood, Washington, February 25, 2017. For more, see Roger Daniels, *Prisoners without Trial: Japanese Americans in World War II* (New York: Hill & Wang, 1993).

9. Fujiko Tamura-Gardener, interview by Andrew Dunn.

10. "Boy Contemplates Turkeyless Thanksgiving, Gets Surprise," *Minidoka Irrigator* 1, no. 17 (November 11, 1943).

11. H. L. Stafford, "Director Stafford Extends Thanksgiving Message," *Minidoka Irrigator* 3, no. 39 (November 20, 1943).

12. "Thanksgiving Day to Be Observed on November 23," *Minidoka Irrigator* 4, no. 37 (November 18, 1944).

13. Kleinkopf, "Relocation Center Diary," 95–96.

14. "Special Christmas Fund Drive on December 3–5," *Minidoka Irrigator* (November 28, 1942).

15. Kleinkopf, "Relocation Center Diary," 95–96.

16. "Nobu Suzuki Interview, segment 36," *Densho Encyclopedia* ddr-densho-1000-84-36, Nobu Suzuki Interview I Segment 36, Densho Digital Repository (accessed August 16, 2022).

17. "Tsuguo 'Ike' Ikeda Remembers Celebrating Christmas at Minidoka," *Densho Encyclopedia* https://encyclopedia.densho.org/sources/en-denshovh-itsuguo-01-0018-1/ (accessed August 16 2022).

18. Kleinkopf, "Relocation Center Diary," 95–96.

19. Kleinkopf, "Relocation Center Diary," 95–96.

20. Kleinkopf, "Relocation Center Diary," 95–96.

21. Kleinkopf, "Relocation Center Diary," 95–96.

22. Kleinkopf, "Relocation Center Diary," 95–96.

23. "Fumiko Uyeda Groves, segment 23," *Densho Encyclopedia*, ddr-densho-1000-10-1, Fumiko Uyeda Groves Segment 1, Densho Digital Repository (accessed August 15, 2022).

24. Fumiko Uyeda Groves, segment 23," *Densho Encyclopedia.*

25. "Gay Christmas Day Seen as Donations Pour In," *Minidoka Irrigator* (December 19, 1942).

26. "Food Packages Sent," *Minidoka Irrigator* (March 31, 1945).

27. Kleinkopf, "Relocation Center Diary."

28. Fujiko Tamura-Gardener, interview by Andrew Dunn at Lakewood, Washington, February 25, 2017.

29. Kurt Ikeda, interview by Andrew Dunn, August 2022.

30. Kurt Ikeda, interview by Andrew Dunn, August 2022.

CHAPTER 9

Not Everyone Celebrates Christmas

Expanding Your Holiday Horizons

Martha B. Katz-Hyman

D RIVING BY THE LOCAL MALL around Christmas several decades ago, our younger son looked out the window at all the decorations and flags in the parking lot and said plaintively, "Don't they know that not everyone celebrates Christmas? There should be Hanukkah menorahs or dreidels there, too!" That one comment sums up the challenge that historic houses and historic sites face every year in November and December: programming and interpretation that revolves around Christmas, in all its varied manifestations, regularly bring large numbers of visitors to holiday-specific programs and results in significant publicity and needed income.

Yet there are others for whom the focus on this one holiday results in feelings of exclusion. At a time when historic houses and historic sites seek to expand their interpretive reach and include previously ignored audiences, reexamining Christmas programming and interpretation and holiday programming and interpretation to more closely reflect both the site's original residents and the diversity of the surrounding community can yield increased engagement of both longtime and first-time guests. Doing this requires the desire to want to change what may be a "sure thing" into a program that is more complex and nuanced; that interprets more than one holiday celebration (or none at all); and requires an investment of time and money to accomplish successfully.[1]

Today, Hanukkah is the best known of all the other holidays and observances that occur in December. But the ancient rabbis, who surely knew about this observance, and whose discussions and interpretations of Jewish law are recorded in the Talmud, the source of Jewish law, asked, "What is Hanukkah?"[2] In answer to their own question, they described Hanukkah as a joyous occasion that commemorated the divine intervention enabling the overthrow of a foreign power that threatened Jewish religious life.[3] The story of that overthrow is told in the Books of the Maccabees, which describes the battles between those Jews who wanted to become more like the Greeks, and other Jews who insisted on not following that path.[4] But instead of focusing on the military victory, the rabbis of the Talmud chose to emphasize the miracle of the small amount of pure oil found in the Temple in Jerusalem during its cleansing after the defeat of the Hellenizers that could be used to light the sacred lamps and which lasted eight days instead of one.

It is this miracle that is commemorated by the commandment to light oil lamps or candles in an eight-branch lamp with an additional space for one more—the *shamash* (servant) with which the other candles are lit. This lamp is called a Hanukkah *menorah* (lampstand) or a *hanukkiah* (a special lampstand for Hanukkah), and the miracle of the oil is remembered in one of the blessings said while lighting. For centuries, it was the simple lighting of the lamps or candles and the recitation of the blessings that marked the observance of the holiday. Even as these Hanukkah menorahs evolved from simple small clay lamps arranged in a semi-circle to special ones that had oil receptacles around their edges, to elaborate standing lampstands made from silver, the observance centered on the lights, the blessings, and the story of the Maccabees, their victory, and rededication of the Temple in Jerusalem.

Scholars have suggested several reasons why Hanukkah is celebrated at the darkest time of the year in the Northern Hemisphere and varying explanations as to why it is an eight-day holiday. Early texts from over two thousand years ago suggest that it is related to a delayed celebration of the holiday of Sukkot—the Festival of Booths—which occurs in the fall and is eight days long. More modern scholarship connects it to pagan celebrations of the winter solstice, much as many scholars of Christianity connect the observance of the birth of Jesus and the celebrations of Christmas to those same pagan celebrations.[5] What better way to make sure a new holiday became popular among a specific group of people than to associate it with a holiday that was already being observed by a large segment of the population?

As with any holiday, there are many additional customs and traditions that have been added over the centuries by Jews around the world to the simple lighting of the *menorah/ hanukkiah*. For Jews whose families originated in Spain, the Balkans, the Middle East, and North Africa, stories of Judith, an Israelite woman who killed the Greek king, Holofernes, and thus helped to save the Jewish people, are told on the holiday, and the Scroll of King Antiochus, the villain in the Books of the Maccabees is read.[6] Jews whose families originated in Eastern Europe have a tradition—well known in the United States and Canada— of playing a game of chance called *dreidel*, a Yiddish word meaning "spinning top." A *dreidel* has four sides, each one with a Hebrew letter that both tells someone how to play the game but also tells the story of Hanukkah in four words: "A Great Miracle Happened There."

It would not be a Jewish holiday without special foods, and no matter which tradition someone follows, the common characteristic is that the food is cooked in oil, in remembrance of the miracle of the oil that lasted for eight days. Best known are potato pancakes (*latkes*), and, from the Sephardic tradition, fritters (*bimuelos*) (see figure 9.2). For most Jews in North America, *bimuelos* have been joined by jelly doughnuts (*sufganiot*) as Hanukkah treats. There is also a tradition of eating dairy meals, with cheese, during the holiday, in remembrance of Judith and how she gave Holofernes ample cheese and wine that made him unable to fend off Judith's deadly attack.

In addition, unlike the major Jewish holidays of Rosh Hashanah and Yom Kippur, and the pilgrimage holidays of Sukkot, Passover, and Shavuot—the Festival of Weeks—there are no restrictions on working, except while the lights are burning; there are no special services in the synagogue such as those for the major holidays (although there are special prayers and readings from the Torah said over the course of the eight days), and there are no restrictions on the kinds of food that can be eaten, as there are on Passover.[7] The emphasis by the rabbis of the Talmud and those who followed them was on the miracle of God's deliverance from those who sought to destroy Jewish laws and traditions.

Through the centuries after the rabbis asked, "What is Hanukkah?," Jews in communities around the world made Hanukkah their own, either observing it with their own families or with friends, and adding poems, songs, and distinct customs to mark these eight special days. The arrival of over 2 million Jewish immigrants to the United States between 1880 and 1924 accelerated changes in religious observance that reflected the very diverse communities from which these individuals came as well as the challenges of both assimilating into American society while at the same time remaining faithful to Jewish beliefs and practices. For some of these new immigrants, the arrival of Christmas brought back memories of attacks by Christians on Jewish settlements, especially in Poland and Russia.

Hilda Satt Polacheck, who was born in Poland and immigrated to Chicago in 1892, wrote that "Christmas was a day to be feared by Jews in Poland. . . . [P]eople had been taught in their churches that the Jews had killed Christ. So the birthday of Christ was celebrated by murdering Jews, burning their synagogues and destroying their homes." Going to a Christmas party at Hull House helped her realize that, in America, things were very different, and she would not be persecuted or harmed on the holiday.[8] Many settlement houses held Christmas parties; many fewer—and primarily those that were run by Jewish organizations—held Hanukkah parties. One exception was the settlement house run by Jacob Riis in New York City, which in December 1908 held a "Maccabean Festival," but even that was marked by controversy within the Jewish community.[9]

But the issue of Christmas and how American Jews would respond and live with it was not just a problem for new immigrants: The proximity of Christmas to Hanukkah—already difficult to avoid even before the great wave of Eastern European Jewish migration—became an even bigger challenge to those community leaders who fought to preserve Jewish traditions, whether they be the traditionalists or the reformers. Changes to how American Jews thought about Hanukkah and its place in their lives emerged in the mid-nineteenth century as rabbis and community leaders faced the problem of how to make Judaism and Jewish traditions relevant in a country where religious leaders did not have the influence and authority that they had once enjoyed.

In a place like the United States, where Jews had freedoms that were rare in other countries, it was next to impossible for rabbis and Jewish community leaders to make their congregants adhere to Jewish laws and customs that had been followed in the countries from which they had emigrated. Traditionalists urged their communities to follow those practices; reformers sought to modify or even change those practices to better accommodate changing beliefs about the role of religious practice in American Jewish life. Emphasizing the story of Hanukkah and the Maccabees, of the triumph of traditional Jewish practice, along with the military victory of the Maccabees over those who sought their defeat, served each side of this debate. Traditionalists could point to the adherence of the Maccabees to Jewish law as an argument for continuing to follow those laws and customs even in a new land. On the other hand, reformers emphasized the military might of the Maccabees and their ability to conquer a much stronger foe and compared the ancient struggle to the American values of liberty and independence. The efforts of both sides had the effect of raising Hanukkah and its observance from a minor holiday to a major part of the Jewish holiday calendar.

At one end of the spectrum, some Jewish families adopted Christmas as an American civic holiday, with elaborately decorated trees, festive parties, and stockings put out on Christmas Eve for Santa Claus.[10] They felt that Hanukkah, with its simple ceremonies and observances, was no match for the bright lights, shiny ornaments, and lavish gifts that marked Christmas in America and that adopting Christmas just made them more American, not less Jewish. Other Jewish families celebrated Hanukkah in some way, lighting the candles in the Hanukkah menorah, having family Hanukkah parties, and decorating their homes with Hanukkah decorations, echoing the home decorations for Christmas that were a hallmark of the holiday. Still others ignored Christmas entirely, focusing on the story of Hanukkah and its observance, but regarding it as the minor holiday it was.

By the mid-twentieth century, the transformation of Christmas from an observance specific to one religion into a public holiday for all people, of whatever faith, was accepted as part of the December holiday season. When Jews began leaving the former Soviet Union in great numbers in the 1990s, the custom they had of having a decorated tree—which they saw as secular and not religious—came with them, and in the American Jewish community, decorated trees at Hanukkah—often called "Hanukkah bushes"—continued. Whether Hanukkah began and ended before Christmas, overlapped with Christmas, or started after Christmas, the tensions between the two holidays were smoothed over.[11]

However, by the end of the twentieth century, changing ideas about ethnic and religious representation—the belief that downplaying or even concealing one's heritage was no longer necessary or even desirable—resulted in public lightings of Hanukkah menorahs, increased incorporation of Hanukkah programs or at least aspects of Hanukkah observance in public school settings, and an understanding of the importance and place of Jewish holidays other than Hanukkah (see figure 9.1). It is indeed paradoxical that a holiday that once was so minor that even the ancient rabbis had to ask, "What is Hanukkah?" has become the vehicle through which most Americans have learned about Jewish life.

There are, of course, historic houses and historic sites that have excellent interpretive programs that focus on December holidays and events other than Christmas. The Tenement Museum in New York City, which tells the stories of Americans and immigrants of many ethnicities and traditions who lived in one apartment building on the Lower East Side of

Figure 9.1.   The small town of Postville, Iowa, is the home of Agri Star Meat & Poultry, a kosher meat-processing facility owned by Orthodox Jews. Most of Agri Star's workforce is not Jewish, but a very large Hanukkah menorah stands on the roof of the plant's entrance to fulfill the commandment to publicize the miracle of the holiday. Photograph by Carol M. Highsmith, Prints and Photographs Division, Library of Congress.

Manhattan between the 1860s and the 1930s, is an important example of a historic house that thoroughly integrates programming for all those who lived in the building.

Jews were among those who lived there, and so Hanukkah is one of the holidays that is interpreted at the museum, along with the holidays of the other families who lived there during the course of seventy years.[12] On the coast of New Hampshire, Strawbery Banke Museum in Portsmouth interprets a range of families and traditions associated with the fifteen houses that are open to the museum's visitors.[13] These houses, which range in date from 1695 to 1955, include the Shapiro House, which interprets a Jewish family who lived there in 1919 (see figure 9.2). There, too, Jewish traditions and holiday observances are fully interpreted to visitors who choose to enter the house.[14]

But these are large organizations that interpret sites with a history of Jewish residents and traditions. Interpreting Hanukkah or other Jewish holidays like Passover, or the Jewish New Year (Rosh Hashanah) or the Day of Atonement (Yom Kippur) comes naturally to them, because museum staff know Jewish holiday traditions and how to present them to both Jewish and non-Jewish audiences. These are also organizations that regularly offer programming and interpretation that focuses on the other residents of the site, whether it is the earlier and later immigrant families who lived in the buildings that became the Tenement Museum, or the houses at Strawbery Banke Museum and the ways in which

Figure 9.2.   Hanukkah's central theme focuses on the miracle of the oil that lasted eight days, and so the foods eaten during Hanukkah—whether from Eastern Europe or India—involve cooking in oil. At Strawbery Banke in Portsmouth, New Hampshire, visitors often see the first-person interpreters portraying Mrs. Shapiro preparing latkes (potato pancakes) at the stove when they visit during Hanukkah. Courtesy of Strawbery Banke Museum.

the residents of the various houses observed (or did not observe) Christmas over the centuries.

The challenge for those who plan December holiday programming, and those who are charged with implementing it, is to consider what Christmas meant to the people who lived in these places, how it was observed (or not), and then use that information as the basis for what visitors see and learn, rather than choosing interpretation and programming that may be seasonal but which does not reflect the people who lived there. Even more important is to consider how to engage audiences that do not observe Christmas but who come to the house wanting to know more about its residents and what their lives were like, including how holidays were celebrated. This does not mean adding programming or interpretation that does not fit the house's history. What it does mean is expanding that seasonal programming to include aspects of the winter season that do not focus on one holiday to the exclusion of the routines of daily life or even discarding holiday programming to present a more accurate interpretation of a specific place and a specific time.

Acknowledging that there are different ways to think about holidays and observances in December gives historic houses a way to shift programming from an exclusive focus on Christmas to programming that is more inclusive. There are other cultural and religious traditions that are often observed during the last quarter of the secular year. Diwali, a Hindu festival, is most commonly celebrated in October or November, according to the Hindu lunar calendar. In some years, Eid al-Fitr, which marks the end of Ramadan, the Muslim holy month of fasting, is in December. It varies from year to year because the Muslim calendar is also a lunar one and so the month of Ramadan's observance—and thus, Eid al-Fitr—changes accordingly. Similarly, the Chinese New Year, observed according to the Chinese lunar calendar, incorporates elements of light into its celebrations.[15]

There are also those whose religious traditions, although Christian, do not include the Christmas celebrations that most think of as traditional. Among them are the Amish, the Mennonites, Quakers, and Jehovah's Witnesses. By considering different communities and their seasonal observances as well as seasonality in general, historic house staff can enlarge visitors' perspectives and help them understand how the advent of winter changed what people wore, the kinds of food they ate, the types of activities they did, and how they worked at their occupations. Shifting this programming does not mean abandoning programs and interpretations focused on Christmas. What it does mean is being more aware of the community in which your historic house or historic site is located and how your site can best interpret its own history rather than simply adopt generic seasonal programming.

The Ken Seiling Waterloo Region Museum and Doon Heritage Village in Kitchener, Ontario, provides an excellent example of how programming for the holiday can focus both on Christmas and its observance and on the wider community and other seasonal events and practices. The site, located in southwest Ontario, includes a living history village (Doon Heritage Village, formerly called Doon Heritage Crossroads) and a modern museum (the Ken Seiling Waterloo Region Museum).

Doon Heritage Village is a sixty-acre living history site that focuses its interpretation on 1914 and includes nineteen buildings that were either relocated from their original sites in the Kitchener/Waterloo area or built on-site to replicate buildings that could not be moved or had disappeared before they could be moved.[16]

Prior to 2022, a two-hour school program in the museum, "Family and Community Traditions," looked at four other winter celebrations/festivals/holidays: Lunar (Chinese) New Year, Eid al-Fitr, Hanukkah, and Diwali (from two perspectives). The program was developed in consultation with local representatives of these faith and community groups. Whenever possible, volunteers who were familiar with one of these celebrations were recruited to deliver and personalize their half-hour segment of the program. The program looked at the origins of the holiday, when it takes place, the food eaten, if gifts are given, and customs. The students made or did something with each program segment: made a Chinese decoration; painted a clay diya and worked together to make a rangoli; were given a temporary henna tattoo to take home to apply; and played dreidel. The segments took place in different parts of the museum and each location was decorated in suitable style. The students learned about different calendars at each location to explain the dates for each celebration. From mid-November to mid-January, general museum visitors could take part in a variety of activities focusing on Diwali, Hanukkah, Eid al-Fitr, the Lunar New Year, and the Newfoundland Christmas tradition of Mummering.[17]

In the village, different homes focused on the different ways that Christmas was celebrated in 1914. The Old Order Mennonite home presented a religious and noncommercial observance, while the commercial excess and somewhat secular celebration of that year was reflected in the Dry Goods and Grocery Store. Two homes presented celebrations that reflected their ethnic origins: visitors learned about the Scottish tradition of Hogmany in the McArthur home; while in the Sararas home, visitors found a German-inspired celebration with the traditions of the Advent wreath and Christ candle in the window. English/British traditions were highlighted in the Seibert House with a focus on the tree and food and gifts of the era. There were evening events for the general public as well as a Christmas-based student education program that included visits to the various locations noted above, along with activities and treats. Although in-person programming was canceled in 2020, modified programming in the village returned in 2021, with activities taking place outside, including tours in which visitors could view decorated homes from outside, and, also outside, tables with various games and activities.

Still another model for winter/Christmas interpretation is one that is part of the annual programming at Henricus Historical Park, in Chester, Virginia, south of Richmond. The park was created in 1985 to interpret early Virginia history during the period 1611–1622, when the location was one of the English settlements upriver from Jamestown. It is a living history museum overseen by a partnership among the Henricus Foundation, Chesterfield County, and Henrico County.[18] Although the site is anchored in the seventeenth century, its history extends through the post–Civil War period (several battles took place nearby), and World War I (the 80th Division trained at an Army camp nearby). The site combines these time periods—seventeenth, nineteenth, and twentieth centuries—with the period of the American Revolution to provide visitors different perspectives on how Christmas observances changed, depending on the political changes in England, the desire to return to some semblance of normalcy in Virginia following the Civil War, and how Virginia soldiers experienced a Christmas in France in 1918 while they waited to return home.[19]

Some sites, understanding that their histories do not include what most visitors might consider a "traditional" Christmas, change their programming during December accordingly.

Prior to 2017–2018, interpretation at the Morgan Log House in Kulpsville, Pennsylvania, focused on the ancestors of Revolutionary War general Daniel Morgan and frontiersman Daniel Boone. There was little to no documentation or sourcing, and interpreters relied on stories and legends about the site's early owners. However, careful review of the history of the site and the people who lived in the house in the last half of the eighteenth century led to a major change in how Christmas is interpreted. Instead of a generic "Christmas of the past" that had been their traditional program, new research revealed that the Mennonite and Quaker families who lived in the house during the eighteenth and nineteenth centuries observed Christmas quietly, if at all, while going about their usual daily activities. The program now focuses on winter and winter preparations as well as the important idea that the past was a place of diverse and different beliefs and practices.[20] These changes in how Christmas is interpreted have led to changes in non-holiday interpretation, emphasizing the varied experiences of those who lived there, including one family who were conscientious objectors during the American Revolution.[21]

The Ken Seiling Waterloo Region Museum, Doon Heritage Village, Henricus Historical Park, and Morgan Log House are examples of historic houses and historic sites that both acknowledge Christmas and its deep roots within their respective communities but use the history of those communities and the recognition of their diversity to construct interpretive programs that are site and audience specific. They incorporate diversity: diverse audiences, diverse communities, and a recognition that the past really is a different place, with beliefs, traditions, and expectations that sometimes are very different from our contemporary ones. These programs also are very site specific: they help audiences understand the people who lived in their regions and how these people chose to celebrate—or not celebrate—these holidays.

Acknowledging the diversity of our audiences is key to making them feel welcome during a time of year when feeling excluded is all too common. We must be mindful of this other audience, with programming that recognizes the community in which they all live and the daily events that mark their lives. There were other things going on in December besides Christmas: interpreting those can give a much fuller and nuanced view of what a house's residents experienced in the last month of the year and the richness of the community in which they lived.

Notes

1. My thanks to Dr. Jonathan Sarna, Joseph H. Braun, and Belle R. Braun, professor of American Jewish history at Brandeis University, who generously shared with me sources and suggestions for this chapter.
2. The Hebrew word חֲנֻכָּה is spelled in English in several different ways: Hanukkah, Ḥanukka, Chanukah, or Chanukkah. It means "dedication," which refers to the rededication of the Temple in Jerusalem that existed until its destruction by the Romans in 70 CE (Common Era). Today the name of the holiday is most commonly spelled in English as "Hanukkah."
3. Dianne Ashton, in her book *Hanukkah in America: A History* (New York: New York University Press, 2013), thoroughly details the history of the holiday over two thousand years ago and

goes on to discuss how that observance changed in the following centuries and its emergence as a major Jewish holiday beginning in the late nineteenth century.

4. The Books of the Maccabees were written after the structure of the Torah and the additional books of the Jewish Bible were codified, and so they are not included there.

5. For a basic explanation of Sukkot, go to "Sukkot 101," https://www.myjewishlearning.com/article/sukkot-101/ (accessed February 7, 2022); Dianne Ashton, *Hanukkah in America*, 15–16.

6. See Ty Alhadeff, in "New Light Shed on Sephardic Sources for Hanukkah Heroes," for more information on the story of Judith and the Scroll of Antiochus: https://jewishstudies.washington.edu/digital-sephardic-treasures/sephardic-sources-for-hanukkah-heroes/ (accessed February 2, 2022). Both the story of Judith and the Scroll of Antiochus were translated from their original languages (Hebrew and Aramaic) into Ladino, the language spoken by Jews of Mediterranean origin, and incorporated into prayerbooks used by congregations that follow Sephardic traditions. Ladino is a mixture of Hebrew, Spanish, Turkish, Arabic, and French, and in much the same way that Yiddish—a mixture of Hebrew, Middle German, Aramaic, and Slavic languages—was used by Jews of Eastern Europe in their daily lives, Ladino was used by Jews of the Mediterranean in their daily lives.

7. For a basic explanation of Shavuot, go to "Shavuot 101," https://www.myjewishlearning.com/article/shavuot-101/ (accessed February 7, 2022).

8. Hilda Satt Polacheck, *I Came a Stranger: The Story of a Hull House Girl*, ed. by Dina J. Polacheck Epstein (Urbana and Chicago: University of Chicago Press, 1989), 9, 51–52.

9. See Jeffrey S. Gurock, "Jacob A. Riis: Christian Friend or Missionary Foe? Two Jewish Views," *American Jewish History* 71, no. 1 (September 1981): 29–47, for a discussion of Riis and how his work was viewed by various groups within the New York City Jewish community.

10. For example, in the early years of the twentieth century, the Haas family of San Francisco, who arrived in the United States from Germany in the mid-nineteenth century, held elegant Christmas parties to which they invited their fellow German Jewish friends. But a century later, the trappings of Christmas had disappeared from these December family gatherings, to be replaced by the observance of Hanukkah and the Sabbath. See Joshua Eli Plaut, *A Kosher Christmas: 'Tis the Season to Be Jewish* (New Brunswick, NJ: Rutgers University Press, 2012), 10–13.

11. Because the Jewish calendar is both a lunar and a solar calendar, the dates of Hanukkah observance change from year to year in the secular calendar. Thus, it can begin as early as the end of November and sometimes—though rarely—coincides with Thanksgiving in the United States, or it can begin just after December 25 and last until the first days of the new year. For a more complete explanation, go to "Jewish Calendar: Solar and Lunar," https://www.myjewishlearning.com/article/jewish-calendar-solar-and-lunar/ (accessed February 11, 2022).

12. For examples of past Hanukkah programming and Hanukkah-related blog posts, see the links on this page: https://www.tenement.org/?s=Hanukkah (accessed March 30, 2022).

13. For a list of the houses open to visitors, including links to individual pages about them, see https://www.strawberybanke.org/houses/historic-houses.cfm (accessed March 30, 2022).

14. For a history of the house and of the Shapiro family, see https://www.strawberybanke.org/houses/shapiro.cfm (accessed March 30, 2022).

15. See Rabbi Arthur O. Waskow, "Hanukkah and the Winter Solstice," My Jewish Learning, for a fuller explanation of why Hanukkah may be associated with the winter solstice: https://www.myjewishlearning.com/article/hanukkah-and-the-winter-solstice/ (accessed February

18, 2002). For Diwali, see Lizz Schumer, "What is Diwali? The History behind the Important Holiday": https://www.goodhousekeeping.com/holidays/a37680263/what-is-diwali-history-story-celebration-facts/ (accessed February 21, 2022). This article includes a link to "Diwali Toolkit" published by the Hindu American Foundation and intended for educators and parents, which includes a history of the holiday, lesson plans, and activities: https://www.hinduamerican.org/diwali#:~:text=Download%20Diwali%20Toolkit (accessed February 21, 2022). For Eid al-Fitr, see "Eid al-Fitr," History.com, https://www.history.com/topics/holidays/eid-al-fitr (accessed February 21, 2022). For the Chinese New Year, see "The Lunar New Year: Rituals and Legends," Asia for Educators, http://afe.easia.columbia.edu/special/china_general_lunar.htm#preparations (accessed February 23, 2022).
16. Region of Waterloo Museums, "Doon Heritage Village" (Kitchener, Ontario), https://region-ofwaterloomuseums.ca/en/visit/doon-heritage-village.aspx (accessed February 25, 2022).
17. These programs were described by Carolyn Blackstock in personal email messages to the author, December 16, 2021, and February 25, 2022.
18. Henricus Historical Park (Chester, Virginia): https://henricus.org.
19. Information on these programs was provided to the author by John Pagano, historical interpretation supervisor at Henricus via email, March 17, 2022.
20. A chancery court case from Loudoun County, Virginia, in 1815, illustrates this point. On January 11, 1813, William Lewis and Elijah Reticor agreed to pay John Beveridge $30 on December 25, 1813, for the hire of Winney, an enslaved woman, for the year 1813. Such hiring agreements customarily began on January 1 and ended December 31, and paying Beveridge at the end of the year for Winney's labor was normal. For the three men, the fact that December 25 was Christmas was not a deterrent to fulfilling their legal obligation to pay the agreed-upon hiring amount. Lewis sued Beveridge over a disagreement on the amount of interest that Lewis and Reticor had to pay Beveridge over and above the $30. Loudoun County (Virginia) Chancery Causes, 1815. Loudoun County, Chancery Causes, 1815–023. Local Government Records Collection, Loudoun County Court Records. The Library of Virginia, Richmond, Virginia: https://www.lva.virginia.gov/chancery/case_detail.asp?CFN=107-1815-023 (accessed June 30, 2022).
21. This change was described by Tim Betz, former executive director, in a personal email message to the author, December 15, 2021, and in personal conversation, March 9, 2022.

CHAPTER 10

Kwanzaa

A Teachable Moment for All Ages

Kelly Elaine Navies

MY EARLIEST MEMORIES of Kwanzaa begin in early childhood. Our family celebrated it almost as soon as we arrived in the California Bay Area in 1969, just three years after the founding of Kwanzaa in 1966 by Dr. Maulana Karenga. I have vivid recollections of standing in a circle of people passing the Unity Cup and shouting, *Harambee* seven times. I know now that *Harambee* is Swahili for "let's all pull together." In those moments, I felt as if I were in a very warm and safe space surrounded by love and wonder. Wherever we might be on that particular evening—in a home or a cultural center—the aroma of good soul food filled the air with the promise of a joyous *Karamu* or feast.

You may wonder why a chapter on Kwanzaa is included in a book about Christmas. Unlike Christmas, Kwanzaa is not a religious holiday. However, it does intentionally fall during what has been traditionally understood to be the season of Christmas. To be more precise, Kwanzaa starts the day after Christmas, December 26, and lasts for the seven days ending on New Year's Day. Kwanzaa was designed to fall between these two popular holidays. Such timing allows it to exist as a nonreligious alternative, while also capitalizing on a time when many families are already gathering.

Back in 1966, during the height of the Black Power Movement, Dr. Maulana Karenga created Kwanzaa.[1] Based in Southern California, where he is the chair of the Africana Studies Department at California State University–Long Beach, Karenga is a scholar activist and renowned author of many works on black studies, including the standard text, *Kwanzaa: A Celebration of Family Community and Culture*. Karenga developed this holiday not just for

African Americans or black people in America but for the entire African diaspora to celebrate their rich history and culture and pass important values on to the next generations.[2]

Although Kwanzaa is a relatively young holiday, it did not emerge out of thin air. Kwanzaa is based on traditions and principles that are intrinsic to cultures throughout the Africa continent. The ideas and concepts of Kwanzaa are expressed in the Swahili language, which is one of the most widely spoken languages in Africa.

The seven principles that form its core were drawn from communitarian values found throughout the African continent. These principles are *Umoja* (Unity), *Kujichagulia* (Self-Determination), *Ujima* (Collective Work and Responsibility), *Ujamaa* (Cooperative Economics), *Nia* (Purpose), *Kuumba* (Creativity), and *Imani* (Faith). The word Kwanzaa comes from the Swahili phrase, *matunda ya Kwanza*, which means "First Fruits," as the holiday is rooted in first-fruits celebrations found throughout Africa in both ancient and modern times.

First-fruits celebrations are traditions that allow a community to come together and reinforce values of unity, gratitude, and reverence. Such traditions have been recorded as early as ancient Egypt and are found in contemporary African cultures, as well. In Southeastern Africa, first-fruits celebrations take place in late December/early January. The Zulu first-fruits celebration, *Umkhosi*, is celebrated around the same time as Kwanzaa and lasts for seven days as well.[3] Thus, the structure of Kwanzaa is heavily influenced by these and other similar traditions throughout the continent of Africa.

As mentioned earlier, Kwanzaa is not a religious holiday; it was specifically designed to transcend religious divisions and thus facilitate a space where black folk can come together and celebrate shared culture and values, whether they practice Christianity, Islam, Buddhism, or some other religion or spiritual belief. For over fifty years, Kwanzaa has evolved from a niche holiday observed by a few to an event with international cultural impact. In fact, it is currently observed by people on almost every continent. In 2020, at the height of the pandemic, the founder of Kwanzaa, Maulana Ron Karenga, held the first virtual international Kwanzaa celebration.

The mission of the National Museum of African American History and Culture (NMAAHC) is to tell the American story through an African American lens. Further, the museum is committed to the Smithsonian goal of facilitating the "increase and diffusion of knowledge." To sum it up, as a cultural heritage institution, the museum is dedicated to engaging the public through the telling of African American stories in a multiplicity of formats. The core principles of Kwanzaa, such as *Kuumba* (Creativity) and *Nia* (Purpose), support this mission, thus it is a natural fit for our museum to acknowledge Kwanzaa and offer education and programming to our audience about this holiday.

Indeed, Kwanzaa is a seven-day teaching moment, and provides our institution with many opportunities to do what we do best—create relevant, informative, and dynamic educational programming (see figure 10.1). The structure, symbolism, and tenets of Kwanzaa enable our museum to draw upon multifaceted and multimedia resources to teach the public about Kwanzaa while also introducing them to our rich collections and related cultural themes that are already highlighted in the museum.

Similarly, other cultural institutions can also draw creative and programmatic inspiration from Kwanzaa—particularly if they desire to highlight the culture of the African

Figure 10.1. Museum staff explaining the symbolism of the items on the Kwanzaa table at the Robert F. Smith Family History Center. The fruit, or *mazao*, signifies the community's collective harvest, expressing gratitude. The straw mat, known as *mkeka*, represents the foundation upon which we construct our lives. The seven-candle holder, or *kinara*, symbolizes the community's African roots. Courtesy of the National Museum of African American History and Culture.

diaspora. In fact, the Anacostia Community Museum in Washington, DC, which opened in 1967, has hosted in-person Kwanzaa workshops and celebrations almost as long as it has been around. For a museum rooted in its community-identity, such as Anacostia, Kwanzaa is a fitting tradition. In addition to celebrations that immerse community members in the culture of the African diaspora, Anacostia also offers Kwanzaa workshops for teachers, high school students, and young children. In 2008, Kwanzaa was featured in the museum's exhibition, "Jubilee: African American Celebration."[4]

When the pandemic hit in March 2020, NMAAHC staff met the challenge by creating a vast array of digital offerings that included the celebration of Kwanzaa. An important component of this programming is that it was designed to appeal to all ages. And like most of our programming, the goal is to both educate and entertain. Programming for Kwanzaa at NMAAHC had to be as dynamic as the other programs and exhibitions to which our patrons have grown accustomed. Rather than an obstacle, shifting our emphasis to digital programming during the pandemic provided us with an opportunity to draw upon the strengths of our staff in curatorial, education, and public affairs to develop content. In this way, our staff exemplified the principle of *Ujima*, Collective Work and Responsibility. An example of how programming was implemented is the Kwanzaa blog that was launched in December 2020. Other institutions may find inspiration in these program ideas.

It was the first winter holiday season after nearly the entire world shut down due to COVID-19. All of the Smithsonian units, including NMAAHC, closed their doors. The year 2020 was also when the world was rocked by the violent deaths of unarmed African American George Floyd and others.[5] Families were looking for ways to understand the heightened racial tensions in their communities and for ways to nurture hope and healing for their children. Smithsonian staff were compelled to telework and even more significantly, to develop creative ways to engage our attentive and disquieted audience during these trying times.

As the winter holiday season approached, NMAAHC staff from throughout the museum collaborated on a wide range of virtual programming designed to teach our audience about Kwanzaa and share ways they might practice this holiday with their families. Our "virtual" Kwanzaa programming took many forms. There was an offering called "Around the Table" that featured renowned food historian Jessica B. Harris sharing a recipe for each day of Kwanzaa in a short video. The video for the first night is the longest as she describes in detail the contents of her Kwanzaa basket, which includes foods from around the world that have meaning for her and for African American people. For example, she explains why she includes black-eyed peas, which originate in Africa and are eaten for good luck in the New Year by African Americans throughout the United States.

Another feature of the virtual Kwanzaa was a daily blog that highlighted a song, a "thought for the day," a recipe, and a children's activity. Each culturally significant item was carefully curated to illustrate the principle of the day. In this blog, the first day, Umoja (Unity) was represented in this way:

- Song: "Worth His Weight in Gold (Rally Round the Flag)" by Steel Pulse
- Thought For the Day: Excerpt from the novel *Beloved*, by Toni Morrison. "Baby Suggs Sermon in the Clearing"
- Recipe: Dates, Figs, Milk
- Children's Activity: A link led users to a page with an activity that invited children to draw a picture of a meal they enjoy making and eating with people they love, to talk about unity, and finally to sing "Come Together" with John Legend and Sesame Street friends (another video link)

Each item/activity would reflect the principle of the day and be an example of the culture of the African diaspora. We hoped that families would supplement their observance of Kwanzaa with these literary and cultural offerings. The virtual programming also explored the meaning of Kwanzaa with short videos of people conducting Kwanzaa ceremonies and explanations of the various symbols, such as the *Muhindi*, which are ears of corn that represent the children in the family and the future of the family and community; and the *Kinara*, which holds a candle for each of the seven days. This candle holder is symbolic of the African roots of people of the African diaspora; and of course, *Zawadi*, otherwise known as the Gifts. In Kwanzaa, gifts are given to children, as in some other holidays, but a significant difference is that these gifts should have a cultural and educational theme and are ideally handmade. The virtual offerings included many examples of arts and crafts, particularly those that children might enjoy.

Figure 10.2.   Storytelling is a feature of cultures of the African diaspora and was part of Kwanzaa Family Day in 2019 at the Robert F. Smith Family History Center. Courtesy of the National Museum of African American History and Culture.

The Early Childhood Education team contributed to virtual Kwanzaa programming, as innovatively as the rest of the NMAAHC staff. They developed an online Kwanzaa activity guide for four- to eight-year-old children that included information about each principle, an object that connects to the principle, discussion questions, and a suggested music, art, play, or writing activity. This guide was offered in both English and Spanish. In 2021, they created a video series to accompany the above-described guide. In each video, an educator lights a candle on the *kinara*, explains the day's principle, and talks about an object in the museum's collection that relates to that principle.

The NMAAHC Early Childhood Education Team held their first in-person Kwanzaa Family Day at the museum in 2019. They developed a variety of hands-on learning activities and used museum objects to introduce youths of all ages to the principles of Kwanzaa. Throughout the day, families were invited to various activities:

- Interactive storytimes featuring a Kwanzaa principle-inspired book or an African folktale, like Ananse the Spider
- Djembe (West African drum) lessons taught by a local music educator
- An Adinkra (Ghanaian graphic symbols) symbol art project
- A community-building project inviting families to add their own links to a paper chain by sharing their answers to questions like "How do you show your creativity?" and "What do you love about your community?"

- An exhibit project using Kwanzaa gallery guides that help children make connections between art and objects in the collection to principles like Ujima, Kuumba, and Umoja.

Families were also able to access a resource table and mini library, where they could learn more about black children's books and even take a book home. Finally, there was also a Kwanzaa demonstration table, where families could see how to set up their own Kwanzaa table and learn the purpose and meaning behind items like the *kinara*, *mkeka* (straw mat), and unity cup. It is easy to see how this multifaceted, in-person program drew upon and illuminated the meaning of the seven principles of Kwanzaa.

The seven principles of Kwanzaa lend themselves to an array of creative expressions and allow the museum to use its multifaceted and multimedia approach to public education, both in person and remotely. The challenges of the pandemic motivated museum staff to search for ways to create a virtual atmosphere akin to the warmth of a home decorated with red, black, and green candles and Kente cloth. They could achieve this with robust and dynamic programming that ranged from delicious, African-inspired recipes and accessible crafts, to intellectually stimulating activities and literary excerpts.

As I stated earlier, Kwanzaa is a seven-day teachable moment that enables an institution like NMAAHC to fulfill its mission to teach essential lessons about African American history and culture, while entertaining, inspiring, and introducing a new generation to a culturally relevant holiday. It is a holiday that has the power to transcend religious distinctions and bring communities together in *Umoja* (Unity). Other cultural institutions can surely look to the above examples in seeking to implement Kwanzaa programs of their own. The keywords in Kwanzaa programming are community and culture. Your institution can design its own celebration while simultaneously nurturing community outreach. Identify key individuals in your community who already observe Kwanzaa, and ask them to collaborate on a public program.

The NMAAHC has reopened and is welcoming thousands of visitors again. All of the staff are eager to put their energy and skills back to in-person programming, but now a rich array of online offerings will complement their programming. The demands of the pandemic era have forever changed the way museums approach outreach and programming, and this change directly impacts Kwanzaa content as well. Now, in addition to "Kwanzaa Day" the public can count on blogs, video series, and live streams.

When I was a little black girl with an Afro, growing up in the California Bay Area in the 1970s, celebrating Kwanzaa with a close-knit family and circle of friends in homes and cultural centers, never did I imagine Kwanzaa would enter the digital age, an age where a child in the United States can experience the African diaspora without leaving the comfort of their home. Families can embody the principles of Kwanzaa by merely accessing programming from NMAAHC and take advantage of the myriad resources and activities available on our website.

In the future, I know the celebration of Kwanzaa will continue to evolve and be incorporated into programming at other cultural institutions. From *Umoja* (Unity) to *Imani* (Faith), the seven principles represent the best of the human impulse and offer myriad possibilities for educational programming. Americans of all cultures and backgrounds are yearning for a

template that brings them together rather than tears them apart. I suggest we look to Kwanzaa for inspiration. May all of our children have safe spaces filled with love and wonder.
Harambee!

Notes

1. The Black Power Movement was a political movement expressing a new racial consciousness among blacks in the United States in the late 1960s. See Kwame Anthony Appiah and Henry Louis Gates Jr., *Africana: The Encyclopedia of the African American Experience* (New York: Basic Civitas Books, 1999), 262.
2. The African diaspora refers to the voluntary and involuntary movement of Africans and their descendants to various parts of the world. See Horace R. Hall, "African and Black Diaspora as Curriculum" (published online, March 25, 2021) at: https://doi.org/10.1093/acrefore/9780190264093.013.1581.
3. For more discussion of first-fruits festivals that inspired the development of Kwanzaa, see Maulana Karenga, *Kwanzaa: A Celebration of Family, Community, and Culture* (Los Angeles: University of Sankore Press, 1998).
4. See Emily Niekrasz, "Celebrating Kwanzaa at the Anacostia Community Museum" (Washington, DC: Smithsonian Institution Archives, 2019), https://siarchives.si.edu/blog/celebrating-kwanzaa-anacostia-community-museum.
5. George Floyd was killed on May 25, 2020, during an arrest for passing a counterfeit $20 bill. Officer Derek Chauvin was convicted of the murder. His death sparked a worldwide uprising against police brutality, led by the Black Lives Matter movement in the United States.

Resources

Appiah, Kwame Anthony, and Henry Louis Gates Jr., eds. *Africana: The Encyclopedia of the African and African American Experience.* New York: Basic Civitas Books, 1999.

Harris, Jessica B. *High on the Hog: A Culinary Journey from Africa to the United States.* New York: Bloomsbury, 2011.

Karenga, Maulana. *Kwanzaa: A Celebration of Family Community and Culture.* Los Angeles: University of Sankore Press, 1998.

PLANNING

CHAPTER 11

'Twas the Year before Christmas

Planning Your Event and Protecting Resources

Laurel A. Racine

WHO DOESN'T LOVE a festively decorated house complete with food, music, and entertainment thrown wide to the neighborhood? Of course, we all do—except, maybe, when it is *your* historic house museum filled with irreplaceable site-associated art and history objects preserved from four generations of the family.

My first experience with Christmas in a historic house was as a graduate student erecting artificial trees in the courtyard for Winterthur's Yuletide display and then giving tours for visitors. Soon thereafter I joined the National Park Service's Northeast Museum Services Center regularly working with curators from eighty national park units from Maine to Virginia. While not common to all parks, I heard often enough about the challenges of planning for holiday events that I convened a conference call (before video meetings!) to investigate the topic and for a time hosted a "Holiday Historic House" information-sharing and support group.[1] At first I tried to pull back from the holiday theme thinking there must be other occasions for decorating houses, but I found the main focus is truly Christmas decorating.[2] I have since expanded my inquiry to include house museums that decorate for the holidays in other parts of the country.

Holiday tourism of historic houses is wildly popular as people seek wholesome, family-friendly events to share with friends and relatives during the Christmas season. A well-decorated historic house can effectively connect with people through all their senses and teach them about the past while they enjoy the season's sights and sounds. Lights, food, music, and entertainment are the natural extensions of the holiday celebration, sometimes leading historic sites to relax their policies to further promote the festive feel of the events. The challenge for historic house museum staff is to remain focused on resource protection among all the fun, goodwill, and festivity of holiday events.

Planning and Logistics

If your site already hosts a Christmas event, you know the planning is a year-round activity. You put away the decorations, analyze the event, and start planning for the next year. As the advocate for the museum collection, it is your job to both envision the worst-case scenarios and develop workable solutions.[3]

If you are new to planning a Christmas event at your site, the collections manager at Reynolda House in Winston-Salem, North Carolina, recommends you start small and be sure the staff who cares for the museum collections are in the conversation early so the event is safe and realistic for objects and visitors.[4] Your site can build confidence and skills before attempting a larger event.

Written policies can provide helpful ground rules for planning a Christmas event. Lilly House at Newfields in Indianapolis, Indiana, has established policies regarding food, drink, flowers, and plants they adhere to even at Christmastime. Longfellow House–Washington's Headquarters National Historic Site in Cambridge, Massachusetts, excludes glitter from all crafts and decorations to avoid spreading the abrasive grains through the house.[5] Conservators at Winterthur Museum Garden and Library in Winterthur, Delaware, test all new faux materials to approve them for display.[6] Stains and pests do not take a holiday, so neither should the policies protecting your resources. The director at the Campbell House in Saint Louis, Missouri, encourages establishing an understanding of the irreplaceable nature of site-associated objects so staff, volunteers, and the board understand why a historic house museum cannot follow through on every crowd-pleasing suggestion.[7] It should not be (or be perceived to be) the caprice of the curator; there are best practices in the museum profession for solid reasons.

An important policy for all, written or not, is to report any accidents or damage as soon as they occur to increase the likelihood of cleaning it or a successful repair. It is easier to remove a stain if the substance is known and only freshly spilled. It is easier to repair a broken vase if all the pieces are located. Staff should make notes and take record photographs of all damage.[8] Having a form for recording damage prepared ahead of time helps capture all the relevant information.

Planning adequate time to execute your Christmas decorating is essential for the safety of museum collections because accidents happen when people are rushed or tired.[9] Planning ample time can also help you spread out the number of people in the building at once if you have multiple contractors or, like the curator at the Theodore Roosevelt Inaugural National Historic Site, members of several garden clubs who need to install decorations. For some sites like Andrew Jackson's Hermitage in Nashville, Tennessee, staying after hours to finish decorating is not an option because there is not enough lighting in the historic rooms for people to safely work, especially with museum collections.[10]

Some sites close rooms or buildings to decorate for Christmas, so the public need to know of the closures, while others decorate only on days they are regularly closed to the public. Staff at Andrew Jackson's Hermitage is strategic about when and where they decorate. They do not close to decorate for Christmas but work in the public areas (e.g., halls) before the house opens so they do not impede the visitor flow. During public hours they decorate the furnished rooms where visitors do not walk but can see them in process through acrylic barriers. This allows the site to stay open and visitors to have a behind-the-scenes experience. With a less defined barrier between the public and the furnished rooms, Winterthur closes rooms and Hampton National Historic Site in Towson, Maryland, closes the house entirely when they decorate for Christmas.[11] Collection objects are more vulnerable when they are in transport or waiting to be installed and there are staff, packing materials, and equipment taking up valuable space.

Elaborate displays like those at Lilly House and Winterthur require the year to plan and weeks to execute. At Winterthur, staff create a work order for every object to move in or out of each room including very precise locations. Lilly House closes for two weeks. It takes three trained staff an entire day to clear the furniture, rugs, and small objects out of the rooms they plan to decorate. A contract decorating company spends half a day setting up the "backbone" of the display including trees, garlands, and wreaths. It then takes eight days for eight to ten staff and volunteers to decorate the rooms. Breakdown of the decorations is much faster taking three days followed by carpet cleaning and reinstallation of collection objects. Even the more moderate display at Campbell House entails moving furniture, clearing mantels, setting up multiple trees, bringing thirty boxes up from the basement, and setting up a sixty-piece crèche.

There are reasons to plan for even more installation time. The Homestead Museum in City of Industry, California, recently lost 40 percent of their staff, so they need to plan for fewer people to carry out the work over a longer period.[12] Keep in mind the physical nature of the work to lift, carry, and build decorations when planning both people and time for tasks. Andrew Jackson's Hermitage and Lilly House also recommend building in time (sometimes substantial!) to clean up needles shed from the faux greens and glitter shed from ornaments.

There are practical logistics to consider. If contractors, volunteers, or staff need to bring items into the building, define which door(s) and what routes they can use to safely navigate boxes, furniture, or trees through the house. Staff or volunteers should monitor entrances if there are multiple trips in and out. Never prop a door open for convenience because it is a security breach and will change the nearby temperature and humidity levels. There should be a method for signing people in and out of buildings for both security of the collection and safety of people in case the building needs to be evacuated.[13]

Live musicians inside the historic house can add to the ambience of a special event, but you must consider where they will perform and store belongings. Hampton hires choirs and carolers who need a separate, secure place in which to store coats, hats, purses, and more while they perform to avoid having historic furniture used for this purpose. If an instrument is large or heavy, you will need to plan a safe path for it to travel through the house, what section of the house is large and robust enough to support the weight, and any buffer or cap needed under piano wheels or spikes on the bottom of double basses. A string quartet should perform at a distance from collection objects to give space for the arms and bows.[14] At Andrew Jackson's Hermitage, musicians play in the public area, not in the historically furnished rooms. Longfellow House hosts a harpist in the library. This is their largest room, but they still need to move chairs to accommodate the instrument. The harpist sits on a non-historic chair. They hire the same musician each year because she is sensitive to the historic setting. One year they hired a vocalist who wanted to wander singing through the house, which the staff did not allow for the safety of the objects.

For a new event, check that the electrical service in the building is up to code and able to support any additional lights or electronic decorations you are contemplating. Threading electrical cords through rooms or overloading the meager number of outlets can be unsightly and dangerous. Winterthur only uses a strand of lights for two or three years then allows staff to take them home to avoid worn cords and a strand burning out mid-season. For simplicity, should a strand burn out, they unplug it, remove visible bulbs, and run a new strand alongside it. Staff at Lilly House minimize the complexity of turning on lights as much as possible. They can control most of the interior lights with a single button. Lights plugged into outlets are controlled with seven-day digital timers. A few specific lights such as LED candles or fairy lights are operated by remote control.

Christmas lights are a key ingredient in many historic houses decorated for the holidays. Consider the types of lights and how close they are to collection objects and even new decorations. Increasing the light levels in a room for even just a season could irreversibly damage fragile organic objects.[15] When possible, use lights that do not give off heat such as LEDs. Until there is a replacement with the correct appearance, Winterthur uses C-6 and C-9 bulbs with an opaque ceramic finish to represent the mid-twentieth-century era of H. F. duPont's family. These lights produce heat, so use added precautions including no paper or cellophane ornaments nearby, dimmers to bring down the heat, and timers to ensure lights are not left on accidentally.

Weather

Depending on your location, opening for the holidays in the late fall or early winter can present weather-related challenges for the safety of visitors and cultural resources alike. Well before the holiday event or season, you should consider safety and security concerns related to precipitation, ice, and opening the house after dark. Think about how rain and snow might affect the site and visitors. Depending on the weather, staff might need to clear snow and treat ice for visitor safety. The Homestead Museum cancels their holiday event when it rains because there are unpaved walkways between buildings, which would be unpleasant for visitors and lead to mud in the historic houses. All museums should be prepared to cancel or close early due to weather and have a public notification plan in place, since forecasts can change swiftly and dangerous conditions appear. Recently, Holidays at Hampton closed an hour early because high winds cropped up.[16]

With many visitors arriving for popular holiday events, the door to your museum will hopefully open frequently, which is a challenge for maintaining the temperature and humidity levels inside. If your building does not have a permanent, historic vestibule, it might be worthwhile to consider a way to temporarily mitigate environmental differences. In the past Hampton would seasonally build a weather vestibule on the large front porch that visitors enter before opening the main door to the house. Currently, they use an ante-room as an airlock (only one door opens at a time) between outside conditions and the rooms where collection objects are.

Lilly House has a historic vestibule that they supplement with a twenty-foot awning with sides that covers the sidewalk to the front door. For aesthetics, they chose an awning with a curved top and side windows, and they provide welcoming signage to encourage visitors to come in. The enclosed awning mitigates the environment inside the house and protects waiting visitors from the wind. Covering the sidewalk also saves the staff from shoveling and salting as well as gives plenty of runway for visitors' shoes to dry off and shed grit.

For evening events, assess the exterior lighting to ensure there is adequate illumination for safe access to and security of the site after dark. For year-round security most sites have strategically placed spotlights to light the property around buildings and dispel dark corners where perpetrators can hide. Hampton augments their usual lighting with a tall, generator-run light tower to provide extra general illumination to the grounds and paths. They put it on a side road outside the visitors' main viewshed. Many sites delineate paths between buildings with festive luminaria. Longfellow House places real candles in sand-filled, fire-proof bags along the paths. They spend about twenty staff hours setting them up while breakdown (including extinguishing the candles in water) is faster. The Pioneer Museum in Fredericksburg, Texas, switched from traditional luminaria to placing LED lights in quart and pint fruit jars along the paths between their nine buildings. This approach is less labor intensive, requiring about one and a half hours to execute.[17]

Visitors

Some sites enjoy their heaviest visitation during holiday events and need to consider the flow of visitors to and through their buildings. Despite the desire to accommodate all visitors as soon as they arrive, you need to manage the number of people who can safely and securely be in a building at any one time to maintain a quality visitor experience and protect the building and collection objects. The number and timing of visitors in a building will vary depending on its floor load, means of egress, visitor proximity to sensitive objects (including wallpaper), the size of the smallest space a group must pass through, and the sight lines for monitoring visitors as they walk through open exhibit areas. You will want to identify pinch points and places where visitors pass especially close to displays and remove collection objects from those areas.

There are some strategies for managing the number of visitors entering your buildings. First, you need to determine what a safe number is, advocate to management, and communicate this to staff. No one wants a visitor embarrassed because they jostled a vase off a table in a crowd. You are doing no one a favor if they can come inside but cannot move around or see anything. Numbers matter to everyone.

One option is a reservation or timed ticket system that requires a robust communication strategy so walk-in visitors are not disappointed. Longfellow House experimented with reservations but returned to a first-come, first-served policy. Managing the line and capacity limit requires staff and/or volunteers to track how many people are inside and when they depart so more people can be invited in. These folks need breaks so they can stay alert, and be sure to set expectations in advance, so no one leaves their station without a replacement. Radios or cell phones facilitate communication among everyone providing customer service and security.

To spread visitors out and give them more to do, sites often augment the furnished house experience with offerings on the lit grounds. Longfellow House hosts refreshments and crafts in the neighboring carriage house. Some years Hampton has a Victorian Santa for children to visit in the reconstructed orangery. Lilly House has an extensive illuminated landscape people can explore including gift and food vendors. When Winterthur could not have visitors to their interior Yuletide display in 2020, they developed a popular range of outdoor activities including a wine walk, mulled cider station, and a Santa tram around the grounds. They found they needed to clearly mark what paths were closed to visitors so they would not wander into unlit areas. If you decide you need tents to house outdoor activities, take care not to attach tents to historic building fabric or place stakes in sensitive landscape areas such as historic gardens or potential archaeological sites.[18]

When visitors enter, you will want to consider coats and bags. Is your space large enough to accommodate them or should visitors leave them at the entrance? If you are lacking a dedicated coat closet in an ancillary space (many of us are!), you might consider a temporary coat rack in a non-exhibit area or a volunteer-run bag/coat check to keep big coats, bags, and packages out of the furnished spaces.

Your visitation at Christmas is likely different from the rest of the year. You probably have more visitors, they want to browse, and they are not expecting a long tour. Staff and volunteers are key to monitoring visitor flow and the security of collections even if you have a camera and security system. For some sites, the tour guide leading a group is the primary security measure. Other sites such as Hampton opt for a more free-flow approach with personnel stationed in strategic locations to both monitor the collection and provide interpretation to or answer questions for otherwise self-guided visitors.

Protecting Collections

While visitors enjoy the open display of furnishings in historic houses, especially when there are no barriers in the way, museum curators know collection objects are at risk of damage or loss in this type of exhibit. The unusual circumstances and increased visitation of holiday events exacerbate the already vulnerable situation of objects in a historically furnished house. Lilly House and Winterthur use formal stanchions to define the visitor path while Longfellow House has had success with visitors staying on carpet runners. Longfellow House also places ribbons across the seats of chairs to remind people not to sit. The Homestead Museum minimizes barriers for an immersive experience. Hampton removes the fragile

Federal seating furniture from the Great Hall, which would be otherwise unprotected in this busy space, where the site stages small musical performances.

In the past, Reynolda House displayed a fully set dining room table but monitoring the silverware was a cumbersome task. They were right to be vigilant as another site acknowledged the theft of a fork. Today Reynolda House displays a historic tablecloth and an arrangement of candlesticks in the dining room while a vitrine containing a full place-setting is on permanent display in the nearby kitchen.

Holiday decorating often entails moving objects off exhibit to remove them from reach of visitors or to make way for decorations. All staff and volunteers entrusted with moving collection objects should receive training on how to handle the types of objects they will be touching. The objects are irreplaceable, and untrained people can cause unintentional harm. Winterthur requires watching a training video and taking a test before anyone can handle objects. Most sites limit the number of people who handle the collection objects to the collections care staff and a small crew of trained volunteers or staff from other departments. Limiting those with responsibility to move objects promotes the safety, security, and accountability of each object.[19] Annual training enhances the effectiveness of participants as does inviting the same individuals to participate every year. There are important roles for volunteers and staff who do not handle collections including setting up Christmas trees, decorating trees with new ornaments, and setting out fake flowers and new decorations on non-historic surfaces.

When you need to move objects off exhibit, plan for where they will go. Even a temporary move needs to be carefully planned to ensure the continued safety and security of each object. Your strategy can vary depending on the length of the event and storage options available. Reynolda House staff move objects into on-site storage; storage within the same building is ideal to minimize exposure to outside weather. Campbell House's event is a single evening, so they place the objects on carts and wheel them into another room to be returned the next day. In reverse, the curator at Longfellow House waits until the day of their evening event before he places small collection objects on display and usually returns them to storage immediately or the next day unless there is a special tour. He watches the site-associated toys under the Christmas tree for the duration of the event.

It is also important to consider collection objects when you are adding Christmas decorations to a display. It is essential to place a protective barrier such as Mylar under decorations to avoid scratching the surfaces of objects and furniture. Paintings hung on the wall over tables and mantels are a special consideration. Reynolda House is careful not to place any holiday decorations on tables with paintings over them to ensure nothing touches them. Theodore Roosevelt Inaugural National Historic Site had custom Plexiglass barriers created to place in front of the portraits over the mantels to protect them from all holiday decorations. Winterthur has designated containers in its collection where they can arrange faux flowers in a very controlled way. The faux flowers are each wrapped in Mylar. They are then threaded through a grid of fine tape at the top of the container and supported with a "frog" (round disk with holes or prongs) at the bottom.

Moving objects on or off exhibit can lead to the temporary loss of an object. You need to plan and carefully record any collections moved for the night or the season so they can be safely returned later without fear of being lost.[20] The director of historic preservation at Lilly

House strives to update the locations for all objects before the site reopens to the public so he can provide frontline staff with an illustrated inventory checklist. For especially complicated spaces without museum collections such as the kitchen, he includes photographs of the room so staff can do a quick visual scan to ensure the decorations are all in place.

Protecting Buildings

Increased visitation, precipitation, and anti-slip treatments for walkways and stairs can threaten your historic floors and floor coverings with water, chemicals, and abrasives. Lilly House employs the many strategies possible to mitigate such damage.[21] They place an eight-foot-wide water hog mat in the vestibule to absorb as much moisture as possible (even after people have been under the twenty-foot awning). Inside the front door is a non-historic wool carpet they cannot protect because of the door swing height, so they plan for its deep cleaning every January. They place runners on the other carpets. In the library they remove the large rug and place runners on the hardwood floor. They have two sets of carpet runners so they can swap out a set to dry and vacuum, as needed.

Like barriers between collection objects and holiday decorations, it is necessary to protect mantels, shelves, walls, trim, architectural elements (decorative and otherwise), and floors from decorations and their attachments. It is essential to place a protective barrier such as Mylar under faux greens and other decorations to avoid scratching mantels, shelves, and other surfaces. The curator at Lilly House covers the entirety of each mantel with Mylar, which he weighs down so he can attach adhesive hooks to the Mylar instead of the mantel. The hooks hold Christmas stockings while the Mylar prevents decorative greens from scratching the mantel.

At the Theodore Roosevelt Inaugural National Historic Site, the curator works with a group of garden clubs to decorate the historic house each year. She distributes a detailed policy to them that specifies they cannot apply any decorations to the structure or furnishings with adhesives, wires, or nails.[22] Letting decorators know the ground rules in advance avoids surprises on installation day.

Staff at Andrew Jackson's Hermitage are especially careful to ensure that Christmas decorations do not touch historic architectural details, wallpaper, mirrors, furniture, or decorative objects. They place decorations strategically or place buffering materials between the decorations and historic objects to prevent any scratching, marking, or other damage. They wrap the historic banister in archival polyester sheets before wrapping faux evergreens around it (see figure 11.1). There also is a security railing parallel to the historic railing to provide for visitor safety without handling the historic railing. Wrapping the banister takes a couple hours.

The Pioneer Museum hosts a very popular children's event, Kinderfest, in early December each year. In the past children could hang their stockings on the large fireplace in the Kammlah House. Staff filled the stockings with traditional goodies while the children went to a program. To decrease the wear on the hearth and accommodate more children, the museum now builds a hearth and chimney set in its social hall to serve this purpose, keeping the spirit of the event alive while preserving the resource.

Figure 11.1.   The Hermitage's historic banister under the generous faux greenery to the left is wrapped in archival polyester sheets before the greens are installed to avoid damage. Visitors use the security railing to the right of the historic railing, which indicates the amount of wear a popular historic house receives. Courtesy of Andrew Jackson's Hermitage, Nashville, Tennessee.

Threats

Fire

It goes without saying that fire code and policies must be observed during Christmas events as they would any other time of year. If you have a no smoking policy or restrict smoking to a designated area, the additional volunteers, contractors, and visitors must observe it. Fire exits must remain clear. Double check that all fire extinguishers are in place and fully charged, should they be needed.

Loss of museum collections to fire is a heightened concern during holiday events. Holiday decorating in historic houses, especially for evening strolls, often entails the use of candles. Replace burning candles with one of the currently available authentic-looking electric candles. These might be more expensive than traditional candles, but they can be used for years and are infinitely safer for visitors, the collection, and the building. Or Hampton displays a late nineteenth-century-type tree with real but unlit candles that they illuminate with a spotlight from across the room. Live burning candles can be dropped, knocked over, or contact curtains, clothing, wood, or another combustible fuel with potentially disastrous results. They also can be a nuisance producing smoke that might set off a smoke detector or wax that can stain nearby surfaces. In a similar vein, the Pioneer Museum replaced kerosene lanterns with LED lanterns of the same appearance for its historic buildings. They also use LED bulbs in the fireplaces to replicate the appearance of fires without the danger of live fire.

Many historic sites also discourage the use of open flames such as cooking or heating fuel in historic buildings for similar reasons (see discussion of food below). Lighting fires in disused historic fireplaces also can be very dangerous because old chimney flues can contain combustible creosote, or a crack in the brickwork could allow sparks to contact wood and start a fire. Sparks are also apt to jump past the hearth and cause injury to visitors or museum collections.[23] An unattended fire is more dangerous than one actively monitored by a trained interpreter during an open-hearth cooking demonstration.

Two other possible ignition sources that might emerge during the holiday tour season are the decorations and space heaters. Both the Homestead Museum and Pioneer Museum have identified the early use of live Christmas trees as an issue. The trees often became excessively dry and brittle before Christmas, increasing their potential to ignite. In fact, the fire-retardant material sprayed on them sped up the drying process, making the problem worse. They both use faux greens now. Many museums choose to decorate with faux greens and trees (see discussion of biological infestation below), but you need to ensure these are made of flame-retardant materials so as not to increase the fire load of dangerous materials in the building just when crowds of visitors are there as well. If the historic house is unheated or poorly heated, it might be tempting to use space heaters to take the chill out of the air for visitors, but avoid using them for safety's sake.[24]

Food and Drink

During normal operation, most historic sites prohibit food and drinks in exhibit areas, but the holidays can bring pressure to relax standards. However, stains and pest infestations can cause the staff headaches for months or years afterward. The Pioneer Museum had issues with visitors spilling wine on their unfinished pine floors. For visitors, food and drinks should be served in an ancillary structure (e.g., historic outbuilding, visitor center, or outside tent) or not at all. The Homestead Museum and Longfellow House both serve refreshments in a separate building and ensure no food or drink enter the furnished historic buildings. Likewise, staff, contractors, and volunteers installing holiday decorations or displays should only eat in designated areas. When food is involved at a museum, staff must perform vigilant housekeeping before, during, and after the event. Staff should remove all food waste from areas next to collections and period rooms frequently. All food, disposable cups and plates, and other waste should be removed from the buildings immediately after the event.[25]

Another way that food (followed by stains and pests) can enter the furnished rooms is via the decorations in the form of fruit, candy, cookies, and nuts. Use artificial food instead of real food when displayed with collections or in period rooms (see figure 11.2). The Homestead Museum enjoys using realistic faux food to provide visitors with an immersive experience. The Pioneer Museum had a long tradition of using edible decorations such

Figure 11.2.   The Lilly House kitchen is decorated with a fantasy of faux desserts from fruit to cakes. Courtesy of Indianapolis Museum of Art at Newfields.

as fruit, popcorn, candy, and cookies, but these attracted rodents into the buildings. They discontinued the use of edibles a few years ago and are replicating the appearance with faux food instead. Several years ago, Winterthur experimented with dried and freeze-dried foods. The dried-fruit pyramid became infested with worms. They found the freeze-dried food worked at first, but the baked goods rehydrated over time and again became a threat to the collection.

Plant Materials

Pests can also enter a historic house in fresh flowers and live plants. May Cassar, Environmental Adviser to the UK's Museums and Galleries Commission, reminds us that using plant and flower materials in museums "carries a heightened risk of damage to museum objects from pest infestation, pollen staining and from localised [sic] increase in humidity as well as scratches and chips when pots and containers are placed on museum objects, such as furniture."[26] However, many historic sites allow or encourage the use of fresh or dried plant materials in holiday decorations while mitigating some of the potential issues.

As much as possible, flower arranging should take place off-site or in a designated on-site location. Arrangements should have a low center of gravity, be of a size that can navigate through the house safely, and not large enough to contact other surfaces. If possible, flowers should be in a moist oasis instead of water and avoid misting or spraying arrangements.[27] Flowers should be commercially grown in a greenhouse only with no flowers cut from the landscape. According to English Heritage, museums should avoid the following because they are apt to cause stains: geraniums, peonies, berries and soft fruit, and the stamens of lilies and other flowers with staining pollen. For the latter, the stamens can be removed off-site and the flowers used. Also avoid spray-painted foliage or arrangements with glitter and other loose decoration.[28]

Winterthur has specific tables approved for flower arrangements because it is an acceptable risk if they get wet or otherwise damaged. Flower arrangements require staff time. Winterthur has staff with object handling training who groom the flowers each day including weekends. If the museum is closed for a day, the floral arrangements are moved to a cooler the night before.

English Heritage discourages museums from using live plants because there is a high risk of insect infestation.[29] Knowledgeable staff should inspect plant materials as they arrive for any signs of infestation or potential staining. Lilly House staff inspect even the plants coming from their own greenhouse. If an infestation becomes apparent later, the plant should be bagged, tied, and disposed of outside the building as soon as possible.[30] Winterthur uses potted plants sparingly to avoid insects and mold spores, for example, one narcissus for fragrance or a couple poinsettias for pops of color. The curator at Lilly House highlighted how poinsettias and cyclamen require daily care including watering, picking up leaves, and rotating out ailing plants. Only the greenhouse staff water the plants with narrow-spouted watering cans to manage the flow of water.

Most museums I spoke with eschew live greens in favor of artificial greens. The Pioneer Museum cited dry greens and trees as an unattractive fire hazard; Winterthur added how they can cause allergic reactions among visitors; Longfellow House used laurel garlands many years ago and they still find tiny leaves in the house. If you choose live greens, they should be fresh to minimize falling needles. For fresh or faux greens, you can cover floors with drop cloths while moving decorations in and out to catch material before it drops on rugs and carpets.

You should place a barrier such as Mylar under floral arrangements, live plants, and all greens to avoid scratching or dampening the furniture or architectural elements. The director of historic preservation at Lilly House places Mylar on the entire surface of a table, not just a circle under the vase, to catch any sap or nectar dropping from an arrangement. The curator at Longfellow House forbids decorating the light fixtures because greens scratch the gilded surfaces.

Planning for a holiday event might sound (or feel) like preparing for the seven plagues: inclement weather, crowds of visitors, broken objects, lost objects, fire, stains, and pest infestations but once the policies are in place and everyone is trained (including management), it might be possible for you to enjoy the event as much as the visitors do.

Special thanks to Margaret Breuker, Conservator and Project Specialist, National Park Service, Lowell, Massachusetts.

Notes

1. National Park Service Northeast Region Curatorial Conference Call, Sponsored by the National Park Service Northeast Museum Services Center, February 25, 2009.
2. We would have liked to explore this topic using a variety of religious traditions as examples; but to our knowledge, to date, the National Park Service does not decorate any of its historic structures, particularly in the Northeast Region (Maine to Virginia excluding the greater Washington, DC, area), for holidays other than Christmas.
3. Gretchen Anderson and Rebecca Newberry, "Seasonal Affective Disorder: Caring for Collections during Seasonal Special Events," Slide Presentation Sponsored by Connecting to Collections Care, December 3, 2015, slides 27–28. Available at http://www.connectingtocol lections.org/wp-content/uploads/2015/09/Seasonal-Affective-Disorder-.pdf.
4. Katie Womack, Collections Manager, Reynolda House, Winston-Salem, North Carolina, phone conversation with author, November 17, 2021.
5. Jean-Luc Howell, Director of Historic Preservation, Newfields, Indianapolis, Indiana, video conversation with author, November 22, 2021; David Daly, Curator, Longfellow House–Washington's Headquarters National Historic Site, Cambridge, Massachusetts, video conversation with author, October 12, 2021.
6. Deborah Harper, Senior Curator of Education, Winterthur Museum Garden and Library, Winterthur, Delaware, video conversation with the author, October 13, 2021.
7. Andrew Hahn, Director, Campbell House, St. Louis, Missouri, video conversation with author, November 10, 2021.
8. Nicky Ingram, *Practical Conservation Guidelines for Successful Hospitality Events in Historic Houses* (Swindon, England: English Heritage, 2004), 5, 10. Available at http://www.english -heritage.org.uk.
9. Ingram, *Practical Conservation Guidelines*, 5.

10. Jennifer Schmidt, Collections Manager, Andrew Jackson's Hermitage, Nashville, Tennessee, phone conversation with author, November 30, 2021.

11. Gregory Weidman, Curator, Hampton National Historic Site, Towson, Maryland, email to author January 4, 2022.

12. Paul Spitzzeri, Director, Homestead Museum, City of Industry, California, video conversation with author, November 16, 2021.

13. Ingram, *Practical Conservation Guidelines*, 4.

14. Ingram, *Practical Conservation Guidelines*, 8.

15. Ingram, *Practical Conservation Guidelines*, 4.

16. Weidman, email to author January 4, 2022.

17. Evelyn Weinheimer, Archivist and Historian, and Lacey Lebleu, Curator, Pioneer Museum, Fredericksburg, Texas, phone conversation with author, November 22, 2021.

18. Ingram, *Practical Conservation Guidelines*, 8.

19. *National Park Service Museum Handbook, Part III, Museum Collections Use* (Washington, DC: Park Museum Management Program, National Park Service, US Department of the Interior, 1998–2000), 6:17.

20. *Museum Handbook, Part III*, 1:45–1:46.

21. "Curatorial Safety: Safe Walkways during Inclement Weather," National Park Service Museum Management Program, January 2003. Available at https://www.nps.gov/museum/safety/pdfs/Safe-Walkways.pdf (accessed December 27, 2021).

22. *Museum Handbook, Part III*, 6:17; Lenora Henson, curator, Theodore Roosevelt Inaugural National Historic Site, "8th District Federated Garden Clubs of N.Y.S. Suggestions for Victorian Christmas 2007" (unpublished, 2007).

23. "Curatorial Safety: Special Tour and Open House Fire Safety," National Park Service Museum Management Program, January 2003. Available at https://www.nps.gov/museum/safety/pdfs/Special-Tours.pdf (accessed December 27, 2021).

24. "Curatorial Safety: Space Heater Safety," National Park Service Museum Management Program, January 2003. Available at https://www.nps.gov/museum/safety/pdfs/Space-Heaters.pdf (accessed December 27, 2021).

25. *Museum Handbook, Part III*, 6:16, 7:35.

26. May Cassar, "Fact Sheet: Using Cut Flowers and Potted Plants in Museums" (London, England: Museums and Galleries Commission, 1999), 1. Available at https://collectionstrust.org.uk/wp-content/uploads/2017/01/Museums-Galleries-Commission-Using-Cut-Flowers-and-Potted-Plants-in-Museums-Aug-1999.pdf (accessed December 27, 2021).

27. Ingram, *Practical Conservation Guidelines*, 9.

28. Ingram, *Practical Conservation Guidelines*, 9.

29. Ingram, *Practical Conservation Guidelines*, 9.

30. Cassar, "Fact Sheet: Using Cut Flowers."

CHAPTER 12

Decking the Halls

All You Need to Know to Decorate Your Historic Site

Andrew W. Hahn

ONCE YOU HAVE DEVELOPED a plan for accurately interpreting Christmas at your site and have established procedures to protect your collections and buildings, you are now ready to put it all into action by acquiring the needed decorations, implementing a decorating scheme, and ultimately storing it all away during the off season.

Over the last twenty years, I have coordinated and expanded the Christmas displays and programs at the Campbell House Museum, an 1851 townhouse in downtown St. Louis, Missouri, which is interpreted to the year 1885. Christmastime at the Campbell House has become the most visited and profitable season of the year (as much as 20 percent of our annual attendance can occur during the last four weeks of the year) because of a combined offering of period- and site-appropriate decorations, special tours, and other events. It is a season we are constantly promoting throughout the year. We invite all visitors to Campbell House to come back and experience the "magic of an old-fashioned Christmas."

Each year the "magic" begins in mid-November with the setup of the bulk of the Christmas display over two days (a Monday and Tuesday as those are days the museum is closed). For the next eight weeks, the story of Christmas at Campbell House and some unique St. Louis Christmas traditions are told as part of the regular guided tour (the museum only offers guided tours). We have found that even after January 1, many people are still eager for the Christmas experience, so we do not put Christmas away until mid-January. In addition to an increased number of group tours, Christmas is also the season for joint evening tours with other St. Louis historic houses.

Decorations are central to the Christmas season's celebrations and this chapter will offer ideas and sources for making and buying Christmas decorations, tips on installing them, and practical advice on packing and storing them until the next Christmas season.

Acquisition

Fresh Decorations

Your Christmas decorating plan should include all the locations of your site—both inside and out. While real trees, greens, fruits, and flowers are historically accurate, they are usually not practical or safe for the interiors of most historic sites and house museums, but they are the natural choice for the outside. Exterior decorations will include wreaths for doors, windows, and railings. Greens are, after all, the oldest and most traditional of all the Christmas decorations. Since ancient times greens have been used at Christmastime as a sign of hope during the darkest season of the year. Wreaths or garlands are an ancient symbol; worn on the head by the Greeks and Romans, they signified victory and celebration. No one is sure when wreaths went from the head to doors and walls, but by the seventeenth century they were firmly in use as part of Christmas celebrations.

If your site sits on even a modest-size piece of ground, there are no doubt plant resources available that can be easily and sustainably harvested to create your own exterior wreaths and garlands. Look around the grounds of your site—evergreen boughs, holly sprigs, ivy lengths, and even dried herbs (rosemary, lavender, and sage especially) are just a sample of the wide variety of plants that can be incorporated in making beautiful and period-appropriate wreaths and garlands. The collecting of greens and herbs can also be beneficial for the plants. There are many helpful tutorials on YouTube that provide step-by-step directions to staff or volunteers willing to make wreaths and garlands for your site.[1]

Fresh decorations will fade. Depending on your climate, that could happen quickly. If your Christmas season includes a special event or tour, remember to inspect fresh outside decorations to make sure they look good for that day.

While creating wreaths and garland can be quite time consuming (make full use of your volunteers to help with this job), visitors to your site will notice and appreciate the use of natural materials in your decorations. This also helps your site make an especially good first impression at Christmastime.

If you cannot source fresh greens from your site, local florists can help you find fresh materials. Alternatively, you can buy plain evergreen wreaths, boughs, and garland from your local Christmas tree lot and make them unique to your site by adding your own extras like bows and greens, such as ivy, holly, and herbs.

Fake Greens, Trees, and Lights

While your site may use some fresh decor inside, this will not be practical or safe for most sites and collections. Thankfully, there is easy access to high-quality fake trees, wreaths, garlands, and even food that will make your interiors shine at Christmas.

House museums in larger cities can shop in person at wholesale floral supply companies that service the floral trade. These companies are not open to the public and stock an unbelievably large variety of high-quality fake trees, wreaths, greens, and ribbons. To set up an account, provide your organization's federal tax identification number and, if applicable, your state tax exemption certificate. There are, of course, an endless number of online resources where you can buy trees and greens, but to create the perfect display nothing beats being able to see and handle all the options.

It is best to buy completely plain (no lights, bows, glitter, frosting, or other additions) fake trees, wreaths, and garlands so you can tailor them to perfectly suit your decorating plan. Plain greens not only offer the most flexibility but are often among the lowest in price. If a historic fake tree (feather tree) is appropriate for your site, Dresden Star Ornaments still makes them by hand for a reasonable cost.[2] Even at wholesale cost, good decorations can be expensive, but think of your Christmas purchases as an investment that with proper storage will last for many years.

Fake food and flowers might be the perfect Christmas touch needed for a dining table or sideboard. Your plan will dictate what variety of fake flowers can be used, and they can be bought from the same floral supply companies where you purchased greens. Many sites already use fake food, be it simple vegetables and breads or more complicated desserts and candies. Fake food in a room is an appropriate part of almost any Christmas decorating plan as the season has always been celebrated with food. Online commercial suppliers of fake food can be sources for simple things like breads.[3] Alternatively, you can make your own fake food based on the look of a specific recipe associated with your site or region. There are also individuals who can make custom food displays for you.[4] Fake food can be an excellent investment because it can be used throughout the year.

Lighting can be an important part of setting the Christmas scene at your site. While you never want to use real candles inside, there are very real-looking alternatives. The technology behind "flameless" candles has developed dramatically in the last decade. Battery-powered LED taper candles are made from wax and come in a variety of lengths and are startlingly realistic. The best ones have moving, flickering "flames" and often come with a remote control, which not only makes turning the lights on and off easy but can even adjust the brightness and color. There are even wired versions of these LED candles that can be clipped on Christmas tree branches. Even just a few LED candles can completely transform the look and feel of a room, and they can be used in candlesticks at your site year-round. Small LED spotlights that sit on a tabletop or in the corner of a room can also help you highlight your Christmas display; however, make sure the light output is within the parameters of any collection policies.

Objects: Toys, Books, and Ornaments

Most Christmas plans will call for objects to decorate a tree or to create a display of gifts. The first place you can look for some of these items is your site's accessioned collection, but be sure to follow any collection policies and procedures you have in place when using collection items.

There are many options for tree ornaments. Consider making ornaments for your tree. This is not only economical, but often historically accurate as many early decorations were homemade. Paper, fabric, and wire can all be used to craft appropriate tree ornaments.[5] For tree garlands or swags, it is best not to use real food (popcorn, berries, and nuts) as they can attract pests. However, there are readily available excellent fake alternatives to these edible tree trimmings.

Genuine manufactured glass ornaments from the nineteenth and early twentieth centuries can be expensive and hard to find. But no matter if you are looking for early glass Kugel ornaments or the later and more colorful glass ornaments, the original designs have been copied extensively and reproductions are generally not costly and are readily available.

Toys are the most obvious items to display from your collection. Dolls (along with their associated clothes, dishes, and furniture), doll houses, games, banks, and musical instruments are all appropriate. Even non-toy items from your collection can be incorporated into a Christmas gift display under a tree or mantel, especially if it has a presentation box.

Books were a favorite Christmas gift a century ago. Your site may already have titles in your collection that would have been appropriate gifts presented at your site. There were also thousands of titles published in the nineteenth and early-twentieth centuries specifically to be given as Christmas gifts. These Christmas titles often have festive decorative covers and bindings. Consider acquiring some of these for your Christmas display. Online sources like eBay can help you pinpoint books appropriate in the period to your site. If you simply search for "Christmas book," you will get thousands of titles. However, if you use eBay's category selector and choose "Antiquarian and Collectible" and even the decade range of your site (e.g., 1800–1849 or 1850–1899) you can find period titles appropriate for your site. Even though these books are antiques, they can be quite affordable, often less than $40.

Do not forget Christmas cards and postcards. Your site's collection may have period cards that can be scanned and printed for display. Vintage designs in the public domain can also be easily downloaded from the internet and printed to decorate trees and packages, set on mantels or to decorate a tabletop.[6] A small special exhibit of Christmas cards is not only festive and visually appealing, but is also relatively easy to put together.

Lastly, for sites on a budget there are options. As already discussed, you can make some decorations like ornaments. For trees and greens, secondhand ones can be modified to suit your plan. Seek donations by making a wish list to circulate among staff and volunteers. Check your local thrift store. Right after the holiday season they will have an impressive supply of trees, greens, and everything else for Christmas.

Installation

Unless your site has a large staff or a budget for contract workers, volunteers will be critical in implementing any Christmas decorating plan. Involving all your staff and as many volunteers as possible is not only a practical way to get it done but can also be a lot of fun.

Every year in mid-November, four days are dedicated to setting up Christmas at Campbell House (see figure 12.1). Day one involves preparation by two staff members to sort

Figure 12.1. Volunteers setting up the circa 1890 tree in the Campbell House parlor have everything they need to get the job done: ladders, work tables, and a photo guide to emulate. Courtesy of Campbell House Museum, St. Louis, Missouri.

Box 12.1. Campbell House Christmas—Parlor Setup Schedule

Friday

1. Pull and sort parlor decoration boxes from basement storage and ready on carts to go upstairs—32 boxes/bags (staff).

Monday Morning

1. Move Parlor center table and associated collection items to Morning Room (staff).
2. Move Christmas tree platform from Carriage House and setup in Parlor (staff).
3. Move and stage boxes/bags in Entry Hall (staff and volunteers).
4. Setup three worktables, one 8-foot ladder, tools, and trash can (staff and volunteers).
5. Assemble tree and decorate according to photo guide in this order—tree topper, angels, ornaments, beads, and ribbons (staff and volunteers).
6. Take lunch orders and eat.

Monday Afternoon

1. Skirt tree platform (staff and volunteers).
2. Setup Creche set on platform according to photo guide (staff and volunteers).
3. "Fluff" and hang four wreaths (staff and volunteers).
4. Add greens and fake fruit to mantels (staff and volunteers).
5. Store empty boxes under the tree platform (staff and volunteers).
6. Remove tables, ladder, trash, and then vacuum the room (staff).

boxes in the basement Christmas storage area and stage them for delivery upstairs. Over the next two days about a dozen volunteers (docents, board members, and others) come together to decorate six rooms (entry hall, parlors, dining room, library, and carriage house) and the gift shop. These two days begin with the moving of all the bagged (trees and wreaths) and boxed (mantel greens, garlands, bows, flowers, fake food, toys, and a large crèche set) items from a storage area in the basement to the rooms. This is followed by the storing away of any collection items and the moving of furniture and carpets. Finally, over two days boxes are opened and the decorating occurs according to a written schedule and photo guides. On day four the staff does any needed "fluffing," stores away the empty containers, and lastly sweeps and vacuums the decorated spaces. Check the floor for any large pieces of greens to prevent vacuum cleaner clogs and repairs.

Educate your staff and volunteers about the plan you have developed for Christmas (have a printed copy for everyone to read). Share how specific decorations were chosen because they are accurate to the period of your site and/or to the site's history. This knowledge will also give staff the leverage to explain why suggested ideas may not always be appropriate. It is also important that volunteers fully understand the rules of handling collections and how things are to be moved, stored away, or incorporated into your Christmas plan.

Be sure every volunteer knows their assigned tasks. It is helpful to have a typed schedule of jobs assigned to a specific person. Also ensure that each volunteer has everything required for their job, which could be as simple as ornament hangers, a ladder, or folding table on which to work.

The key to efficiently setting up Christmas is organization. Boxed and bagged items in storage are all clearly labeled so staging is a breeze. For example, boxes with greens and fake food for the dining room are labeled "Dining Room Mantel," "Dining Room Table," "Dining Room Sideboard," "Dining Room Cakes," "Dining Room Tarts," and "Dining Room Mantel Wreath." Campbell House recently added an elevator so moving things from storage is quite easy for volunteers using carts. However, in the past staff did most of the hauling of boxes upstairs to save volunteers the effort. Try to save your volunteers from too much heavy lifting.

Every year photos are taken of the completed decorated rooms with detailed shots of each mantel and table. This not only serves as documentation for the history of the museum but is also an important visual record that can help in the decorating for the next year. Printed copies of pictures of each decorated area (mantel, tables, trees) are taped to the top of each storage container or bag as a visual guide for decorating that area.

To make decorating days fun and festive, play Christmas music, and, if possible, provide snacks or lunch. In my experience a fed volunteer is a happy volunteer that is ready to work. This is a small price to pay for the labor your volunteers provide, and it will also help you retain a core group of Christmas volunteers that will return in January to take it all down.

Lastly, consider that you may be able to enlist the help of a local professional to implement your Christmas plan with staff supervision. Local florists, interior decorators, or even garden clubs are often looking for service projects to give them visibility. If you are successful in getting the help of a professional, it must be made clear that they follow the established Christmas plan because it is based on research of the period, local community, and the people associated with your site.

Storage

The storage of Christmas decorations can be just as big a challenge as buying and decorating for the season. Museums rarely have enough storage space and this is especially true for historic houses and sites, which often must rely on attics, basements, and under beds for storage. The purchase of proper storage containers should be included in any budget for Christmas decorations.

To store Christmas, begin by acquiring a supply of plastic storage boxes with lids (Rubbermaid are among the most durable and stackable). These boxes will protect the contents better than cardboard, will last longer, keep out moisture and pests, and, most importantly, they stack neatly and securely. Label each box on both ends and the top so you can read the contents no matter what side is facing out. Your labels should note the specific location for the contents of each box (e.g., "Dining Room Mantel").

For items that do not fit in boxes, buy bags to hold wreaths and long lengths of garland. If your budget allows, you can buy bags (or even wreath-shaped boxes) made specifically

Figure 12.2. Christmas decoration storage area in the Campbell House basement. All the decorations are stored together in one room and each box is clearly labeled on the end and top for easy identification. Courtesy of Cambell House, St. Louis, Missouri.

to hold Christmas wreaths. Heavy-duty trash bags with drawstrings also work well. When packing wreaths with bows, we take the extra step of stuffing the bow loops with tissue so they do not get smashed during moving or storage. When finding a storage space consider hanging the wreath and garland bags. This will stop these items from becoming compacted when stored. Again, we label all the bags with the item's location.

If possible, do not disassemble fake Christmas trees. It is more difficult to move trees still assembled, but it will save a lot of time during set up next year (it is very time consuming to assemble and straighten the branches on fake trees). If you need to disassemble trees there are large storage bags with sturdy handles that are designed specifically for Christmas tree storage. And, like the boxes, make sure wreath and tree bags are properly labeled with the location of each item.

Next, find an appropriate space to store Christmas in the off season. Ideally it will be a space where all your Christmas decorations can be stored together (see figure 12.2). If that is not possible, at least try to store all decorations for a particular room together. This will make setting up next year easier. Do not store your Christmas decorations and other props in your historical accessioned collection storage area. This separation will minimize confusion and will safeguard your collection during the chaotic Christmas setup.

Some sites will have to store Christmas at an off-site storage facility. In this case, make a numbered inventory of all your Christmas boxes and bags to ensure that everything makes it back to your site for decorating day.

During the Christmas season, store all the empty boxes and bags nested together. You may even find a space in your period rooms to store these empties—perhaps under the dining room table.

Interpreting Christmas is a major commitment of time and resources but with proper planning and help from staff and volunteers, it can be easy to source, decorate, and store Christmas each year.

Notes

1. Royal Horticultural Society, "How to Make a Christmas Wreath" (2018), https://www
.youtube.com/watch?v=wxeghj2tu7k; Proven Winners, "Make Your Own Holiday Garland"
(2016), https://www.youtube.com/watch?v=V8w7nKDKvNE.
2. Dennis Bauer, "Feather Trees" (Ferndale, CA: Dresden Star Ornaments), https://victorian
ornaments.com/feather-trees/.
3. Commercial manufacturers of quality fake food items include Iwasaki Images of America
(http://iwasaki-images.com) and Display Fake Foods (https://displayfakefoods.com).
4. Stephanie Burt, "How Museums Make Their Fake Foods Using Real Recipes" (Atlas
Obscura, August 12, 2019), https://www.atlasobscura.com/articles/who-makes-fake-food-for
-museums.
5. Sew Historically, "20 DIY Victorian Christmas Ornaments with Historical Sources" (December 25, 2020), https://www.sewhistorically.com/20-diy-victorian-christmas-tree-ornaments.
6. Free vintage illustrations are available from Elissa Capelle Vaughn, "Free Vintage Christmas
Cards in the Public Domain," https://freevintageillustrations.com/free-vintage-christmas
-cards-public-domain.

CHAPTER 13

Decorating for Christmas

Collaborating with Garden Clubs

Lenora M. Henson

ITE-SPECIFIC PREPARATIONS for the installation of holiday displays and related events depend on many factors: How many spaces are involved? How big are those spaces? What is being installed? Are you adding holiday-specific objects from your collection or installing (non-collection) decorations? What sort of "prep work" needs to be done prior to installation? What (if any) collections objects should be moved? Where will those objects be placed?

The following should also be considered: Who is doing the installation (e.g., staff, volunteers, outside groups)? What sort of help or supervision is necessary? When will the displays and/or decorations be installed? Will the site be open to visitors during the installation process? Will any clean-up be necessary in the immediate aftermath of installation? And, don't forget the post-holiday piece of the puzzle: When will the displays be removed? Who will remove them? Will all or part of the decorations need to be stored for next year? If so, where? Your answers to these and other related questions will naturally guide your planning process—from the time you spend, to the partners you involve, to the specific concerns that wake you from a sound sleep at two o'clock on the morning of D[ecorating]-Day. The following case study will illustrate how one historic site has addressed some of these issues and point out several successful planning strategies.

The Theodore Roosevelt Inaugural National Historic Site preserves the home in Buffalo, New York, where Theodore Roosevelt was sworn in as the twenty-sixth president of the United States in September 1901. The "TR Site"—as it is known by locals—is a Greek Revival structure that has survived many changes since its oldest section was built circa 1837. Today, the museum has public areas on its first and second floors, including three restored rooms and approximately six exhibit spaces connected by central hallways and various staircases. A connected, two-story visitor center (built on the footprint and with the same massing and scale of a carriage house that existed at the time of TR's inauguration) welcomes visitors arriving from the parking lot behind the building and those who approach from the columned porch that dominates the western facade.

The TR Site has hosted an annual event called "Victorian Christmas" since 1974. For many of those years, Victorian Christmas was the TR Site's biggest annual fundraiser and deemed crucial to its financial stability. Integral to the event, and much-loved by the community, are the decorations installed by members of local garden clubs. Each year, more than a dozen areas in and around what was once the home of Ansley and Mary Grace Wilcox are festooned with holiday trimmings. This includes the museum's restored rooms, visitor center, front porch, and central hall/stairway.

Coordinating the decorating efforts of multiple garden clubs, while protecting the historic resource, requires considerable planning and cooperation (see figure 13.1). For the TR Site, the foundation of this process is the long-standing and solid partnership it has developed with the 8th District Federated Garden Clubs of New York State. Institutional records show that individual members of several garden clubs provided floral arrangements and wreaths for the TR Site's very first Victorian Christmas. These modest beginnings apparently paved the way for greater collaboration; by the next year, clubs were participating as groups and expanding their contributions.[1] In recent years, a dozen (or more) garden clubs have regularly participated in decorating the museum. As curator of the TR Site, I oversee the process and work closely with two volunteer coordinators from the 8th District. These volunteer chairs serve as indispensable liaisons between the two groups and provide a first point of contact for individual garden clubs interested in decorating the TR Site.

Planning for Victorian Christmas and decorating gets underway when I (and sometimes other TR Site staff) meet with the 8th District chairs in February of any year. The meeting has several goals: to review the previous year's successes/challenges and to choose a decorating theme/color scheme for the coming year. Reflecting on the previous year's decorating experience is an important step. It allows for (typically minor) course corrections that can better protect the historic site, address garden club concerns, and/or improve the visitor experience. The changes that come out of this meeting most often deal with refining the number/type of decorations to be installed in a specific museum space. For example, typical visitor flow was disrupted when particularly elaborate and eye-catching decorations were installed in a stair landing window one year; as people stopped to get a closer look or take photographs, the area quickly became congested and potentially dangerous. Since then, the garden club responsible for decorating the stair landing window has been asked to provide only a "simple wreath." My subsequent conversations with the club reinforce this message and explain the reason behind the request.

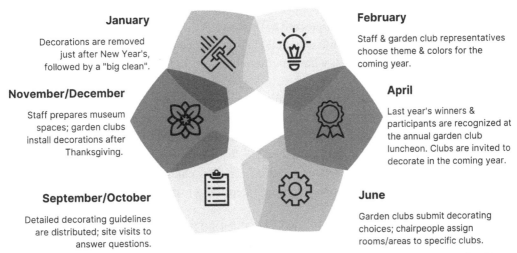

January

Decorations are removed just after New Year's, followed by a "big clean".

February

Staff & garden club representatives choose theme & colors for the coming year.

November/December

Staff prepares museum spaces; garden clubs install decorations after Thanksgiving.

April

Last year's winners & participants are recognized at the annual garden club luncheon. Clubs are invited to decorate in the coming year.

September/October

Detailed decorating guidelines are distributed; site visits to answer questions.

June

Garden clubs submit decorating choices; chairpeople assign rooms/areas to specific clubs.

Figure 13.1.   The Christmas decorating process begins nearly a year in advance at the Theodore Roosevelt Inaugural National Historic Site.

Fine-tuning the rooms/areas of the TR Site to be decorated for Victorian Christmas is usually the easiest part of the first planning meeting. Choosing a decorating theme and a color scheme takes more time and conversation. In that they encourage a coordinated look among the various garden clubs' decorations; however, the theme and colors are important and have been eagerly anticipated since being incorporated into the event during the early 1990s. I compiled a list of themes and colors that have been used in the past by searching through the TR Site's institutional files and I shared this with the 8th District chairs in advance of our meeting. By the time we get together, each of us typically has at least one or two possible themes and color combinations to offer for consideration. Most of the time, a consensus choice emerges from the ensuing discussion relatively quickly; once in a while, however, all of the initial ideas are abandoned, and more brainstorming is required.

Decorating themes have embraced the traditional (*'Twas the Night Before Christmas*) as well as more modern classics (*Winter Wonderland*) that would have been unfamiliar to both TR and the Wilcox family. Occasionally, the theme celebrates relevant milestones; for example, the centennial of Buffalo's Pan-American Exposition was anticipated by *Victorian Christmas in the City of Light*, and the teddy bear's one hundredth anniversary inspired *A Merry Beary Christmas*.

In terms of color schemes, traditional reds and greens are used in heavy rotation, although accent colors vary from year to year. Based on evidence gleaned from the society pages in turn-of-the-twentieth-century Buffalo newspapers, Victorian Christmas color schemes have also regularly made use of pinks and even the occasional blue.[2] One particularly memorable year, garden clubs were asked to decorate using "iridescent jewel tones (teal, violet, gold, green), like those . . . [found] in a peacock feather"; that year's very appropriate theme was *Feathered Finery*.[3]

Once those decisions are made, I put together and complete a packet of information that serves as an invitation to decorate. This includes the following:

- a letter from the TR Site's executive director,
- a set of decorating guidelines that all clubs are expected to follow,
- a link to an online form, where garden clubs can indicate their decorating preferences, and
- a list of requested decorations (number/type) according to room or area.

The information is distributed to all the area garden clubs at the 8th District's annual spring meeting and luncheon; it also gets posted on the 8th District's website. The spring meeting is the perfect opportunity to reengage with the garden clubs and share this information, since I am generally on hand to present awards stemming from the previous year's Victorian Christmas decorations.

Over the course of the next several months, the 8th District chairs work with individual garden clubs to determine which club will decorate each room or area at the TR Site. This makes sense because the chairs are familiar with not only the garden clubs, but also the possibilities and limitations of the TR Site. For instance, if two garden clubs have their hearts set on decorating the same area, the 8th District chairs are much better positioned than I am to negotiate an agreement. Or, if a small garden club, with only a few members and even fewer resources, would like to get involved but is daunted by the predefined decorating areas, the 8th District chairs can work with me to divide an area appropriately or find an alternate solution. Generally, by the end of the summer, all of the rooms and areas have been claimed or assigned, and the 8th District chairs provide me with a list of garden clubs and the museum spaces they will be responsible for decorating.

In early September, I contact each participating garden club via email. This message repeats some of the information that was shared with the garden clubs in the spring, but also contains new information—some of which is tailored to the area each club will be decorating. Specifically, the early fall mailing includes:

- a cover letter reminding garden clubs to schedule an in-person preview of the area they will decorate;
- logistical details regarding "Decorating Days" (note: in 2020–2021, this included restrictions in response to the coronavirus pandemic);
- individualized decorating tips and special considerations focused on protecting collection objects and floors in each museum space (see box 13.1);
- when available, architectural drawings with commonly requested measurements;[4]
- an announcement regarding the annual Curator's Choice Award;[5] and
- excerpts from the previously referenced research detailing Buffalo Christmas decorations (1896–1906).

The fall email typically leads to in-person, on-site meetings with representatives of the various garden clubs. These preview meetings are invaluable. They not only provide the garden club with a chance to see, photograph, and measure their space, but also allow me to

Box 13.1.   (Sample) Decorating Tips/Special Considerations Pertaining to Specific Spaces

Morning Room

- For the long-term preservation and safety of our historic spaces and artifacts, only six (6) people will be permitted to work in this room at a time.
- If your garden club would like anything (furniture, knickknacks, etc.) moved, please discuss it with [the curator] in advance. In order to reduce the chances of damaging/breaking historic items, we are happy to move fragile items before your garden club arrives.
- No decorations on/around the desk (southwest corner).
- The candelabra on the mantel are part of the room's furnishings and will not be removed for Victorian Christmas. However, they can be moved temporarily to facilitate decorating. We are happy to move them for you.
- This area is not secure—visitors have free access to the room.
- If you plan to use candles as a part of your decorations, please trim the wicks so they cannot be lit.

Visitor Center Windows (Exterior)

- This area is not secure—please remember this as you plan your decorations.
- Brightly colored ribbons draw attention and prevent the decorations from getting "lost" on the large façade.
- The TR Site will provide hardware to hang the wreaths.
- TR Site staff will be happy to hang predecorated wreaths at our convenience.

(Restored) Dining Room

- Any chandelier decorations must be discussed in detail and cleared with [the curator] in advance. Because the chandelier is original and extremely fragile, [the curator] will install any/all of those decorations *before* any other decorations are placed in the room.
- No street shoes are allowed in the dining room. Feel free to bring your own inside-only slippers. Alternatively, shoe covers will be provided.
- If the small round table (in front of the windows) needs to be moved out of your way temporarily, please ask [the curator]!

---

work with them to find solutions to the dilemmas created by the restrictions (no tape, bare wires, etc.) imposed by the TR Site. I take copious notes to remind myself which (if any) artifacts need to be moved before garden clubs arrive and have found that these meetings make the chaos of Decorating Days more manageable. I have also found it useful to establish myself as the single source of answers for decorating questions. If I am the only person who can (or will) provide answers, there is not much room on Decorating Day for a conversation beginning with the assertion that "another staff member told me it would be fine to ..."

In the weeks leading up to Decorating Days, the collections manager and I are working diligently behind the scenes to prepare. Over the years, we have developed a checklist that is very useful and keeps us on track (see box 13.2). We make sure that our supply of Mylar, shoe covers, fishing line, and garbage bags is adequate; we check the stock of authentic-looking candles that are available for the garden clubs to borrow (plus charge the batteries used to operate them); and ensure there is enough space in our collections storage area for any furnishings/objects that will be removed during Victorian Christmas.

Decorating Days at the TR Site are the Monday, Tuesday, and Wednesday after Thanksgiving, and while it is impossible to anticipate every challenge that will crop up during Decorating Days, experience suggests that it is best to face the process with as much information as possible. Garden clubs are required to let me know which day and what time they plan to decorate. This gives me a sense of how many garden clubs expect to be in a particular area of the museum each day. On the rare instance that four clubs ask to decorate entire rooms at the same time (rather than smaller, less intense "areas"), I can proactively reach out and suggest another day; this not only protects the historic resource and safeguards our staff but also ensures a much better decorating experience for all of the garden clubs.

Armed with my notes from preview meetings and the schedule, I can face Decorating Days with confidence. Garden clubs may decorate between the hours of 9:30 a.m. and 4:30 p.m., which provides a "cushion" for behind-the-scenes tasks at the beginning and end of each day. Typically, this is when some objects are moved into temporary storage and others are protected in place. For example, to prevent mantel decorations from coming into contact with paintings that hang above several of the TR Site's fireplaces, we install custom-made acrylic barriers.[6] Temporary worktables are set up before the garden clubs arrive while ladders, garbage bags, and shoe covers are also staged in appropriate areas. The TR Site has also chosen to suspend its regular public tour schedule while decorating takes place.[7] This has eased pressure on several fronts and helps by making additional staff resources available to focus on Decorating Days.

Although members of the various garden clubs do most of the actual decorating, the TR Site's collections manager and I keep a very close eye on the process. We are available to troubleshoot, protect surfaces, and install decorations that do not use nails, tape, glue, or bare wire. We monitor activity in the museum's restored rooms especially closely; this includes enforcing established occupancy rules (for example, no more than six people are allowed in the Morning Room at a time) and simply being aware of how people are moving around in the space (this might, for example, prevent someone from bumping into a table and knocking over a lamp). The garden clubs usually finish decorating on Tuesday, allowing staff to clean and complete other Victorian Christmas–related tasks on Wednesday. This is also a good time to document all of the decorations; the photographs become part of our institutional history and are important promotional tools as well.

There is an enormous sigh of relief and the pace slows down when Decorating Days are over, but holiday decorations remain in place at the TR Site throughout the month of December. I try to walk through all the decorated spaces daily. If I find anything amiss (e.g., perhaps gravity has been unkind to some decorations), I can remedy minor trouble or contact garden clubs as necessary. Early in the month, a panel from the 8th District stops by

Box 13.2. Collections Department Victorian Christmas Task List[1]

Before Decorating Days Begin

- Rearrange/clean up collections storage area to allow for storage of furniture and silk flower arrangements removed from the restored rooms.
- Remove furniture from the west end of the restored library.
- Rotate selection of unaccessioned/framed vintage Christmas postcards; hang in the rotating exhibit room.
- Move the [unaccessioned] Xmas collection toys, ornaments, decoration boxes, and so on from the third-floor (attic) storage to the first-floor/front hallway closet.
- Stash supplies in the first-floor/front hallway closet (mylar, blue cloth, shoe covers, scissors, fishing line).

During Decorating Days

- Remove faux flower arrangements from the restored rooms, front hallway, and the Exploration room mantel.
- Monitor activities of the garden club members to ensure the safety and security of the house and the furnishings; make sure decorators adhere to the decorating guidelines.
- Re: (Restored) Dining Room
    - If requested by the garden club, remove tableware, move table, and install decorations on the chandelier; reinstall (as needed) after decorating is complete.
    - Temporarily move chairs from around the table during decorating; reinstall once decorating is complete.
    - As needed, trim plastic sheeting to fit and install (mantel, dining table, round table, and sideboard).
    - As needed, assist with hanging decorations on the windows, doors, and picture rail.
    - Vacuum/sweep room once decorating is complete and garden clubs have left.

- Exploration Room
    - Move TR bust to the archives.
    - Assist with decorating as necessary (e.g., install wreath over fireplace, offer mantel weights and/or corner guards).

(continued)

Box 13.2. (*continued*)

De-Decorating Days (early January)

- Assist with the removal of decorations, monitoring the garden club members and ensuring the safety and security of the house and the furnishings.
- Deep clean the restored rooms, including removing all Victorian Christmas debris from surfaces and furniture, dusting all mantels and woodwork, sweeping and vacuuming rugs.
- As needed, reinstall tableware in the restored dining room.
- De-decorate the Christmas tree in the restored library, wrap ornaments, place in plastic totes, and return to third-floor storage.
- Reinstall furniture in the west end of the library.
- Remove exterior decorations and salvage materials as requested by the garden clubs.

Note

1. Special thanks to the TR Site's longtime collections manager, Amy Sanderson, whose assistance is invaluable, particularly during Victorian Christmas. Amy is the one who took the time to type up the comprehensive "To-Do List" that guides us in the weeks before/after Decorating Days. Note that the full document is approximately four pages long; it has been excerpted to provide a general idea of the kinds of tasks we undertake in relation to decorating and Victorian Christmas.

to judge the decorations against garden club criteria. All visitors to the TR Site are invited to vote for their favorite decorations.[8] Winners of the Visitors' Choice Awards, as well as the 8th District awards, are announced at the garden clubs' annual spring meeting. Modest checks accompany the awards.

Because the garden clubs are also responsible for removing their decorations, I like to stay in touch during December. I often send a quick message in the middle of the month to express my thanks for their hard work and note how much our visitors are enjoying their decorations. Sometimes, however, those ideas are incorporated into an end-of-the-year reminder about the "De-Decorating" schedule (usually January 2, 3, or 4). As with decorating, the clubs are asked to let me know when they will arrive to remove decorations. The de-decorating process is much quicker and involves far fewer members of each garden club, but there is considerable clean-up that needs to be done afterward and it takes several days to get everything back to "normal" at the TR Site. At that point, Victorian Christmas is officially over, and staff can take a short break, before the process begins all over again in February!

My tenure at the Theodore Roosevelt Inaugural Site has spanned all or part of more than twenty Victorian Christmases. Decorating can differ from year to year, but it seems to work best when communication is clear, open, ongoing, and consistent. Further, while it is difficult to overstate the benefits of organization and preplanning, it is at least as important to reflect on what is and what is not working. Taken together, I have found these elements go a long way in mitigating many of the stressors associated with holiday displays and events at historic sites.

Notes

1. Theodore Roosevelt Inaugural Site Foundation collection (641.015.001).
2. Bryan J. Sajecki, "Buffalo Christmas Decorations/Celebrations, 1896–1906" (Spring 2010), Theodore Roosevelt Inaugural Site Foundation, curator Lenora M. Henson's files.
3. Victorian Christmas 2016 communications, Theodore Roosevelt Inaugural Site Foundation, curator Lenora M. Henson's files.
4. Stephanie L. Goris, who was an architecture student at the time, volunteered to create measured drawings of spaces that are typically decorated during Victorian Christmas. However, garden clubs are reminded that the drawings should not be considered a substitute for an in-person preview.
5. Established in 2010, this award recognizes the garden club whose decorations "best capture the spirit of turn-of-the-century Christmas decorations in Buffalo, *while following the established guidelines for decorating at the TR Site.*" It is presented at the 8th District's annual spring meeting, along with the Visitors' Choice Awards.
6. The barriers are approximately six inches high and custom fit according to the width/depth of the artwork and frame.
7. Admittedly, this decision was made easier because visitation was generally low after the holiday weekend.
8. Although it has never been quantified, anecdotal evidence suggests that this friendly competition between garden clubs helps to drive visitation during December. It is not uncommon for garden club members to return with friends or to hear from a visitor that a friend/garden club member encouraged them to visit (and vote!).

CHAPTER 14

The Ghost of Christmas That Never Was

The Evolution of the Annual Holiday Event at Lindenwald

James McKay and Patricia West

EBENEZER SCROOGE yields to the lessons of his spectral visitors by declaring, "I will honour Christmas in my heart, and try to keep it all the year. I will live in the past, the present, and the future. The spirits of all three shall strive within me."[1] This captures a meaningful goal for a historic site holiday event, to use Christmas as a way to understand the past in the present as we face the future. Yet what if there *was* no documented Christmas at a historic house?

When Freeman Tilden formulated six foundational principles of interpretation, he might have considered adding a seventh. The cynics among you are probably already thinking, "Ah yes, principle seven, historic houses MUST host an annual Christmas event despite limited historical evidence to support it." Having had long careers as a house museum curator and a chief interpreter, we can be as cynical as anyone about the ubiquitous "historic" Christmas event, but that is not the principle we have in mind. Our proposed seventh principle is "research-based interpretive planning for events can be a tool for promoting the protection of resources and cultivating a deeper understanding of history."[2]

Skilled planning can use the popularity of a holiday event to highlight the very purpose and necessity of our institutions, providing an opportunity for our audiences to explore the nature of history and how it is constructed. After years of wrangling an annual candlelight open house, this became the winning concept that allowed us to manage the event with relative success. Through trial and error, a set of planning tenets emerged facilitating the development of holiday events that reduced the danger of resource degradation, presented site-related history in an exciting manner, and kept the event fresh for the public, staff, and volunteers.

The canvas for this work was Lindenwald, the mid-nineteenth-century mansion of eighth U.S. president Martin Van Buren, located in Kinderhook, New York. The National Park Service (NPS) site began hosting its holiday event there in the 1980s, coinciding with the annual commemoration of Van Buren's birthday on December 5. The heavily attended open house featured historic furnished rooms illuminated by burning wax tapers and elegantly festooned with Christmas greenery and floral arrangements created by enthusiastic Kinderhook Garden Club volunteers.

Admiring crowds were led to believe by implication that Van Buren held spectacular twentieth-century-style Christmas parties. It was really beautiful and utterly inadvisable from a preservation perspective. Significantly, it was just bad history. There was no historical evidence that such displays had ever occurred in Van Buren's home; the crowds were unmanageable; the floral and food arrangements so attractive to the eye were even more attractive to mice; and the candles were a flat-out existential threat to the house and museum collection. Change was required, but there was an engaged constituency to consider, as the event had become a treasured part of the community's celebration of Christmas.

Initiating Reform

"Assure me that I yet may change these shadows you have shown me by an altered life?"

As detailed in a 2014 article in the journal *Collections*, a gradual revision process for this event began in the late 1990s with a delicate pruning away of some of its most vividly problematic features.[3] A series of initial adjustments were made to address immediate preservation concerns. Simultaneously a foundational refocus began with the cultivation of a critical awareness that there was no evidence of any Christmas celebration having occurred at Lindenwald in the historic period. Consultation with a scholar of the history of the Hudson Valley Dutch confirmed that Christmas was, relatively speaking, not a heavily celebrated holiday in Van Buren's Kinderhook, in contrast with New Year's Day.[4] The Dutch did, however, rather quietly celebrate St. Nicholas Eve, conveniently for our purposes on December 5, Van Buren's birthday. This historical information gave us the platform to use interpretive planning and historical research to shift the focus substantially without entirely rejecting a holiday event.

First and most urgently, we instituted a long overdue ban on open flame, purchasing what were at the time the most realistic low-voltage electric candles available, albeit at substantial expense (now thankfully superseded by relatively inexpensive battery candles). This was a necessary starting point because we were initially dealing with an entrenched attachment to the idea that this was a "candlelight event."[5]

Next we eliminated the use of actual food in the displays (fruit, nuts, candies, etc.) and began a long period of purchasing high-quality faux food to loan to the garden club volunteers to use in their arrangements.[6] Other action steps included eliminating the use of water in floral arrangements to avoid spill risk, and while we still allowed fresh flower arrangements for the two-day span of the open house, we more aggressively managed the safety of the collection. For example, we discontinued all use of the collection as part of the displays by simply removing vulnerable items in advance.

In addition to these and other explicit preservation measures, our first attempt at using an interpretive strategy to harness the event was to guide the garden club volunteers to make the floral arrangements more historically accurate.[7] Our thinking was that the arrangements could continue as the highlight of the event, while the interpretive goal would be to historicize Christmas by demonstrating how plant materials and holiday celebrations were different in the mid-nineteenth century. We engaged a botanical historian to treat the garden club to lectures and guidance, and at first most were delighted by the challenge. However, these sharply limited arrangements featuring a strict list of historically accurate plants meant the event became repetitive.

Historical accuracy became even more difficult as we communicated the fact that there was no evidence of Christmas having been celebrated at Lindenwald. But because December was aligned with Van Buren's birthday and St. Nicholas Eve, it seemed possible to revise the interpretive focus of the event without risking loss of its claim as the start of the community's Yuletide festivities.

However, this popularity meant that the sheer volume of visitors in the open house format was an enormous problem as revelers brushed against the painstakingly restored nineteenth-century wallpaper and accidentally kicked chair legs. Further, the thick crowding did not allow for proper visual security monitoring, resulting one year in a minor theft, which was clearly a red flag. A dynamic tension arose between the need for change and the wish not to alienate a community with palpable attachment to the event. While recognizing that steps needed to be taken to manage the crowds, we did not want that decision to damage goodwill toward Lindenwald.

Trial and Error

"Without desire to cramp these people's opportunities of innocent enjoyment."

Thus began several years of experimentation with a reservation system for an event featuring theatrical vignettes. Using this interpretive technique was intended as a way to control the size and flow of the crowd because we felt that people were accustomed to making reservations in that genre. The theater event model allowed us to develop a reservation system of thirty-minute "seatings." Groups of twenty visitors were led from a festive reception area in a tent outside the historic house to view the decorations and enjoy dramatic vignettes featuring accurately costumed historical characters in each room.

The event was publicized indicating that reservations were being taken by telephone using a manual reservation system, and we held our breaths, concerned about possible negative feedback. But launched together, the theatricals, the reserved seatings, and the reception area worked well. Visitors were pleased to make a reservation and enjoyed the smaller crowd. Happily, after the first year of taking manual reservations, we switched to a free online reservation system that made the change even more appealing to the public. The reception area held temporary exhibits to prepare guests for the historical cast and dialogue in the vignettes, and holiday treats that were not permitted in the historic house were served there, which enhanced the event's social dimension. The revised event was well received and allowed far better control of the number of people in the house at any one time.

Yet despite the success of the reservation system, the theatricals themselves were not completely successful. For our first attempt we hired several local actors to portray historical characters but discovered that professional actors often require the firm hand of a knowledgeable director, in this case one attuned to the history objectives of the event. As a result, the following year we worked on our own with staff and volunteers. We quickly learned that the production of quality, historically accurate, theatrical-based events was beyond our capacities. While the interpretive staff had experience presenting programming in period clothing, it was primarily using third-person interpretation. We had been careful to craft short vignettes of just several lines of dialogue per character, but the quality of the vignettes was still unsatisfactory.

With a few noteworthy exceptions, the performances by earnest volunteers and staff, however well received by empathetic visitors, proved uneven and problematic. Particularly memorable were episodes of forgotten lines and recovery attempts consisting of ad lib gaffes. Further, the historically accurate costuming, makeup, and hair styling were costly and difficult to procure. We concluded we did not have the skill or time to create theatricals, particularly those based on historical characters and events.[8] The fates had stirred us in another more favorable direction.

In the routine post-event debrief with staff and volunteers, we resolved we needed to change the model again. By 2013, we tried an alternative approach that explicitly focused on one central interpretive topic that the evening would highlight. Relying on historical research delivered using interpretive tools, we turned toward selecting a single topic germane to the site's mission. In its most basic expression, the formula was "Martin Van Buren, verb, noun." The unifying theme selected for the first experiment with this model was "Martin Van Buren had a daughter-in-law from South Carolina." The dynamic topics accessed through a focus on Van Buren's daughter-in-law Angelica Singleton Van Buren, a southern plantation heiress living in Lindenwald, where the antislavery Free Soil Party was founded in 1848, proved interpretively rich.[9]

Staff and volunteers were immersed in researching antebellum culture and used the interpreter's toolbox to create temporary exhibits and explanatory handouts that established the historical context of slavery and pre–Civil War society.[10] Importantly, we guided the garden club away from the sharply limited "realism" of mid-nineteenth-century floral arrangements and instead offered them opportunities to learn about the life of Angelica Singleton and create arrangements expressing that theme. Van Buren's experiences at home with his family were presented in a way that offered historical perspective on his place in time; visitors would be introduced to the idea that Van Buren had a close family member from South Carolina at a time of escalating sectional tension over slavery.

We kept the visual drama of featuring a few interpreters in period costume but eliminated the acting and rehearsal dimensions. It was, of course, a great relief to eliminate the risk of historical faux pas arising from well-intentioned ad libbing, particularly with this topic. Angelica Singleton herself was the evening's hostess, not merely as eye candy, but to vivify that the focus was on antebellum American life.[11]

It was an explicit objective to use the interpretive tools at our disposal, such as orientation exhibits and interpretive training, to reveal that Angelica Singleton not only grew up in a wealthy South Carolina family, but she also inherited a plantation and enslaved people upon her father's death in 1852, a story further complicated by the fact that she lived at Lindenwald with a father-in-law who was the 1848 presidential candidate of the Free Soil Party. (And we thought our holiday family discussions were politically fraught!) The less formally dialogic approach proved engaging to the public, volunteers, and staff, and facilitated an event that could also support key interpretive goals in a manner that allowed visitors to at minimum know something significant about the dynamic family and racial dimensions of the pre–Civil War era.[12]

We tried this model again the following year, when we chose another family topic that could be approached without substantial new research: "Martin Van Buren had grandchildren."

By organizing the event around the Van Buren grandchildren we once again had a topic that was familiar yet had many associated topics that could be used to craft a visually appealing and historically informative event. The interpretive and museum staff explored not only the biographies of the grandchildren, but also the history of child-rearing in antebellum America, and the garden club was asked to incorporate the theme of antebellum childhood into their arrangements. The grandchildren also facilitated the historicization of Christmas through the display of Dutch St. Nicholas Eve traditions, such as children placing a wooden shoe with a (faux) carrot as a treat for St. Nick's horse, hoping the next morning to find the carrot replaced by treats.

Once more we developed temporary exhibits and explanatory handouts to detail how differently the correct upbringing of children was perceived in this period. For example, an exhibit incorporated several quotes from an essay by Professor George Whippel that appeared in *The Mother's Assistant* in 1845. The essay, titled "Dangers of Childhood, and Means of Obviating Them," asserted, "The first danger lies in an unsubdued will. The first and indispensable duty of every parent is, in the strength of God, and with fervent prayer, completely to subdue the child's will. There is no alternative."[13]

The exhibit certainly raised eyebrows and showed historical change over time. Professor Whippel was not the star of the show, however. That was Bob the Squirrel. Excerpts from *The Travels and Extraordinary Adventures of Bob the Squirrel,* a children's morality story published in 1847, were read by interpreters as visitors moved from room to room. The technique was a way to create continuity and build interest in exploring the exhibits on childhood, the Van Buren grandchildren, and Bob the Squirrel himself at the end of the tour.

By now we were convinced that we could draw meaningful topics from the wellspring of existing historical research while maintaining an event that had a familiar holiday air, retaining and even expanding our audience. Another example was built on the fact that Van Buren's secretary of war was South Carolina congressman and diplomat Joel Roberts Poinsett. Before becoming the secretary of war for Van Buren, Poinsett had served in the John Quincy Adams and Jackson administrations as the country's first ambassador to the newly independent Republic of Mexico. While in Mexico, Poinsett, an amateur botanist, became familiar with a plant known locally as the Christmas Eve flower. He sent the plant home to South Carolina where it became known as the "Poinsettia."[14]

The simple formula was applied to establish the topic "Martin Van Buren's secretary of war introduced the poinsettia to the United States from Mexico," which inspired some excellent programming that attracted a new audience to the event. The interpretive staff chose to focus not on Poinsett himself but on the meaning of the *Flor de Nochebuena* derived from a Mexican folk story emphasizing themes of hope and family.[15] The staff worked with the local school district to create a pre-event activity in which an NPS ranger read Tomie DePaola's illustrated version of the story in both English and Spanish.

The students were then asked to create poinsettia-themed artwork illustrating their own messages about the meaning of the holidays to be used in exhibits at the site during the upcoming event, to which the children and their parents were given special invitations. The story's message was appealing but also explicitly inclusive, drawing attendance from the Kinderhook area's largest local minority group in an authentic way that was neither manufactured nor pandering.[16] Using the principle of good historical research and universally engaging messaging, the event was a huge success. The garden club decorations featured newly meaningful masses of crimson flowers in creative arrangements, while excited children and their parents, many of whom had never been to the site before, eagerly searched the displays for their own contributions.

The Power of Reflexive History

"Tonight, if you have aught to teach me, let me profit by it."

Perhaps the most adventuresome use of interpretive tools and historical research as foundations for the event was in 2016, the year of the centennial of the establishment of the National Park Service. The yearlong celebration of the creation of the NPS provided an opportunity to creatively engage in what Seth Bruggeman describes as "reflexive history," a historic site's awareness of its own institutional history and the role it has played in the way the site has been interpreted and preserved.[17] Using the theme of the agency's history illuminated the beliefs and practices of those who created it in the context of the Progressive Era. And, from a holiday perspective, because it was going to be 1916, the garden club could finally have its period-appropriate faux Christmas tree. Indeed, the Christmas tree, as well as the opportunity to use novel content from the early twentieth century in their creative designs, was met with great enthusiasm from garden club volunteers.

Five salient topics were selected to place the establishment of the NPS within the larger context of the social and political foment of 1916. Once again displays and interpretive literature were developed that identified key topics: Women's Suffrage; African American Activism; Temperance; Political Reform, and World War I. We also included exhibits that revealed the lasting change wrought by the Progressives through the sixteenth, seventeenth, and nineteenth amendments to the Constitution, and highlighted the history of the family that owned Lindenwald for the longest time in the twentieth century and did much to

Figure 14.1   Using "reflexive history" highlighting the Progressive Era origins of the National Park Service allowed garden club volunteers to create arrangements based on twentieth-century Christmas customs. Interpreters included a suffragist, Woodrow Wilson, a WWI doughboy, a temperance advocate, and W. E. B. DuBois. Courtesy of National Park Service.

help preserve it. That the family purchased the property in this period allowed guests to understand the story of Lindenwald in a completely different historical context than its usual presentation.

Finally, because we had a faux Christmas tree at last, we created a tabletop exhibit historicizing this special seasonal adornment. The reception area featured large, colorful wall-mounted displays highlighting Progressive Era constitutional change. We placed additional tabletop displays inside Van Buren's home to underscore the story of the early-twentieth-century owners of Lindenwald. Handouts provided detail and references for those wishing to explore topics in depth. The objective was to historicize and vivify the context for the establishment of the National Park Service and the post–Van Buren history of Lindenwald.

The tour of the house was structured around the five topics using skilled staff and volunteer interpreters in period clothing presenting first-person interpretation. As visitors walked from room to room, they encountered a suffragist, a temperance worker, a World War I doughboy, President Woodrow Wilson (who signed the legislation that established the National Park Service) and W. E. B. DuBois, who offered copies of his singular *The Souls of Black Folk* (see figure 14.1).[18]

Dramatic free-standing panels placed alongside the interpreters emphasized each of the Progressive Era topics. Through the coordinated efforts of the interpreters, the exhibits and handouts, and the creative floral arrangements supporting each room's topic, visitors learned about the goals of Progressive Era reformers and how the founding of the National Park Service was a part of those efforts, all while celebrating the Christmas season. Our work to present "reflexive history" resulted in not only a unique holiday event (with a tree!), but also one that showed that the site itself has a rich and meaningful history beyond its association with Van Buren.

Among some of the other topics explored using the Christmas event formula were the history of Irish servants at Lindenwald, Van Buren's relationship with Queen Victoria (with an emphasis on the evolution of Christmas during her reign), and since Van Buren's family ran the Kinderhook village tavern, the role of taverns in community life in the early republic. It should be mentioned that a key component of the success of the events was the development of a written operations plan that covered the logistics, scheduling, and safety requirements, as well as a basic outline of the topic and learning objectives. This compact package of information was extremely useful in keeping staff not directly involved in the planning of the event (such as administrative staff and volunteers) fully informed. Also critical was a briefing meeting held prior to the event as well as a debriefing evaluation that staff from all work groups participated in within a week after the event.

Using the Past to Face the Future

"Ghost of the Future . . . I fear you more than any spectre I have seen."

The events described here are a sample of how the full range of history associated with Martin Van Buren and Lindenwald seen through a reflexive lens were used as grist for what was recast as the annual "Winter Celebration." Doing so resulted in a popular community event that not only allowed for greater protection of resources, but also helped to thread the needle between fictionalizing a phantom historic Christmas event that had never occurred, and one that too rigidly applied concepts of historical accuracy since evidence was lacking. Finding a way in the present to be authentic about site history while still celebrating the community's holiday was critical.

As we know from the research of Thelen and Rosenzweig, people trust the history that they learn at historic sites more than from any other institutional source.[19] The role of the public historian is therefore an important one deeply pertinent to our current cultural crisis.[20] So why does it matter if historic sites, by virtue of the ubiquitous and beloved Christmas event, create a past that never existed? In an age of fevered, unrestrained, and frequently nefarious use of media to communicate to the masses, skilled planning for an event of this nature goes to the very purpose and necessity of our institutions in promoting an educated citizenry capable of self-rule. To return to the inspiration for our "seventh principle," Tilden elegantly advised that interpretation is "an attempt to reveal the truths that lie behind appearances," not unlike the purpose of Scrooge's ghostly visitors.[21]

In reflecting on the potential power of historic sites to energize (or suppress) social action, Clint Smith quotes Frederick Douglass: "The duty of today is to meet the questions that confront us with intelligence and courage."[22] This noble goal requires us to "live in the past, the present, and the future," in the words of the enlightened Scrooge. Armed with this perspective we can go forth and face the challenges and possibilities of the historic site Christmas. In that effort, "God bless us every one."[23]

Notes

1. Charles Dickens, *A Christmas Carol in Prose* (Boston: Ticknor and Fields, 1869), 102.
2. This is an extension of Tilden's paraphrase of a National Park Service directive: "Through interpretation, understanding; through understanding, appreciation; through appreciation, protection." Freeman Tilden, *Interpreting Our Heritage,* ed. R. Bruce Craig (Chapel Hill: University of North Carolina Press, fourth ed. 1957; 2008), 65.
3. Laurel A. Racine, Gregory R. Weidman, Lenora M. Henson, and Patricia West, "The Curator's Role in Crowd-Pleasing Events: Maintaining Safety, Accuracy, and Security in the Excitement of It All," *Collections: A Journal for Museum and Archives Professionals* 10, no. 1 (Winter 2014): 47–66.
4. Personal correspondence, Ruth Piwonka, Municipal Historian, Kinderhook, New York, 2012.
5. A critical step toward improving the safety of the event was to shift it from evening to the well-lit afternoon. It helped that in the years after the establishment of the Lindenwald event the local community and the county tourism office separately instituted large evening events in the village of Kinderhook and in the county seat of Hudson, New York. Each year the two other events grew in size and scope and conflicted with Lindenwald's "candlelight event," justifying its time shift.
6. This turned out to be a relatively easy sell, since they were all well aware of the issue of mice in rural homes from personal experience. We also purchased faux greenery with berries so we could ban any real greens having that messy red feature so prone to falling off and lodging in the loops of Brussels carpet.
7. Patricia West in Racine et al., "The Curator's Role in Crowd-Pleasing Events," 62–63.
8. See, for example, Tessa Bridal, *Exploring Museum Theatre* (Lanham, MD: Rowman & Littlefield, 2004); and Stacy F. Roth, *Past into Present: Effective Techniques for First Person Interpretation* (Chapel Hill: University of North Carolina Press, 1998).
9. On the significance of Lindenwald to the establishment of the Free Soil Party, see United States Department of the Interior, "National Register of Historic Places Registration Form: Martin Van Buren National Historic Site" (2012): 20–24.
10. We had particular enthusiasm for Thavolia Glymph's *Out of the House of Bondage: The Transformation of the Plantation Household* (Cambridge and New York: Cambridge University Press, 2008). Our staff and volunteers were accustomed to working with scholarly texts through a history book club run by the park interpreters.
11. Great care must be taken with the topic of antebellum plantations not to lapse into any degree of toxic romance, as we have learned most recently from Clint Smith's analysis in *How the Word Is Passed: A Reckoning with the History of Slavery across America* (New York: Little, Brown and Company, 2021).
12. See Amy Murrell Taylor, *The Divided Family in Civil War America* (Chapel Hill: University of North Carolina Press, 2005).
13. George Whippel, "Dangers of Childhood, and Means of Obviating Them," in *The Mother's Assistant* (February 1845): 25–30.

14. It became clear that Poinsett is overdue for new scholarly analysis. Had it been published in time we would have benefited from the fascinating insights of Prof. Mark Schmeller, who described Poinsett's "imperious meddling" in "The Conspiracy-Fueled Origins of the Christmas Poinsettia" in the *Washington Post* (December 2019).

15. J. M. Taylor, R. G. Lopez, C. J. Currey, and J. Janick, "The Poinsettia: History and Transformation," *Chronica Horticulturae* 180, no. 3 (September 2011): 23–28; Tomie DePaola, *The Legend of the Poinsettia* (New York: Penguin Putnam Books for Young Readers, 1997).

16. U.S. Census Bureau, "Kinderhook, Columbia County, New York." Accessed December 27, 2021.

17. Bruggeman has long used his scholarship to uncover the value of historic sites understanding their own histories, beginning with *Here, George Washington Was Born: Memory, Material Culture, and the Public History of a National Monument* (Athens, GA: University of Georgia Press, 2008); and most recently in *Lost on the Freedom Trail: The National Park Service and Urban Renewal in Postwar Boston* (Amherst and Boston: University of Massachusetts Press, 2022).

18. W. E. B. DuBois, *The Souls of Black Folk* (Chicago: McClurg, 1903).

19. Roy Rosenzweig and David Thelen, *The Presence of the Past: Popular Uses of History in American Life* (New York: Columbia University Press, 1998), 21–22.

20. See Anne Mitchell Whisnant, Marla R. Miller, Gary B. Nash, and David Thelen, *Imperiled Promise: The State of History in the National Park Service* (Bloomington, IN: Organization of American Historians, 2011).

21. Tilden, *Interpreting Our Heritage*, 163.

22. Frederick Douglass quoted in the epigraph of Smith's *How the Word Is Passed*.

23. Dickens, *A Christmas Carol*, 111.

CHAPTER 15

'Tis the Season

A Religious History Framework for Interpreting Christmas and Other Holidays

Susan Fletcher, Barbara Franco,
and Melody Smith

MUSEUMS AND HISTORIC SITES often participate in the December holiday season through programs and events that interpret Christmas. As with many holidays, Christmas has multiple layers of meaning, including religious practice, popular culture, and family traditions. Museum audiences may engage with Christmas through many pathways. Some may derive meaning from popular culture, such as their favorite movies or music; others may value time spent with loved ones and family holiday traditions. Visitors may also find meaning in the theological significance of Christmas through religious practice. Some museum visitors may not celebrate Christmas and instead engage with coexisting holidays such as Hanukkah, Kwanzaa, or Diwali, or decline to take part in holiday celebrations altogether.

What role should religion play in holiday programming? When approaching the Christmas season, museums and historic sites fulfill a mission or serve an audience that compels them to consider religion in their holiday preparations. A historic house museum may interpret a family who celebrated Christmas as a religious holiday. Some museums may serve a significant local population that honors other religious winter holidays.

Interpretive strategies for Christmastime programs and events may raise questions about the role of religion in a program's intended impacts. How do institutions talk about religion without conflict or controversy? How can programming include religion without being exclusive? As members of American Association for State and Local History's (AASLH) Religious History Affinity Group, we developed a list of best practices to consider when interpreting Christmas at museums and historic sites through a religious history lens. This list should serve as a framework for heritage organizations to plan programs that intersect religion and Christmas while honoring their mission and audience.

1. Define Your Approach

When planning how your museum or historic site will interpret Christmas, establish a framework for how your institution will approach religion. Beginning this process can be challenging because religions encompass a variety of experiences, even within a single tradition. It is important to understand that there is a difference between the history of a formal, organized, and institutional religious tradition, and the less formal ways in which individuals use religious beliefs to structure and make meaning in their lives.

Scholars recognize that religion has two intertwining (and inseparable) dimensions: belief and practice. Theology mainly focuses on belief while the study of practical theology seeks to understand how belief is enacted in practice. Religious studies scholars, while certainly interested in the content of belief, often work more like anthropologists. They are interested in how religion operates, analyzing where and how religion intersects with other aspects of human life, such as economic or social interaction. For museums and historic sites, a religious definition that incorporates all aspects of lived practice usually makes the most sense for programming or events.

Interpreting religious practice—showing what Americans have made and done as they lived out their religious faiths—is more straightforward and less controversial than a strictly dogmatic approach. It is easier to re-create a practice's outward expressions than to explain complex theological beliefs, which may vary significantly from person to person even within the same religious tradition. For many Americans, the outward expression of spiritual practice at Christmas may include gift giving, decorating living spaces, going to houses of worship, spending time away from routine, and expressing generosity. These are common avenues for meaning making, as evidenced by the recurrence of these themes in Christmas popular culture. It is much more difficult to analyze how Americans feel about these traditions and how they intersect with their personal worldview. In individual American homes that celebrate Christmas today, there may or may not be an overt spiritual dimension, which may or may not be backed by a religious institution, commandment, or creed.

Focusing on lived religious practice does not mean that interpretation should ignore the theological or philosophical bases for the practice. If visitors see a religious practice interpreted without an explanation of the beliefs that shaped it, they only receive half of the story. When a program or event does not communicate the meaning behind a lived practice, it does not help visitors understand why the practice matters. Museums excel at depicting the specific details of human lives. When visitors' curiosity takes them beyond the material details of the object or action presented to them, they ask questions such as the following: Why is that done? Why are they dressed like that? Why are their preparations and actions significant? Why is it so different from what I am used to? Although such "Why?" questions never have a simple answer, religious or spiritual beliefs often play a role. If heritage sites only present what people do and fail to include why people do it, audiences miss important learning opportunities.

The best way for heritage sites to define the approach for their organization is to begin program planning by setting goals that align with institutional strategic plans and audience needs. Program planners should ensure that their program concept and methods reflect the institution's mission, vision, and values and will meet the needs of their community. Once an institution has established goals for the program or event, it can approach specific content and development considerations.

2. Never Assume

Museums and historic sites should avoid making assumptions about the religious beliefs and practices of their audiences and community. Instead, museums should assume the audience has a "baseline non-familiar" background about religion to accommodate people outside of a specific target audience. One cannot speculate about what knowledge all visitors bring to a religious topic. Working off assumptions can lead to further controversy and confusion.

One of these assumptions is that America is continually undergoing secularization and that audiences approach heritage sites through a secular lens. In truth, many museum visitors bring a sacred lens to the museum shaped by their own belief structure. Planners and interpreters should know that a visitor's experiences with religion outside the historic site or museum will inform their experiences within the site. By acknowledging that visitors' private and public lives may cause powerful feelings concerning religion, museums and historic sites can equip themselves to anticipate how their audience's religious (or nonreligious) identities will interact with museum content during the December holiday season.

Conducting audience evaluation and investing in community engagement can greatly enhance program planning and the impact of program outcomes. For example, an executive at a regional history museum wanted to ensure their event planning did not conflict with holidays on the Jewish calendar, such as Yom Kippur or Rosh Hashanah. However, the museum did not know if anyone in their audience observed these holidays. They assumed that if they reached out to their audience and asked about their religious observance, audience members would be offended. So the question of scheduling remained unresolved. A best practice would be to avoid these holidays without asking the museum audience. Rosh Hashanah, Yom Kippur, and Passover are major communal Jewish holidays observed in the synagogue rather than at home. Like all Jewish holidays, they begin the evening before the day marked, so any evening event scheduled at those times would exclude a part of the audience. A list of Jewish holidays is available online at HebCal.com. Consulting with Muslim, Hindu, or other faith leaders would yield guidelines regarding scheduling conflicts with other religious observances.

If the institution included elements of religious observance into their ongoing evaluation, situations like the one above would not seem so intimidating or unmanageable. Engagement teams can ask visitors more exploratory questions regarding religion in focus groups or through a program's summative evaluation. Asking open-ended questions about what holidays they celebrate, what special traditions their family follows, what special foods they prepare can provide more nuanced data and authentic knowledge that can help guide museums to craft interpretations tailored to audience needs and increase the impact of their mission.

Personal religion or spirituality is one of the central ways that people identify themselves, both as individuals and as part of a group. The American religious landscape reflects cultural and spiritual diversity, a factor that museums should integrate into their community engagement. For some Americans, religious identity is a cultural affiliation rather than active religious participation. Some Jews identify themselves as cultural Jews and both Catholics and Protestants may identify with their religion culturally rather than theologically. For non-Western cultures, like the Hmong people and Native American groups, cultural and religious identities may be even more closely interwoven. Therefore, when bringing questions of religious identity into programming, museums need to acknowledge that relationships to a religious tradition can be tenuous and essentially nonreligious, yet still matter deeply. For wide-ranging cultural traditions such as Christmas, this approach takes on special significance.

3. Contextualize

Christmas and other religious-based holidays present a special opportunity for many museums to introduce religious content but including holiday traditions can also raise interpretive issues around authenticity, inclusivity, or appropriateness. An issue that impacts historical interpretations of religion is the inherent conflict between the perceived unchanging beliefs of a faith tradition and history's role in documenting and interpreting change over time. Many present-day practitioners of a faith may assume that their lived religious experience is the same as those who practiced the faith in the past. Because living faith traditions and individual practices do change from place to place and from time to time, it is always important to let visitors know exactly where they are located historically when they encounter a representation of religion. For instance, although a contemporary Jew may readily connect to a museum's depiction of nineteenth-century Judaism, some sense of distance and an accurate historical context will enhance their ability to understand change as well as continuity in their tradition. Especially when interpreting religion in a more immersive fashion, visitors need to know they have traveled to another time.

Historians should search out rigorous documentation for interpretive choices concerning past religious practices to prioritize authenticity. Avoid broad generalizations when interpreting religion, especially when the historical data does not exist to back them up. Documenting how individuals took part in religious practices—whether they are Founding Fathers or ordinary people like tenement families—strengthens interpretation.

Evidence-based interpretation allows visitors to formulate their own questions, rather than presuming that there is a specific agenda or worldview.

Because religion connects to larger questions of geography and identity, crosses boundaries of race and ethnicity, and addresses universal questions of meaning, it can serve as an integrative tool for museum programming. These factors can contribute to a program goal of cross-cultural understanding. By deliberately interpreting different religious practices within the same program, interpreters can implicitly enhance meaning for visitors through comparisons and contrasts.

4. Incorporate Microhistories

Telling individual stories is an effective tool for speaking about religion and can be a helpful interpretive method in Christmas programming. Microhistories are a method of contextualization that communicates larger truths about religious practice. When a historian uses microhistories, they are using instances of a particular event, person, or family's experience to make an argument about the general. By focusing on how a family or community practiced Christmas, museums can help their visitors make a personal connection to religious history while inviting them to consider their own experiences.

This technique also allows museums to sidestep the difficulty of speaking for a faith community: the institution can let adherents of a particular religion speak for themselves. In programs that interpret contemporary spiritual practices, subjects can tell their own stories in person or on screen. Power and agency are given to the individual. For historical subjects, the interpreter must mine the documentary record for details about the individual's experience. Museums and historic sites can also create fictional representative characters based on robust historical research.

A "microhistory" focuses on individual people and groups of the past to articulate larger truths about the variety of religious expressions to museum audiences. However, when employing the "microhistory" approach, avoid oversimplifying complex realities by limiting the number of voices. This can lead visitors to make assumptions or logical leaps that could mislead them or cause them to misinterpret the truth.

5. Collaborate

Christmas programming can lay the groundwork for engaging with religious communities and religious content throughout the year. Museums and historic sites should see the interpretation of Christmas as an opportunity for community outreach and engagement. Many religious groups are already conducting programming during this season and many community members have a personal connection to the holiday. Museums can use these factors to make Christmas an entry point in religious programming, expanding to explore larger questions of religious history within the community.

Partnerships and collaboration are important components of many heritage projects, but they are essential when museums approach under-explored subjects such as religious belief and practice. Employing knowledge from the academic and religious community can situate a program locally. Connecting with spiritual groups and leaders can also help museum staff strengthen their understanding of the religious traditions in their community.

One way to engage with the community is to include someone knowledgeable about local religious history in planning meetings to ensure that programs are created from a place of understanding. Similarly, museums and historic sites can employ local historical fieldwork, academic review, and other research methods in their programming to uncover novel truths about their area's religious practice. Museums can also consult with religious and spiritual leaders to answer questions about theology and belief as they are building their interpretive framework around religious history.

Museums can also explore the idea of bringing historical programming and exhibits into religious spaces during Christmas. A local congregation may welcome a pop-up exhibit about the history of Christmas in your city and clergy may be interested in using your collections or archives for teaching inspiration.

The best practices already covered are excellent starting points to develop and further strengthen community engagement at your institution. Conducting audience evaluation starts a conversation and gives insight into both the community's identity and its needs. When programming takes into consideration the needs and questions of visitors, it acknowledges, validates, and welcomes visitors' personal feelings, connections, and emotions concerning the subject. When the community feels included, they are encouraged to continue the conversation and deepen their connections with the institution, which in turn leads to more effective partnerships.

6. Make Space

For museums and historic sites, creating space for a variety of feelings and perspectives around Christmas is necessary to prepare staff and create a welcoming and impactful environment for visitors. Visitors to a Christmas program at a museum or historic site will come with varying degrees of familiarity or identification with Christianity. Visitor reactions to your museum's interpretation of Christmas may range from profoundly positive to profoundly negative. Additionally, museum staff and volunteers will also have unique perspectives concerning religious knowledge and experience. Navigating the diversity of acquaintance and emotion surrounding Christmas can be challenging for museums.

Balancing the needs of the "insider" and the "outsider" is crucial when interpreting through a religious lens. "Insiders" might be members of a faith community, those knowledgeable about the subject, or those connected through personal experience. "Outsiders" might have little or no knowledge of the subject or have formed assumptions or biases related to the subject community or topic based on cursory experience. To complicate matters, museum staff and volunteers can be insiders and outsiders as well. Both groups might find it difficult to separate their personal thoughts and feelings from the objective historical analysis or contrasting experiences present in the program. Christmas has multiple pathways for meaning making with or without religion. The challenge for museums is to find a delicate balance between welcoming both insiders and outsiders into their programs. With empathy and deep research, museums can find an institutional voice that communicates familiarity and appreciation concerning the diversity of religious experience.

In addition to navigating the delicate balance of insiders and outsiders of a religious tradition, museums should also know Christmas can be an emotionally charged season for their visitors and staff. For some, Christmas is a holiday that inspires emotion, wonder, and enchantment. Christmas may also cause stress, inordinate expectation, and profound grief due to loss. The visitor to your Christmas program may be walking in a season of joy, sadness, anger, fear, or hope. The broad spectrum of emotions that people will bring into museums and historic sites around Christmastime is where the power of interpretation lies. Creating an environment where people feel welcome to bring their emotions and engage with the experience can have a profound impact on anyone involved with Christmas programming. Expecting an array of experiences and anticipating needs through evaluation and community engagement are proactive ways to cultivate a welcoming space where everyone feels their perspective is respected and allowed.

7. Prepare for Conflict

A key component to interpreting Christmas is preparing for and facing inevitable conflict. Amanda Hughes, director of development and strategy at Duke University Chapel, argues that museums should present the differences and disagreements inherent in any discussion about religion, and do so with the input of community members and other consultants to encourage "productive engagement."[1] This approach communicates to the public that the museum has taken a thoughtful and confident approach to their interpretation and that they desire an open and collaborative relationship with stakeholders. Embracing conflict—along with a simple concept, contextualization, community engagement, and a welcoming space—will support religiously related Christmas programming that meets institutional and interpretive goals.

Museums and historic sites might be concerned that visitors will view interpretation that includes a religious perspective as advocacy. Both visitors and museum staff can be very sensitive to any suggestion or appearance that a museum, even a sectarian one, actively promotes a particular religion. Visitors are wary of being "preached" to and museum staff worry that any interpretation of religion may be construed as proselytizing. While there is a distinction between promoting a worldview with partiality and educating about a worldview with fairness, communicating and understanding that distinction can prove difficult. For many Americans, talking about religion objectively without trying to promote one's own views is hard to imagine. Museums and historic sites should be confident in their interpretive strategy and ensure that frontline staff and volunteers understand the goals, intentions, and impacts of the program so that they can communicate them accurately to visitors who might otherwise feel uncomfortable or affronted. Additionally, visitor-facing people should have a method to report visitor feedback about the program so the institution's approach and response can better meet visitor needs.

No matter the intention or planning from an institution, visitors will want to participate in their own way, using different communication strategies as they seek to meet their needs.

A museum or heritage site might be the only place someone is invited to communicate or confront their perspectives on religion; prepare for visitors to accept that invitation and respond. Some museum visitors are eager not just to learn about religion from a guide, but to engage in back and forth dialogue or express their own personal beliefs. Although they may want to learn about other religions, in the process they are trying to understand and show their own religious identities by identifying points of conflict and agreement.

Visitors may seek understanding through dialogue, or they may want to defend their worldview. Some visitors may construe an institution's programming as a secular "attack on Christmas," despite the nonpartisan intention of the program. To meet these challenges, institutions should train visitor-facing staff on not only the program's subject, but on conflict management, de-escalation strategies, openness to dialogue, and personal safety. Institutions should empower their interpreters to end unproductive or aggressive conversations or remove themselves from harmful interactions with visitors.

Museums and heritage sites have an important opportunity to educate visitors both about the subject of religion and how to discuss religion with respect and civility. Preparing for a variety of responses from visitors during Christmas programming builds more avenues for visitors to participate in meaning-making and protects the well-being of museum staff and volunteers.

Note

1. A. M. Hughes, "Radical Hospitality: Approaching Religious Understanding in Art Museums, in *Religion and Museums: Global and Multidisciplinary Perspectives,* ed. G. Buggeln, C. Paine, and S. Plate (New York: Bloomsbury Academic, 2017), 165–72.

Resources

Berns, Steph. "Sacred Entanglements: Studying Interactions between Visitors, Objects and Religion in the Museum" (PhD diss., University of Kent, 2015).

Buggeln, G., and B. Franco, eds. *Interpreting Religion at Museums and Historic Sites.* Lanham, MD: Rowman & Littlefield, 2018.

Buggeln, Gretchen, Crispin Paine, and S. Brent Plate, eds. *Religion in Museums: Global and Multidisciplinary Perspectives.* London: Bloomsbury, 2017.

Harvard Divinity School. "Religion and Public Life for Professionals." https://rpl.hds.harvard.edu/professionals.

Korza, Pam, Barbara Shaffer Bacon, and Michael del Vecchio. *Arts and Civic Engagement Tool Kit: Planning and Designing Arts-Based Civic Engagement Projects.* Washington, DC: Americans for the Arts, 2008.

Moore, Diane L. *Overcoming Religious Illiteracy: A Cultural Studies Approach to the Study of Religion in Secondary Education.* New York: Palgrave Macmillan, 2007.

Ontario Museum Association. *Engaging Your Community: A Toolkit for Museums.* Toronto: Ontario Museum Association, 2015.

Paine, Crispin. *Religious Objects in Museums: Private Lives and Public Duties.* Abingdon: Routledge, 2013.

Simon, Nina. *The Participatory Museum.* Santa Cruz: Museum 2.0, 2010.

Smith, Melody. "A Combined Effort: Why Museums and Visitors Need Religious Literacy." *History News* 75, no. 2 (Spring 2020): 28–33.

The Creative Museum. *Creative Museum Toolkit: Connecting to Communities.* 2014.

Wood, Catherine, "Visitor Trust When Museums Are Not Neutral" (master's thesis, University of Washington, 2018).

Part IV

PUBLIC PROGRAMMING

CHAPTER 16

Have Yourself a Merry Little Christmas Festival

Sandra Smith

WITHOUT A DOUBT, the winter holiday season is replete with traditions shared by family and friends. These traditions take, and have taken, a variety of forms, many of which are addressed in this book.

Characteristics of Festivals

There's no better way to explore the holiday traditions of the past and to build new traditions than through museum and historic site festivals. The word *festival* brings to mind colorful images of multiday parties with thousands of attendees, small-scale events for just a few hundred, outdoor concerts, and even celebrations of local produce in small towns. However, most festivals—especially those at museums—share a few common characteristics:

- *Defined location.* Festivals take place at a specific location rather than an undefined area. The location may be at one or at multiple coordinated museums or historic sites.
- *Defined duration.* While festivals may take place over several days or just a few hours, they are of limited duration. This helps create a sense of urgency in attendees that can be helpful for promotional purposes.
- *Multiple activities or experiences.* Festivals offer several elements, events, or activities that are designed for different ages or audiences. This variety allows attendees to engage in ways that suit them best.
- *Free choice experience.* Visitors are free to move around on their own rather than follow a structured route or plan.

What Makes a Christmas Festival Different from Other Programs?

The winter holidays are a year-end break from the everyday routine, as well as a time to reconnect with family and friends. Many of the same forces at play in planning leisure travel can apply to attendance at holiday programming in museums. As John L. Compton discusses in his classic study "Motivations for Pleasure Vacation," those motivations include deepening family connections as well as seeking novelty (activity outside the norm) and education.[1] Museums are perfectly positioned to meet these needs. Families and friends can spend time together, sharing a novel and educational experience.

Creating a Festival

Why host a Christmas festival at your museum? What can a Christmas festival achieve for your museum? As illustrated in some of the case studies described later, a museum's annual Christmas festival can quickly become part of a family or community tradition and attract audiences that otherwise might not visit. By striking a balance between keeping the core of the event the same while always providing something new to see or do, a well-planned festival can be successful for years.

As with all museum programming, it is important to know what other museums in your community are already doing to avoid unnecessary competition. What is your museum or historic site uniquely positioned to do? Keep in mind your mission and resources when considering what type of event might be best suited to your museum.

One of the most overlooked steps in developing a museum program, including a festival, is understanding its purpose. What are you trying to accomplish? Clearly stating your goals for a program is essential so that all members of the team can allocate resources appropriately in planning and execution, and so that the festival's success can be measured.

Goals can be expansive or modest and will probably change. These may include the following:

- *Attendance.* Attracting audiences to your museum or historic site is a common measure of success; audiences bring revenue through museum admission fees, museum shop sales, or even food sales. In addition, higher attendance means even more channels for word of mouth to spread—free, organic advertising for your museum to build repeat visitation.
- *Revenue generation.* For museums and historic sites, most of which operate on tight budgets no matter their size, the goal of generating revenue during the busy holiday season is both reasonable and necessary. This can be accomplished through increased attendance or through program sponsorships.
- *Audience building.* A Christmas or holiday festival can provide an entry point for people that might not otherwise visit your museum. Because the concept of Christmas is instantly recognizable and understood, programming on holiday themes can overcome the psychological barriers to entry that sometimes plague history

museums. Visitors can see that museums are welcoming to all, that there's something for everyone, and most of all, they can be fun places to spend a few hours. Once the hesitant visitor is in the door, it is easy to build a positive relationship that will help keep them coming back.

- *Didactic goals.* Given the mission of history museums and historic sites, the importance of an educational component almost goes without saying—and yet, somehow, it is during the holiday season that museums seem most likely to lose sight of their educational mission in the name of mass appeal. Consider the mission of your museum and the messages you want to convey, and pull from your story, your community, your local culture. Measuring the success of this goal requires thoughtful visitor evaluation.
- *Creating tradition.* The holiday season, probably more than any other time of year, is about tradition. Families and friends look forward to taking part in the same activities each year. A well-planned and executed Christmas festival can keep visitors coming back year after year. Be sure to keep the essentials of the festival the same while adding or changing elements of it. This offers visitors something new to do or see each year, while still meeting their expectations.

Before deciding that a Christmas festival is right for your museum, first consider a few caveats:

- Return on investment is a simple ratio of revenue versus expense in most businesses, but it can be more complicated in nonprofits, especially museums, where the greatest expense is staff time and effort. It takes years to build a tradition; understand that it will probably take time before you see a financial return on investment.
- Planning and executing a festival can take an enormous amount of work, particularly in the early years when you are still testing the waters, refining the content, and building an audience. There may also be considerable startup expenses as you acquire the needed supplies, equipment, and exhibition materials. These startup expenses can affect the bottom line in the beginning and mask success. Where possible, track startup expenses separately.
- Consider the staffing requirements of any holiday programming. Will your museum be sufficiently staffed when many employees and volunteers travel or take time off to be with family? The week between Christmas and New Year's is often a very busy time for museums as families look for things to do with visiting relatives or children out of school and may even require higher staffing levels than the rest of the year.
- Developing a budget for a program in advance can be challenging, as often expenses do not become apparent until you are already on your way to implementation. Begin by estimating the supplies you will need, being sure to track onetime purchases (startup expenses) separately from expenses that will be incurred annually. How will you market the program? Will you purchase advertising or will you rely on earned media through press releases and media alerts? Estimate the staff time planning and executing the program will take, again being sure to identify which efforts are

onetime versus an annual task. When considering revenue, identify all potential avenues: museum admission, shop sales, food sales, and sponsorships.

Sustaining a Festival

Now that you have planned and executed your festival, the next challenge is sustaining it—keeping audiences returning year after year and continuing to attract new audiences as you grow. As referenced earlier, a major motivation for people attending programs is novelty, essentially finding experiences outside their day-to-day routines. On a larger scale, this keeps them returning each year as well, having the core of the program remain the same, while layering on new experiences and elements. To use a seasonally appropriate image, think of the core elements of your program as a Christmas tree, while the novel or changing elements of your program are the ornaments; some may be used year after year, and some may see only one season. These novel elements—a celebrity guest, new decorations, a new vendor, or demonstration, for example—can be the basis for a publicity hook each year to attract visitors.

The most essential step in building and sustaining a program over several years is reviewing it objectively after each iteration. Be sure to include all stakeholders: program planners, frontline staff, the marketing team, and volunteer representatives, to give a few examples. Using the goals you established while developing the program, review the success of that iteration of the program against each goal. Did your attendance go up or down over previous years? Did the program bring more or less revenue? What did the visitor evaluation tell you? Were you able to earn media attention through your programming? What resources went into holding this program? Were the outcomes of the program worth the investment of time and money? By tracking results year over year, you will be able to spot trends in attendance, revenue, audience satisfaction, media mentions, and more that can help guide your decisions for the future.

Retiring a Festival

Virtually every program, no matter how successful or how well-managed, has a lifespan. Market forces, a change in organizational mission or leadership, or simply declining public interest, can all impact the longevity of a program. When evaluating a program routinely, be mindful of these indicators that it may be time to consider the future of a program:

- *Attendance.* While attendance should rarely be the sole measure of success, comparing attendance to previous years or iterations can help you spot trends. Declining attendance over multiple program iterations can be the canary in the coal mine, an indicator that further objective investigation or evaluation of the program is needed.
- *Media.* Like attendance, waning media attention can be a sign that a program may have run its course. Earned media is essential for most museums as advertising

dollars can be scarce; if a program fails to draw media attention it can have significant negative impacts.

- *Changing Markets.* Museums and their programs are not immune to outside forces. Competition for free time continues to increase and trends change. For example, it was not long ago that escape rooms and axe-throwing were novelties drawing large numbers; now the number of these venues certainly outstrips demand in most cities. It is important to monitor trends and evaluate whether your program still offers something in demand or whether the market is saturated by similar programs or experiences.
- *Opportunity Cost.* When considering the success of a program, be mindful of what your organization is giving up to do it. Programs and festivals, particularly at the holidays, can be labor intensive and expensive. Could those dollars and those hours be put to better use? Could your museum building and the limited space within be used in better, more effective ways, particularly during the very limited holiday season?
- *Return on Investment.* As discussed above, return on investment in program development is more than revenue versus expense. In most nonprofit organizations, and museums in particular, staff time and labor are the greatest expense. As with opportunity cost, could that time and energy be better directed elsewhere?
- *Energy.* Finally, take a hard look at the museum staff and volunteer corps. Are they energized and excited by each iteration of the program, or are they going through the motions each year, depleted and drained? Listen to what the staff and volunteers are telling you—through their words, their energy levels, their participation. Draining your valuable staff and volunteers by holding on to a program or tradition long past its prime is a quick way to lose them.

How do you move on from a long-standing program or festival? Every program, even failing programs, have their proponents. You will no doubt hear from some of them should you choose to take a program off the schedule. Be prepared for this and do not necessarily take it as an indicator that you are making the wrong decision. Do not be fooled by the outcry if audiences are declining.

If possible, offer an alternative to the program to keep audiences engaged while you determine what is next. Use the feedback as an opportunity to communicate with your audiences. Ask what parts of the program they liked best and what they would like to see in future programs. While it is a small sample size, the feedback can be valuable and will strengthen your connection with audiences that felt strongly enough to contact you.

Case Studies

Each of the case studies described are individual interpretations of Christmas festivals—even the two very different iterations of Festivals of Trees. Each has distinct goals and successes, and each was developed specifically to meet both the needs of the museum and the community. They all show how careful consideration of the resources of the museum—including content and context, staffing, budget, and community need—can result in successful annual holiday programming.

Festival of Trees at Indiana Historical Society

The Indiana Historical Society (IHS), founded in 1830, "collects and preserves Indiana's unique stories; brings Hoosiers together in remembering and sharing the past; and inspires a future grounded in our state's uniting values and principles." The IHS's annual budget is approximately $7 million with a staff of around a hundred.

For several years, the historical society had been looking for a signature holiday event or program. Located in Indianapolis, Indiana, the IHS is surrounded by cultural organizations and museums, many of them within walking distance. Following a suggestion by a board member, several of the senior staff visited a museum a few hours away to see its annual festival of trees. As its name suggests, a festival of trees features several Christmas trees, each decorated by a different entity with a different theme. Some of the IHS staff were skeptical, but they agreed to give it a go. The first year featured twenty-five trees, each sponsored and decorated by a different organization or business in the community. In less than a decade, the Festival of Trees at the Indiana Historical Society has become a fixture—a must-do for families each holiday season. While the trees themselves may not necessarily be history themed, the events and activities that are part of the festival are. A perennial favorite series of programs celebrates the holiday film *A Christmas Story*; the author of the book the film is based on is from Indiana.

Over the years, the festival has grown to feature ninety-two trees, the number inspired by the number of counties in the state of Indiana. In 2020 and 2021, due to the pandemic, the Historical Society added a virtual component: a photo of each tree was posted on the website and visitors could vote for their favorite. In order to vote, visitors must provide their email address and are then subscribed to the e-newsletter.

Through this festival, the Indiana Historical Society accomplishes several goals: it is part of an annual tradition for local families; it drives attendance and therefore revenue; and sponsorship of the trees gives the museum an avenue for building connections with the business and philanthropic community. In addition, the core concept of the festival remains the same while allowing novelty; the trees are different each year, so there's always something new to see, and the programming around the trees evolves and refreshes annually as well. For more details, see "Festival of Trees 2020 – 30 Minute Special" at https://youtu.be/rMHfjCjFzsU.

The Carnegie Trees at the Carnegie Museum of Art

The Carnegie Museum of Art, founded in 1895 as the Department of Fine Arts of the Carnegie Institute, creates experiences that connect people to art, ideas, and one another. It is part of the larger Carnegie Museums of Pittsburgh, which has an annual budget of around $60 million and about 250 employees.

The Carnegie Museum of Art in Pittsburgh, Pennsylvania, also features trees every winter (see figure 16.1). Unlike the Indiana Historical Society, the number of trees is small—usually only four or five—and are all funded, presented, and decorated by one group:

Figure 16.1.   The Women's Committee at the Carnegie Museum of Art has annually funded, presented, and decorated Christmas trees since 1961, becoming a key part of the Pittsburgh holiday tradition and a backdrop to revenue-generating public and private events. Photo by Sandra Smith.

the Women's Committee, an organization separate from the museum whose purpose is to promote the museum through significant financial support and community outreach. The Women's Committee has funded the purchase of art for the collections, contributed to the museum's infrastructure and gallery renovations, and participated as a major donor to museum endowment and capital campaigns.

The committee has been presenting the trees annually since 1961, and they have become a key part of the Pittsburgh holiday tradition. The beautiful and massive trees also serve as a backdrop to revenue-generating public and private events as well as family photo sessions, which require a paid permit. For more details, see "Together This Season at Carnegie Museum of Art" at https://www.youtube.com/watch?v=5N0qOAOK_5o.

The St. Louis Holiday Historic House Tour

The Campbell House Museum in St. Louis, Missouri, opened in 1943 and "enlivens the history of St. Louis and Westward Expansion through the story of the Campbell family and their home." The museum has an annual budget of about $325,000 and has two staff members.

A different sort of festival takes place in St. Louis, Missouri. For the past forty years, four historic sites have joined forces every other year to present the St. Louis Holiday Historic House Tour. For five hours, the Old Courthouse, the Field House Museum, the Campbell House Museum, and the Chatillon-DeMenil Mansion open their doors and host several hundred visitors in one evening. Each site offers holiday decorations and activities specific to their interpretation and history, along with light refreshments. A single admission ticket allows entry into each site, and an upgraded ticket provides bus transportation between them. The evening is largely staffed by enthusiastic volunteers due to the small staff at each of the sites and sells out nearly every year. Because the structure of the festival remains the same each year, it requires relatively minimal planning despite the apparent complexity of the event. The festival is a revenue driver and does bring significant revenue to each site, which is especially notable given the relatively small amount of staff time and resources the festival requires.

"A Southern California Christmas" at the Homestead Museum

The Workman & Temple Family Homestead Museum is located in the City of Industry, California, and "inspires visitors to become advocates for history as they explore what life was like in this region from the days of the Mexican ranchos to the Roaring Twenties." The museum is owned and funded by the City of Industry and managed by Historical Resources, Inc. and at the time of this program had an annual budget of $1 million and a staff of nine.

For nearly twenty years, the Workman & Temple Family Homestead Museum in City of Industry, California, hosted a Christmas festival of a very different sort. City of Industry is located in the Los Angeles area of Southern California, and as its name suggests, is home to business and industry and has less than five hundred residents. The museum primarily draws its audience from nearby Los Angeles, Orange, San Bernardino, and Riverside Counties.

The Homestead Museum's "A Southern California Christmas" festival began in the late 1990s as a four-hour outdoor event that took place on a single day in December. It featured bands, local holiday food traditions, and other vendors. It quickly built a regular audience and significant community interest. In short order, the one-day festival grew to two days; the additional day did not significantly add to the cost of the program, and it allowed the museum to add programming and serve a larger audience. At its peak, the festival featured a series of musical and theatrical performances, living history presentations, museum tours, decorations, tamales, piñatas, crafts, and more. The two-day festival drew approximately two thousand people each year, about 10 percent of the museum's annual attendance.

The enormous success of the festival was also its Achilles' heel. Because of its size and complexity, "A Southern California Christmas" took half the year to plan, considerable staff involvement, and significant upfront costs for rentals, vendors, and more. As the museum is owned and funded by the City of Industry, there are no admission fees to visit the museum or attend the Christmas festival, and therefore no way to offset the investments of time and money.

The festival also outgrew the museum's options for a rain plan—the museum itself is small and could not begin to hold the festival vendors and visitors indoors. The first year that rain impacted the festival, the Homestead Museum staff adapted and moved it indoors, hoping that fewer visitors would turn out. That was not the case, however, and the resulting chaos was incredibly challenging. After that, when significant rain was in the forecast, the museum was forced to cancel the event. When this began happening more frequently, the museum staff began rethinking the feasibility of the festival. The sunk costs regardless of the success of the festival, the significant staff time in planning, and the impossibility of a rain plan became insurmountable obstacles, and the museum staff made the difficult decision to end the festival in 2009.

During its heyday, the festival was extremely successful in drawing large audiences, and judging by the outcry and disappointment from the community at its cancellation, it was an important holiday tradition. The festival was also an excellent example of a museum using local culture and history to present very different Christmas traditions.

Handmade Holidays at the Gamble House

The Gamble House in Pasadena, California, aims "to inspire the public's appreciation and understanding of architecture as a fine art through the example of the Gamble House, the most complete and best-preserved work of American Arts and Crafts architects Charles

Figure 16.2.   Vendors line the historic driveway of the Gamble House at the annual "Have a Handmade Holiday" event, which coincides with Museum Store Sunday and kicks off the holiday season at the museum. Photo by Alexandra Rasic.

and Henry Greene." The Gamble House had an annual budget of $1.1 million and a staff of six when the event debuted.

A decade after the final festival at the Homestead Museum, one of the staff heavily involved in planning "A Southern California Christmas" left to become the director of the Gamble House in Pasadena, California, an iconic Craftsman home designed by the firm Greene & Greene. Mindful of the lessons learned with "A Southern California Christmas" and its ultimate cancellation, she took a very different approach when planning the museum's holiday festival.

For marketing purposes, the festival took place on the nascent Museum Store Sunday, which occurs the Sunday after Thanksgiving. The grounds of the museum were opened to picnickers, and the museum offered tours, carolers, a few local craft vendors, and other holiday activities (see figure 16.2). The craft vendors, in particular, were chosen for their thematic ties to the architecture of the Gamble House. In addition, a local cat rescue was featured as a vendor; the museum wanted to do something a little unexpected while making new connections and positioning themselves as supporters of the community. While this smaller Christmas festival could grow larger, it is appropriate to the scale of the museum, is authentic to the museum's mission, and already has deep roots in the community.

Note

1. John L. Compton, "Motivations for Pleasure Vacation," *Annals of Tourism Research* 6, no. 4 (October/November 1979): 408–24.

Resources

Crompton, John, and Stacey McKay. "Motives of Visitors Attending Festival Events." *Annals of Tourism Research* 24, no. 2 (1997): 425–39.

Huber, Kimberly, and Anna Johnson. "Planning and Managing Museum Programs and Special Events." In *The Museum Educator's Manual*, edited by Anna Johnson et al. (Lanham, MD: AltaMira Press, 2009), 95–108.

Martin, Rebecca. "The Nuts and Bolts of Program Management." In *The Small Museums Toolkit Book 5: Interpretation*, edited by Cinnamon Catlin-Legutko and Stacy Klingler (Lanham, MD: AltaMira Press, 2012), 100–132.

Truelock, Gennie, and Tara Richards. "Planning for Special Events" (webinar). Nashville, TN: American Association for State and Local History, October 30, 2018.

CHAPTER 17

"Not a Twinkle Out of Place"

Living History Museums Celebrate Christmas

Sara Bhatia

COMPARED TO SINGLE-SITE historic houses, living history museums are particularly well positioned to mount exceptional Christmas celebrations that transport visitors to a nostalgic past. With their extensive grounds, multiple interpreted buildings, retail shops and dining spaces, living history museums have lots of different levers to manipulate to deliver a robust, multifaceted holiday experience. Some museums make use of their expansive grounds and buildings to host large festival-like Christmas events. Others may self-impose certain rules for their sites—like permitting more modern, festive decor in outdoor spaces while committing to greater authenticity inside historic buildings. Still others take advantage of their large sites to offer a range of experiences, including events with mass-market appeal alongside other programs that are more mission driven and historically authentic.

But while living history museums have certain advantages over house museums, they share common challenges with their smaller peers. Like single-site historic houses, many living history museums wrestle year-round with the challenges of interpreting largely white, elite, Christian communities in a way that feels relevant and welcoming to all visitors. Christmas celebrations can magnify this challenge. Some museums actively seek and embrace diversity within their interpreted community and amplify it during Christmas celebrations—with costumed interpreters depicting a Jewish immigrant family celebrating

Hanukkah, for example, or by exploring religious traditions among enslaved people. Others stage a purely secular celebration, eschewing Christian rituals and symbolism, and replacing the term "Christmas" with the more inclusive "holiday" or "winter."

During the Christmas season, many living history museums also grapple with questions of historical authenticity. It is challenging to incorporate Christmas decor and programming in a way that is both historically accurate and yet still feels festive to a modern visitor. This is particularly so for those museums which interpret the pre-Victorian past, when Christmas was not an occasion for lavish decor or celebration. Today, many living history museums cater to visitors' nostalgic, romanticized ideas about the past by programming an old-fashioned Christmas. While often not historically accurate, these celebrations may convey an authentic *feeling* of a historic Christmas, albeit untethered to a specific historical era or even the museum's usual period of interpretation.

This chapter describes Christmas celebrations at three exemplary living history museums: Old Salem Museum and Gardens (Winston-Salem, North Carolina), Strawbery Banke (Portsmouth, New Hampshire), and Conner Prairie (Fishers, Indiana). While each of these museums offers outstanding, interactive, innovative, and mission-specific programming year-round, they have made very different, but equally valid choices for the Christmas holiday season. For all three, celebrating Christmas involves a delicate balancing act: serving their communities, adhering to mission, preserving historical authenticity, and, perhaps most importantly, contributing to the museum's bottom line.

Old Salem Museum and Gardens (Winston-Salem, North Carolina)

Old Salem Museum and Gardens is a living history site focused on the history of the Moravians, a German Protestant sect, with twenty-five historic buildings interpreted for the period 1770–1819. The complexity of the site—with a traditional museum, dozens of historic buildings, and highly interactive, educational programming—allows a variety of access points and experiences during the holiday season, ranging from a visit with St. Nick to an exploration of the Moravians' miniature crèche-like Christmas displays. Christmas at Old Salem is relatively peaceful and contemplative, a marked contrast with more exuberant, commercial celebrations at other living history museums (see figure 17.1.).

Outdoors, Old Salem's Christmas decor is understated, with ropes of greenery draped on fences and lampposts, simple wreaths garnished with sprigs of dried flowers and herbs, and large planter pots brimming with evergreens. This simplicity is, in part, dictated by the district's Historic Resource Commission's guidelines, which prohibit hanging electric string lights. Indeed, until recently, Old Salem had virtually no external Christmas decor. The traditional greenery is a compromise, straddling the line between authenticity and visitor appeal. While seemingly historic, this decor is not, in fact, authentic. Eighteenth-century Moravians treated Christmas as a single day's event, with perhaps a single sprig of greenery on the mantel or a simple wreath.

While the decorations may not be strictly authentic, they *feel* historic, and are a counterweight to a modern, commercial Christmas. They are also an essential hook to lure visitors.

Figure 17.1.   While the decorations may not be strictly authentic, at Old Salem Museum and Gardens they feel historic and are a counterweight to a modern, commercial Christmas. Courtesy of Old Salem Museum and Gardens.

Unlike many living history museums, Old Salem is embedded in a historic district which includes residents and businesses unrelated to the museum. While Old Salem requires tickets for entry to its historic buildings and museum, everyone is welcome to meander through the district. As a result, Old Salem's Christmas decor and other seasonal sensory delights—the aroma of Christmas strudel at Winkler Bakery, the sounds of local musicians—are accessible to all. In 2019, approximately four hundred thousand people visited Old Salem's historic district; of those, only seventy-five thousand purchased tickets.[1] Converting casual strollers into paying visitors is a challenge. But for historic houses or living history museums in well-traveled neighborhoods, presenting an appealing public face in outside spaces can be a great opportunity to entice paid visitors. To this end, Old Salem's former director Frank Vagnone notes, "I'm doing everything I can to make it feel Christmas-y."[2]

As one would expect for a museum that interprets a religious community, Old Salem's Christmas decor and programming reflect the devout Moravians' Christian rituals. Historic houses include *putzes*, small nativity scenes displayed on a mantel or under a tree. The museum erects a twenty-foot-tall Christmas pyramid, a European precursor of the Christmas tree decorated with lanterns, greenery, and fruit, and a large crèche at the base. But the museum draws the line between *interpreting* the Moravians' religious practices and *participating* in them. For example, the museum refrains from promoting programs sponsored by the local Moravian Church, including a series of December Candle Teas with explicitly religious content, even though the event is held in one of Old Salem's historic buildings.

Vagnone describes this tension as "walking the subtle line of being a peaceful, contemplative, secular site where all people can be comfortable."[3]

Old Salem's secular programming has a serene, even spiritual quality. The museum describes its annual Salem Night as a "time to slow down, leave the busy holiday season behind and start to reflect on family & friends . . . a once-a-season special candlelight evening of open, warm, and inviting Christmas experiences."[4] This evening program features a pianoforte concert and choral singing, and visits to artisans' shops and historic houses, all lit by candles.

Like many living history museums, Old Salem operates in the red all year, and relies on revenues from the holiday season to cover annual operating costs.[5] In addition to Salem Night ($40/adult), a series of intimate Christmas candlelight tours ($65/adult) revolve around an annual theme like "A Baking We Go" or "Crafting Community," with hands-on experiences culminating in a Christmas party. On daytime Saturdays in December, Old Salem augments its regular programming by adding a holiday twist. For example, visitors at the historic Winkler Bakery help bake Christmas cookies; interpreted houses are (lightly) decorated for the holiday and offer hands-on activities like holiday crafts or grinding ginger for baking.

Much of the museum's Christmas programming aligns with its educational mission and interpretive period, but there's some wiggle room, particularly for the retail spaces and one revenue-critical programming event—a photo opportunity for children to meet a Victorian-styled St. Nick. While the Victorian era is well outside the museum's typical period of interpretation, Vagnone notes that under his leadership, the museum has "a more broad sense of the period of significance, and that is how I ground my interpretation of Christmas."[6] Like other Old Salem events throughout the year (Halloween Trick or Treat and the weekly farmer's market) and certain retail establishments (a coffee shop and café/music hall), St. Nick's workshop is intended to appeal to the local community and bring in visitors and revenues. It seems to work. The museum estimates that in 2018, 50–70 percent of visitors to "Salem Saturdays at Christmas" stopped by to visit St. Nick.[7] Flexibility about programming—particularly around Christmas—helps to pay the bills and support the museum's mission. Vagnone is unapologetic about such choices: "I have no problem finding some conceptual, collaborative, intermediate space to find a cooperative way to celebrate Christmas. I'm finding ways to remain true to what we do the rest of the year and still fulfill expectations of holiday visitors."[8]

Old Salem has recently placed a new emphasis on retail sales, which comprise 45 percent of earned revenue.[9] The museum's book and gift shop is stocked with Moravian stars and other Christmas goods and, like St. Nick's workshop, boasts modern Christmas decor including Christmas trees, snowmen, and hanging ornaments. If there's a tension between historical accuracy and keeping the lights on, Vagnone is clear where he stands: "I don't have the theoretical luxury to be completely authentic. . . . I have one hundred employees and making sure I can keep them employed is more important than making sure my Christmas decorations are fully authentic."[10]

Under Vagnone's leadership, Old Salem has expanded its focus from the eighteenth-century Moravian settlers to include enslaved African Americans and Native Americans, and the museum has worked to integrate them into Christmas programming. In 2019, for example, the museum retained Dontavius Williams, a performer known for his first-person historical interpretation of an enslaved man, to share stories about the Christmas and wintertime experiences of the enslaved.[11] In 2017, Old Salem launched an initiative to expand access to the museum for people with physical and cognitive learning challenges, and designates one Saturday in December for visits to St. Nick for children with special needs.

Since 2018, Old Salem has extended the holiday season by hosting a four-day winter fair the week following Christmas. The museum promotes the fair as a post-holiday opportunity for local residents to get out of the house with visiting friends and family.[12] Vagnone describes the fair as a "palate cleanser"—a way to bring in visitors and introduce them to the site without the expectations related to Christmas or even historical authenticity. Some programs are like those on typical Salem Saturdays, but others, like a chainsaw artist and Appalachian folk musicians, offer more modern entertainments. The fair is the museum's biggest ticketed fundraising event of the year.[13]

Strawbery Banke (Portsmouth, New Hampshire)

With picturesque buildings festooned with garlands and costumed carolers in the streets, *Travel & Leisure* magazine quipped, "[Portsmouth, New Hampshire] aspires to be the Christmas Capital of America."[14] Strawbery Banke, a living history museum that interprets the three-hundred-year-old waterfront neighborhood Puddle Dock, is the heart of Portsmouth's annual Christmas celebration. The museum's primary Christmas event is a candlelight holiday stroll, which includes a tour of historic houses.

Strawbery Banke is a ten-acre campus with thirty-nine historic buildings interpreted over three centuries. In December, the village is transformed into a festive Christmas landscape with an emphasis on holiday atmosphere rather than historical authenticity. The museum's director of marketing and communication notes, "I think people—as soon as they step past the visitor's center—really are in a different place. . . . [I]t's a really magical holiday experience . . . a wonderful atmosphere to come and enjoy the holiday."[15]

The museum's "Candlelight Stroll under the Stars" is held on weekend evenings in December. A $32 event ticket includes access to the museum grounds and five historic houses. The museum's ten-acre campus is enclosed by a fence, which allows restricted, ticketed entry on the nights of the "stroll," although the gates are open and holiday lights are lit throughout the holiday season for casual visitors to wander through the grounds. This event is typically sold out and a big revenue booster for the museum—the seven evenings of the stroll account for a whopping 20 percent of the museum's annual paid attendance.

The festive atmosphere evokes an old-fashioned Christmas. Walkways are lined with white lights and glowing luminarias with real candles, wreaths crafted from live greenery and dried flowers hang on doors and windows, and horse-drawn carriages trot along cobblestone lanes. Artisans' shops showcase artisans at work, with some—like a tinsmith making ornamental stars and punched tin lanterns—catering to holiday shoppers. Dozens of costumed interpreters (including a Victorian-era St. Nick) roam the streets chatting

Figure 17.2.   In December, several historic houses at Strawbery Banke are each decorated to different eras and staffed by costumed interpreters, including a modest middle-class house in 1943. Photo by David J. Murray, ClearEyePhoto.com, courtesy of Strawbery Banke.

with visitors. The result is a Disney-like experience. A visitor might encounter women in colonial-era hoop skirts on one block, then turn the corner and see a World War II air raid warden singing Christmas carols.[16]

Five historic houses, each interpreted to a different era, are open during the evening stroll or, alternatively, comprise a ninety-minute tour ($15/adult) for daytime visitors in December. Each house provides a tableau of the holiday season staffed with costumed interpreters in spaces ranging from a wealthy merchant's mid-eighteenth-century Georgian home to a modest middle-class house with an attached general store interpreted to 1943 (see figure 17.2). The houses are meticulously furnished with period-appropriate objects, including holiday decor.[17] Like the museum itself, the tour reflects change over time, and offers some diversity of socioeconomic and ethnic experiences reflecting the diversity of the Puddle Dock community, including a house occupied by a Ukrainian Jewish immigrant family interpreted to 1919, with costumed role players preparing for Hanukkah. While the museum includes native Abenakis and enslaved African Americans in exhibits and other interpretive spaces, their stories are not part of the holiday house tours.[18] In a nod to inclusivity, all activities are labeled as "holiday" or "seasonal" rather than "Christmas." While there's no mistaking the Christmas theme—the village is festooned with Christmas trees and wreaths—it is a secular event.

The Candlelight Stroll also includes events outside the museum's historic mission, including a bonfire, ice skating on Strawbery Banke's outdoor rink, and live contemporary music. Strawbery Banke is a museum dedicated to preserving the history of the Puddle Dock neighborhood, and these activities help foster community today.

The Candlelight Stroll is also part of Strawbery Banke's stewardship program, with benefits for members and donors. There is an exclusive members' preview night with free admission, and the museum hosts a "member house" each evening of the stroll, where members can warm up with complimentary hot cider and donuts inside a historic house.

Strawbery Banke's recently launched sponsor-a-tree program is not a big money maker but allows the museum to engage with the community. About fifty local businesses (mostly small mom-and-pop operations) make an outing to decorate a Christmas tree, with some, like one local insurance company, arriving with wine, packed lunches, and picnic blankets. For many participants, sponsorship prompted their first visit to Strawbery Banke, and some returned for the Candlelight Stroll to show off their decorated tree to friends and family.[19] The relatively low dollar commitment to sponsor a tree ($250 for corporations and $100 for individuals and nonprofits) encourages broad participation and opens the door to membership or future donations. Over time, the museum hopes the grove of sponsored trees will become a draw in its own right. For now, not only does the program generate a little revenue, it cleverly shifts some responsibility for outdoor decor from the museum to the community. Equally important, the program requires relatively little staff effort from the museum—participants trim the trees themselves and provide their own decorations.

Strawbery Banke's sponsor-a-tree program is part of the museum's larger commitment to community engagement. The museum estimates that about 80 percent of holiday visitors are from New England, and about 40 percent from the immediate Sea Coast area.[20] Strawbery Banke partners with the chamber of commerce, the local historical association, and a local concert hall to crossmarket seasonal events. While each organization relies on its own ticket sales, shared marketing benefits everyone and helps attract local media coverage. A city-run trolley connects the various partners' sites to create a cohesive holiday experience, and to ease traffic and parking. For this living history museum, the annual Christmas celebration is about more than just revenues—it is an opportunity to be a good neighbor.

Conner Prairie (Fishers, Indiana)

Conner Prairie, a living history museum that interprets nineteenth-century pioneer life, boasts "there's not a twinkle out of place" at its annual winter festival, "Merry Prairie Holiday." This event, which promises "more lights, more fun, more storytelling," is a family-focused holiday celebration held on weekend evenings in December. Marketing materials for a Merry Prairie Holiday feature an African American woman in a nineteenth-century costume standing side-by-side with an elf, with the two tangled in a strand of multicolored lights. It is a great metaphor for the event—a light dose of history intertwined with family fun, with a conscious commitment to inclusivity.

Launched in 2019, Merry Prairie Holiday is a new event for Conner Prairie, although the museum is well known locally for its festivals. Merry Prairie Holiday is an expansion of the beloved, decades-long "Candlelight" program, an evening tour of the museum's historic Prairietown. But while capacity issues limited Candlelight visitors to about 2,500 per season, Merry Prairie Holiday takes advantage of Conner Prairie's extensive grounds to host 25,000, with room to grow.[21] The expanded event also allows the museum to more fully use its outdoor interpretive spaces, which are otherwise closed from November through early March.

Conner Prairie prides itself on its storytelling, and the museum's motto—"step into the story"—is at the core of all its programming, which includes nature and conservation education along with living history. When Conner Prairie expanded the former "Candlelight" event, Rich Cooper, former vice president and chief program officer explained, "We wanted to bring what Conner Prairie does best as a living history site and put that into the middle of this experience. So we kept those holiday traditions and Christmas traditions and the storylines, and we added more inclusive storylines, along with lots of wintertime fun."[22] Today, costumed interpreters in Prairietown share stories and demonstrate nineteenth-century Christmas traditions inside historic buildings while packs of "rowdies" cluster around campfires and joke with visitors. Costumed tradespeople wander about the village, selling wares and teaching prairie crafts like candle-dipping.

Outside of Prairietown, Merry Prairie Holiday resembles a county fair, with lavish light displays, midway games, carnival rides, live music, and food and drinks served up at Blitzen's Bar. The 1,046-acre site is decorated with massive frameworks wired with lights that form an Instagram-friendly panorama of illuminated tractors, farm animals, and silos, along with Christmas trees, Santas, and snowmen. A barn festooned with supersized ornaments serves as Santa's Workshop, a popular site for "selfies with Santa" and a visit with the elf Trinket Puddingmoon. Conner Prairie takes full advantage of its expansive grounds for family-oriented winter activities. A single $24 admission ticket covers all activities and rides, including a 150-foot long "Polar Bear Plunge" with (snowless) tubing, a carousel, and skating rink featuring sock "skating" on smooth wooden boards.

For the rest of the year, Conner Prairie adheres to historically accurate storylines in authentically furnished historic buildings. But like many living history museums, the rules are a little looser in December. Cooper explains that in contrast with the regular daily programming, "In the evenings, I'm okay with being a little more flexible. Do we have to find elements in history to tell the stories we are telling? One hundred percent. But it is a little harder [to find Christmas stories] in Hamilton County, Indiana in 1836. So are we expanding that idea a little bit? Yes. We are allowing for that stretch to happen for these types of experiences to take place."[23] Flexibility with historic interpretation can open the door to new creative experiences. For example, the museum uses the exterior of the historic Campbell House to screen a very modern 3D projection mapping of the (century-old but well outside the period of interpretation) 1907 version of the children's poem, "'Twas the Night before Christmas."

The museum's commitment to diversity, equity, and inclusion runs through all its programs, and again, Conner Prairie takes some liberties with history to advance these values. For example, the mantel of the historic Campbell House is decorated with ahistorical electric colored lights, a Hanukkah menorah, and a Kwanzaa kinara "because everybody likes to celebrate what they like to celebrate, and everyone should be seen and heard."[24]

The museum works with a local children's theater to do a program about Kwanzaa, and recently introduced to their interpretation an African American family, based on a family of freedmen who settled in Hamilton County in the 1830s. Other inclusive elements include a historic house with a Jewish family playing dreidel, and a historic crankie theater with scrolling panoramas depicting winter holiday celebrations around the world. Cooper notes, "It's important for us to understand that a huge contingent of different cultural groups may not come to this experience. But as a museum, it's still our obligation to talk about the broader stories of holiday traditions in other cultures. We made that a priority, and that has gone over very well for our visitors."

Merry Prairie Holiday is a massive production, requiring extensive work by groundskeepers, the interpretive team, and construction crews. The launch of the festival in 2019 required an enormous capital investment in decor, sledding tubes, LED bulbs, and other equipment. While an expensive endeavor, the museum has found ways to save costs. For instance, a local business donated the massive light installations in return for prominent naming privileges. All exempt employees, including the CEO, work two nights of the event, running the ring toss and staffing the "Selfies with Santa" line. Such involvement helps back-of-the-house employees to keep in touch with the visitor experience while also reducing event-related staff costs.

With the initial investments now made, Merry Prairie Holiday is now profitable and scalable. Cooper comments, "It is well worth our time to do this. While the operational costs can be significant to operate a festival like Merry Prairie Holiday, the profits from admissions and other aspects of the festival far outweigh the operational costs. The festivals also provide opportunities for us to give back to the staff and provide opportunities for us to create new experiences for our visitors."[25]

The revenue benefits are not from ticket sales alone—the festival has brought in new sponsors, and an annual spike in December membership. Alcohol sales are another important component—Conner Prairie has partnered with a local brewery to create specialty beers just for the event, and they also serve up special mixed drinks named for Santa's reindeer. Cooper notes, "The net of the alcohol sales has been incredible. Not only have ticket sales to the event done well, the alcohol sales have done very, very well. And it's been safe. Not once have we had to ask anyone to leave."[26] The availability of alcohol also encourages some visitors to the family-friendly event to reframe it as a date night.

Cooper describes Merry Prairie Holiday as "mission enabling," a high revenue event that helps pay for the work the museum does year-round. While certain elements are well outside the museum's mission—visits with Santa and sock skating, for instance—the repeated emphasis on storytelling is consistent with what Conner Prairie does best. And not only are these festivals more closely mission-aligned than events like weddings, which are commonly hosted at cultural sites—in Conner Prairie's case, they are more lucrative.

With their extensive grounds, multiple interpreted buildings, and retail and dining spaces, living history museums have lots of different levers to manipulate to deliver a robust, multifaceted holiday experience. The three living history museums profiled in this chapter—Old Salem Museum and Gardens, Strawbery Banke, and Conner Prairie—are each exemplary museums with outstanding, historically authentic programming and interpretation throughout the year. Yet they each offer very different twists on celebrating Christmas.

For all three museums, Christmas events add significantly to the bottom line, enabling the museums to do mission driven work year-round. But other benefits are less tangible—an opportunity to experiment with new programming, be a good neighbor, contribute to the community, and expand the museum's reach to attract new visitors, members, donors, and sponsors. While these museums offer exemplary models for creative Christmas programming, living history museums should also ask, "What goals are we trying to achieve at Christmas? What does success look like *for my museum*?"

Additional Ideas for Christmas Celebrations at Living History Museums

- *Black Country Living Museum (Dudley, England)*: This urban open-air museum, which interprets industrial life in England, hosts a "Santa Hunt," a scavenger hunt designed for kids to explore the museum as they search for a missing Santa Claus who has fallen asleep under the spell of magic Christmas dust.[27]
- *Exchange Place (Kingsport, Tennessee)*: Wintertime crafts and trades take center stage at this living history museum that interprets life on a mid-nineteenth-century central Tennessee farm. Skilled artisans demonstrate traditional skills like weaving, spinning, and blacksmithing and sell seasonally appropriate gifts including wreaths, greenery, and fleece products made from the wool of the farm's heritage sheep. The Christmas highlight is the communal lighting of a Yule log, followed by caroling and drinking wassail.[28]
- *Fort Concho National Monument (San Angelo, Texas)*: This preserved late-nineteenth-century frontier Army post hosts a weekend of Christmas festivities in December planned around the "Winter Rendezvous," a campsite featuring hundreds of nineteenth-century military reenactors and traders. On the parade grounds, troops drill, ride, and shoot artillery. Inside historic fort buildings, merchants and artisans sell Christmas goods, and roving musicians perform.[29]
- *Freetown Village (Indianapolis, Indiana)*: This living history museum without walls interprets late-nineteenth-century African American history through the performing arts, using original theater productions and choral groups singing traditional folk songs and spirituals in period costume.[30]
- *Genesee Country Village and Museum (Mumford, New York)*: The museum hosts a culturally diverse holiday celebration, which includes a traditional Polish *Wigilia* Christmas Eve dinner, a Hanukkah celebration, and a reenactment of Watch Night, a New Year's Eve tradition for African American families that began as a celebration of emancipation in 1862, and today combines Christian, Muslim, and African religious and cultural traditions.[31]
- *George Washington's Mount Vernon (Mount Vernon, Virginia)*: Costumed interpreters host an evening of Christmas illuminations, with the mansion and grounds lit with wintery lights and fireworks. The evening includes eighteenth-century music, a sutler's market with period crafts, and patriotic inspirational quotes on the bowling green.[32]

- *Greenfield Village (Dearborn, Michigan)*: The Henry Ford's Greenfield Village is decorated with white lights and greenery to celebrate "Holiday Nights." The districts are filled with carolers and costumed interpreters, as visitors view decorated homes and shops, and historical vignettes furnished for Christmas. Visitors can ride the carousel, ice skate, ride Model-Ts and trains, and attend holiday cooking demonstrations. Evenings end with fireworks and a sing-a-long.[33]
- *Heritage Park (Calgary, Canada)*: Canada's largest living history museum hosts an old-fashioned, family-friendly Christmas celebration, featuring snowshoe races, wood-carving demonstrations, roving carolers, a scavenger hunt, children's maze, and gingerbread decorating. In addition to a Christmas market featuring gifts from local artisans, the museum hosts a "kids only" Christmas store where everything is priced under $20.[34]
- *Maritime Museum of San Diego (San Diego, California)*: In December, the museum hosts a buffet dinner on board an 1898 steam ferryboat with an outstanding view of the privately organized Parade of Lights boat tour in San Diego harbor.[35]
- *Museum of the American G.I. (College Station, Texas)*: Each December, the museum reenacts the historic 1914 Christmas Truce during World War I, when German and British troops laid down arms, emerged from their trenches, sang Christmas carols, socialized, and even exchanged gifts. Additionally, the museum offers military vehicle rides and tours of the trenches on the World War I demonstration field.[36]
- *Mystic Seaport Museum (Mystic, Connecticut)*: For over forty years, the museum has staged annual "lantern light tours" with fully scripted holiday shows using the buildings and grounds of the museum (a re-created nineteenth-century seaport) as its set, with the audience traveling from scene to scene. Some years, the writing process (which begins in the spring) is collaborative; in others, a single writer takes the helm. A crew of paid and volunteer staff include master costume makers and graphic designers.[37]
- *Weald and Downland Living Museum (West Sussex, England)*: This museum interpreting rural life in South East England from AD 950 through the nineteenth century offers a two-and-a-half-hour workshop for participants to craft a wreath out of willow branches.[38]

Notes

1. "Presentation to the Winston-Salem City Council, April 28, 2021, by Frank Vagnone, president and CEO of Old Salem Museums & Gardens," accessed October 26, 2021.
2. Author interview with Franklin D. Vagnone, December 8, 2021.
3. Author interview with Franklin D. Vagnone, December 8, 2021.
4. "Salem Night: Softly the Night Is Sleeping," Old Salem Website, accessed November 9, 2021, https://www.oldsalem.org/events/event/salem-night-softly-the-night-is-sleeping/.
5. Author interview with Franklin D. Vagnone, December 8, 2021. Franklin D. Vagnone, "Running with Scissors (and a Mask!): COVID-19 Responses at Old Salem Museums & Gardens," February 10, 2021, American Alliance of Museums website, accessed October

26, 2021, https://www.aam-us.org/2021/02/10/running-with-scissors-and-a-mask-covid-19
-responses-at-old-salem-museums-gardens/.

6. Author interview with Franklin D. Vagnone, December 8, 2021.

7. "Old Salem President's Update, 4th Quarter 2018," accessed November 11, 2021, https://www
.oldsalem.org/files/2019/08/Fourth-QTY-2018_FINAL-screen-version.pdf.

8. Author interview with Franklin D. Vagnone, December 8, 2021.

9. Franklin D. Vagnone, "Running with Scissors (and a Mask!): COVID-19 Responses at Old
Salem Museums & Gardens."

10. Author interview with Franklin D. Vagnone, December 8, 2021.

11. Author interview with Franklin D. Vagnone, December 8, 2021. "Salem Night: The Chron-
icles of Adam Performances," OSMG website, accessed December 8, 2021, https://www
.oldsalem.org/events/event/salem-night-chronicles-of-adam-performance/.

12. "Old Salem Museum and Gardens to Hold First Winter Fair after Christmas," *Yes Weekly*
website, December 19, 2018, accessed December 8, 2021, https://www.yesweekly.com/news/
old-salem-museums-gardens-to-hold-first-winter-fair-after-christmas/article_ca606924
-0f23-5889-9860-5908e7cc9cde.html.

13. "Old Salem President's Update 4th Quarter 2019," accessed November 8, 2021.

14. Annie Fitzsimmons, "Portsmouth, New Hampshire: Christmas Capital of America?" *Travel
& Leisure*, December 10, 2011, accessed November 3, 2021.

15. Amy Moy, director of marketing and communications, in "Strawbery Banke's Candlelight
Stroll" YouTube video, produced by New Hampshire Chronicle, accessed November 2, 2021,
https://www.youtube.com/watch?v=qcoilNcoRXo&t=1s.

16. "Events > Candlelight Stroll under the Stars," Strawbery Banke website, accessed October 31,
2021, https://www.strawberybanke.org/events/candlelight-stroll.cfm.

17. "Events > Guided Holiday House Tours," Strawbery Banke website, accessed November 1,
2021, https://www.strawberybanke.org/calendar.

18. The museum has recently begun work on two historic homes interpreted to reflect an Irish
immigrant family and an African American family from the 1950s. These two houses will
eventually be included in the tour of historic homes and aid in illustrating the diversity of
the Puddle Dock neighborhood. Author interview with Joe April, director of development,
Strawbery Banke, November 4, 2021.

19. Author interview with Joe April, director of development, Strawbery Banke, November 4,
2021.

20. Author interview with Joe April, director of development, Strawbery Banke, November 4,
2021.

21. In years two and three of MPH (2020 and 2021), Conner Prairie capped the number of
attendees in order to comply with COVID-19 protocols. There's clearly room for attendance
to grow—the museum's most popular festival, Headless Horseman, held on weekends in
October, attracts up to forty-five thousand visitors annually. Author interview with Rich
Cooper, vice president and chief programs officer at Conner Prairie, January 7, 2022. "Conner
Prairie Impact Report 2020," accessed December 3, 2021, https://www.connerprairie.org/wp
-content/uploads/2021/04/CP_AnnualReport_FINAL_COMPRESSED.pdf.

22. Author interview with Rich Cooper, vice president and chief programs officer at Conner
Prairie, January 7, 2022.

23. Author interview with Rich Cooper, vice president and chief programs officer at Conner
Prairie, January 7, 2022.

24. Shawnte Jackon, interpreter of "Old timey lady," quoted in "Conner Prairie—A Merry Prairie Holiday 2021—BTS Commercial Shoot," accessed December 3, 2021, https://www.youtube.com/watch?v=MgHxZa0H_ww.

25. Author interview with Rich Cooper, vice president and chief programs officer at Conner Prairie, January 7, 2022.

26. Author interview with Rich Cooper, vice president and chief programs officer at Conner Prairie, January 7, 2022.

27. "Santa Hunt," Black Country Living Museum website, accessed May 2, 2024, https://bclm.com/visit/2024-events/

28. "Christmas in the Country," Exchange Place website, accessed July 5, 2022, https://exchangeplacetn.org/?page_id=105.

29. "Christmas at Old Fort Concho," Fort Concho National Historic Landmark, accessed July 5, 2022, https://fortconcho.com/home/events/christmas-at-old-fort-concho/.

30. "Freetown Village," Freetown Village website, accessed July 5, 2022, https://www.freetown.org/.

31. "Yuletide in the Country Tours and Dinner," Genesee Country Village and Museum website, accessed May 2, 2024,, https://www.gcv.org/event/yuletide-in-the-country-tours-dinner/.

32. "Christmas Illuminations at Mount Vernon," Mount Vernon website, accessed November 12, 2021, https://www.mountvernon.org/plan-your-visit/calendar/events/christmas-illuminations-at-mount-vernon/.

33. "Holiday Nights at Greenfield Village," The Henry Ford website, accessed July 5, 2022, https://www.thehenryford.org/current-events/calendar/holiday-nights-in-greenfield-village.

34. Elle McLean, "Celebrate an Old Fashioned Christmas at Heritage Park this Month," "Daily Hive" website, accessed July 5, 2022, https://dailyhive.com/calgary/once-upon-a-christmas-heritage-park-2021.

35. "Parade of Lights Holiday Dinner," San Diego Maritime Museum website, accessed July 5, 2022, https://sdmaritime.org/visit/public-events/parade-of-lights/.

36. "Christmas Truce," Museum of the American G.I. website, accessed July 5, 2022, https://americangimuseum.org/events/christmas-truce/.

37. "Forty Years of Lantern Light Tours – Mystic Seaport Museum," Mystic Seaport Museum website, posted December 2, 2019, https://www.mysticseaport.org/news/40-years-of-lantern-light-tours/.

38. "Willow Christmas Wreaths," Weald and Downland Living Museum website, accessed November 17, 2021, https://www.wealddown.co.uk/events/willow-christmas-wreath/.

CHAPTER 18

A Feast for the Senses

Christmas at the National Trust for England, Wales, and Northern Ireland

Katie Knowles

"A glittering display here beyond all dreams, decorations of coloured paper chains and festoons of tinsel, with gay balloons. The great table laden every inch is a sparkle of scintillating lights, silver, glass, dishes, tinsel, candles and crackers . . . as if all those wondrous coloured dishes shown in the illustrations of Mrs. Beeton had slipped from her pages onto this table."
—CHARLES PAGET WADE, FORMER OWNER OF SNOWSHILL MANOR, GLOUCESTERSHIRE[1]

CHRISTMAS PROGRAMMING is a relatively recent phenomenon for the National Trust for England, Wales, and Northern Ireland. For decades historic properties were closed to visitors during the winter months, with the time used to carry out repair work, intensive maintenance, and conservation. Over the last twelve years the National Trust has moved toward year-round opening at many properties, showcasing conservation work in action and developing a strong seasonal visitor program.

A small, nationally based expert team provided a suite of guidance, tools, innovation funding, and inspirational material to support hundreds of properties to develop and deliver high-quality, local programming. This delegated model allows individual property teams to draw on advice or align with overarching seasonal themes, while ensuring their programming is creative, distinctive, and relevant to their place. As the confidence and scale of programming has grown, so have the visitor numbers, from 560,000 visits over an eight-week Christmas period in 2010 to 1.4 million in 2014.[2]

Today this is one of the busiest times of the year for the National Trust; in 2019 we welcomed over 2.9 million visitors to historic sites during that eight-week festive period, around 10 percent of total annual visits.[3] This chapter will explore how the National Trust's Christmas programming has evolved to meet visitor expectations and includes short case study examples of creative and sensory experiences inspired by and rooted in the history of individual places.

The National Trust is Europe's largest conservation charity and over the last 127 years has acquired hundreds of properties across England, Wales, and Northern Ireland, which it looks after for everyone to enjoy. These properties have borne witness to thousands of years of history, from the ruins of ancient monasteries, Norman castles, and Roman villas to grand country houses and estates, industrial heritage, and even the terraced house on a post-war Liverpool estate, which was a childhood home of Sir Paul McCartney.

Each property is run by a dedicated operational team, who draw on expertise and advice from regionally and nationally based teams of curators, conservators, and interpretation and programming specialists. With such a diversity of properties and richly layered histories, the National Trust can offer a huge range of seasonal experiences to its 5.7 million members and millions of annual visitors. From a traditional Tudor Christmas to a 1970s retro celebration or immersive outdoor Winter Lights trails, complete with sounds, smells, and trees drenched in jewel-like color, there is something for everyone in seasonal programming, whether or not they celebrate Christmas.

However, audience expectations of Christmas visits continue to grow. According to research conducted by the National Trust since 2014, a historic property "dressed for Christmas" is now seen as the most basic level of Christmas program visitors can expect.[4] Audience feedback emphasizes the importance not just of authenticity but of atmosphere and spectacle. Visitors still expect programming to have a clear connection to the history of a property, but the primary visit motivations are typically to find backdrops for making memories and spending time with friends and families, getting into the festive spirit or seeking seasonal inspiration. The findings also suggest visitors want to be entertained and to see something different at Christmas to the rest of the year.

There is a recognition that historic furnishings or interiors may temporarily be moved and re-presented, as they would have been when the house was lived in, to create space for decorations, interpretation, and activities. This allows staff to be bold and imaginative when planning programming, giving them some seasonal artistic license to show historic properties and their interiors and collections in a new or unexpected light.

An understanding of the "spirit of place"—what makes a property unique, distinctive, and cherished—underpins and informs our programming approach. A Christmas program is more authentic when it is inspired by and relevant to the multilayered history of the property and the lives of former inhabitants, rather than simply reflecting a generic historic period. The spirit of place can determine *how* a property brings Christmas to life, from the style of the decorations to the traditions that are re-created, or the stories that are shared.

This does not mean a festive presentation must be fixed to a particular point in time or the story of one family or individual. Seasonal visitors to the 450-year-old Nunnington Hall in Yorkshire, for example, journey through time with generations of former inhabitants, experiencing a Tudor feast, a Georgian twelfth-night party, and a 1920s celebration. Yet drawing inspiration from spirit of place can also enable teams to creatively interpret and share aspects of the property's history that may not be fully explored during the rest of the year.

At Hanbury Hall in Worcestershire, for example, the spirit of place is a "stage set or backdrop for the parties, delight, and recreation" of generations of residents (see figure 18.1). An understanding of the property as a place of relaxation and recreation through the centuries inspired the team to create a bold, retro Christmas program that has been successfully running for several years.

Like historic house museums, many properties in the National Trust's care were once homes and places of work and some still retain their original contents, in the places they were made, displayed, treasured, and used. These collections—from internationally significant works of art to humble kitchen gadgets—are often intimately connected with the history of the families who lived, and sometimes continue to live, there. This makes them an excellent research resource for programming and interpretation rooted in place, including at Christmas. At Sissinghurst in Kent, for example, the collection contains the handwritten Christmas lists of former owner and writer Vita Sackville-West, which carefully document which gifts she plans to buy and cards she will send to friends, family, and servants.[5]

Figure 18.1.   Visitors exploring "It's Christmaaas" at Hanbury Hall in Worcestershire, England. © National Trust Images/James Dobson.

Box 18.1. Spirit of Place: It's Christmaaas! at Hanbury Hall, Worcestershire

Hanbury is an early 18th-century country house which was owned by the Vernon family for over 200 years. Few of the original contents remain, but interiors include significant wall and ceiling paintings by baroque artist Sir James Thornhill. It was gifted to the National Trust in the 1950s and was initially let to tenants, with select rooms open to the public during summer months. Oral histories and curatorial research have recently revealed the history of some of the Hall's tenants in the 1970s and 1980s, who were known for raucous house parties. In keeping with the playful spirit of place the team created a winter program based on a Christmas house party. Visitors are taken on a journey from arriving at the party to marveling at the buffet, celebrating on Christmas morning and enjoying a children's sleepover. The house is dressed in 70s and 80s style decorations and small touches make the program feel authentic, from a television playing vintage comedy episodes to the classic toys and boardgames crowdsourced from staff and volunteers. To make the experience more immersive, visitors can buy retro cocktails at the bar, dance to the disco music or soak up the smells of the real food on the buffet. Each year the team build on the experience by opening an additional room and the visitor experience extends across the whole property, including 1980s mirror balls in the garden and welcome areas.

This might seem an unconventional historic house Christmas offer, but it is rooted in an understanding of the history of Hanbury and delivers a bold, temporary visitor experience which contrasts to the typical interpretation and presentation of the property as an 18th-century home. Since it reflects a period in living memory, it also has resonance and relevance for many visitors, triggering discussion and reminiscence about their own Christmases and the foods, toys and music of the era. Over 23,500 visitors experienced the program in December 2021 and repeat visits are high, with many visitors returning with family and friends.

Meanwhile, at Mr. Straw's House in Nottinghamshire, the National Trust looks, after over 1,200 Christmas cards sent and received by the family who lived there between 1888 and 1990. This wonderful archive not only records some of the family's circle of friends and relatives but also the evolution of Christmas card designs over a century. While this small property is usually closed during the winter period, the card collection has been digitized so it can be explored by visitors, used by researchers, and support digital seasonal content.[6]

At the former home of Sir Winston Churchill, Chartwell in Kent, visitors can see the list of presents he received in 1946 and the gift he was given by President Roosevelt, before adding their own suggestions to a Christmas list for Churchill. Visitors can also explore Churchill's artistic relationship with Hallmark greeting cards and create their own Christmas card artwork. As well as collections, many family photographs, diaries, letters, and other documents survive in the National Trust's care, such as the notebooks of former owner Charles Paget Wade at Snowshill, which recall festive celebrations. At Standen in Sussex the team has drawn on accounts of the Christmases enjoyed there by former residents, the Beale family, to create an immersive and authentic experience (see figure 18.2).

Figure 18.2. Christmas decorations in the Dining Room at Standen House and Garden in West Sussex, England. © National Trust Images/Laurence Perry.

Box 18.2. Stepping into Christmas: A Beale Family Christmas at Standen, West Sussex

Standen is an Arts and Crafts family home, designed by Philip Webb and complete with Morris and Co. interiors. The Beales were the only family to live in the property and their memories of life at Standen, are captured in letters, documents (including Christmas present lists) and oral history recordings of visiting descendants. This has allowed the team to recreate a 1930s family Christmas based on real accounts of festive celebrations and an understanding of how the Beales used the rooms, from food fights in the Dining Room to parties and games in the Hall. While the significant Arts and Crafts collection is the main focus of the regular visitor offer, at Christmas these family stories are the perfect basis for a fun, warm and relatable experience.

The interpretation is layered, with short family quotes printed on surfaces or incorporated in displays in each room, but also clever use of lighting and sound. Projections on the window blinds of figures dancing, playing games or getting ready to go tobogganing bring spaces to life. Combining projections with music and laughter creates a sense of movement and energy, as if visitors have stepped into a moment in time. Meanwhile the discarded coats, half-unwrapped presents and empty glasses make it feel as if the family has just left the room. The stylish paper decorations are handmade by staff and volunteers, or carefully sourced to ensure they fit with the Arts and Crafts aesthetic of the rooms and surviving collections.

As well as being rooted in spirit of place and thorough research, a good Christmas program also appeals to the senses. With careful and considered planning, you can use touch, sound, smell, and taste along with dazzling sights to engage and inspire visitors. In 2021 the team at Chastleton House in Oxfordshire dressed the property for a Jacobean Christmas, appropriate to its first owner. The decorations included dried flowers and real greenery from the garden, carefully prepared and displayed with conservation advice to minimize risks to the collection. In addition to the traditional scent of pines, particular scents were incorporated to take visitors on an olfactory journey around the house, including rosemary and ale in the kitchen and the orange, spices, and woodsmoke from the fire in the Great Hall.

At Moseley Old Hall in Staffordshire, the team went a step further, and offered visitors the taste of seventeenth-century Christmas sweet treats made in the brewhouse, while in 2013 mulled perry was offered to visitors exploring a seventeenth-century Christmas inspired by the Dutch collections at Dyrham Park, near Bath. As the installations at Standen show, light and sound can also be used to create drama and atmosphere, allowing visitors to immerse themselves in their surroundings. Projections, soundtracks, and smells have also been used successfully in the popular, sensory Winter Lights program at Anglesey Abbey in Cambridgeshire.

Box 18.3. A Sensory Journey: Winter Lights at Anglesey Abbey, Cambridgeshire

The Winter Lights program has been running at Anglesey Abbey, a Jacobean-style house with spectacular gardens, for the last ten years and is the property's biggest annual fundraiser. Described as an alternative to traditional Christmas experiences, Winter Lights is a 2 kilometer sensory after-dark trail through the grounds, which takes in the house, working watermill and gardens. Members of the property team (including gardeners and curators) and a production company co-create the experience around an annual theme.

In 2021 the program theme 'Nature by Night, Nature by Light' connected visitors with the natural surroundings they walk through on the route and brought the buildings and gardens to life in an eye-catching and thought-provoking way. The team worked in partnership with a local author, musicians and an illustrator, drawing on nature poems and illustrations to create magical projections, sculptures and sounds. The house and mill were dramatically lit with different colors, shapes and graphics, highlighting architectural features and using the buildings as a canvas. The trail was complemented by a carefully crafted soundscape, including soft music, songs, poetry readings, nature sounds and voices talking about the wildlife on the estate. Smells were piped into sections of the trail, allowing visitors to experience the concentrated scent of local flowers, shrubs and trees by night. Sensory experiences can be overwhelming, so visual symbols were used to help visitors understand where sensory points (sounds, smells, bright lights) were located and what to expect. Over 24,000 visitors attended during the three open weekends in December 2021, with further enhancements planned in 2022.

Re-presentation of spaces or movement of collections is often required for Christmas programming, so early involvement of conservation teams in programming plans is crucial. Discussions about the appropriateness of using real or artificial trees, greenery, or candles in historic interiors are also important when deciding how to create drama, atmosphere, and a feeling of authenticity. Where it is appropriate to do so, National Trust properties use sustainably sourced real Christmas trees and foliage. These are natural, authentic, and a strong sensory asset, but real greenery does increase the risk of pests and needs watering or misting to stay fresh. Property teams follow expert conservation advice, placing protective mats or textile felt pads underneath trees and greenery on floors, banisters, and surfaces and implement increased pest monitoring and preventive measures (such as freezing logs or branches before bringing them into the house).[7] However, many properties also have artificial trees and foliage that they reuse annually, and these are also acceptable, provided they are of high quality.[8]

Similarly, LED candles can be used recurrently and with great success to mimic flickering candlelight. In the small, dark rooms at Townend in Cumbria, real candles were judged too great a fire risk, so instead imitation candles were given to small groups of visitors, allowing them to literally shine light on the displays and encourage self-led, candlelit discovery. In contrast, over a hundred real candles were used in 2021 at Hatchlands Park in Guildford, where the Christmas event took visitors through a series of rooms representing different times of the day. Using real candles requires licenses and risk assessments and discussions with conservators about appropriate candleholders, careful positioning, and the need for supervision, but creates a magical and authentic atmosphere as visitors experience interiors and collections by candlelight.

Our winter and Christmas programming is now an established quality program. The National Trust is recognized for excellent standards of presentation and visitors' expectations of warm, festive, and authentic-looking experiences are high. Audience evaluation, conducted through feedback surveys, observation, and interviews, shows that previous experience is one of the primary visit-drivers and that a high proportion of Christmas visitors live locally. Creating programs that can be developed and enhanced annually like those at Hanbury Hall or Anglesey Abbey is therefore very important and gives people reasons to return. The National Trust looks after these properties forever and for everyone, and Christmas programming will continue to develop to meet visitor expectations. Whether visitors want to find out more about historic traditions or the story of a place, feel festive and be inspired, or simply enjoy the spectacle and spend time together with loved ones, creative and sensory Christmas programming inspired by the spirit of the place can offer something for everyone to enjoy.

Notes

1. A description of a Christmas party in the 1890s by Charles Paget Wade, the artist and architect who restored Snowshill Manor in Gloucestershire. This quote comes from Michael Jessup (ed.), *Days Far Away: Memories of Charles Paget Wade 1883–1956* (National Trust, 1996).

2. National Trust visitor figures by property for an eight-week winter period, which includes Christmas (mid-November to early January). Source: National Trust visitor data reports (internal).
3. The number of visits to National Trust properties within a pay barrier was 28 million in the 2019/2020 financial year. There are millions more visits to open access sites. Source: National Trust Annual Report 2019/20, accessed October 2022: https://nt.global.ssl.fastly.net/docu ments/annual-report-201920.pdf.
4. Research was conducted using a mixture of focus groups, in-visit and post-visit surveys, and interviews. The surveys included questions about visiting intentions and comparable Christmas events across the heritage sector, as well as qualitative questions about visitor expectations and experiences.
5. This collection can be explored on National Trust's online collections website by selecting Sissinghurst Castle Garden, Kent, and adding the object type "list": https://www.nationaltrust collections.org.uk/.
6. This collection can be explored on National Trust's online collections website by selecting Mr. Straw's House, Nottinghamshire, and searching "Christmas card": https://www.nationaltrust collections.org.uk/.
7. See also the *National Trust Manual of Housekeeping* (Butterworth-Heinemann, 2005), which provides practical guidance of the care and maintenance of historic houses and their collections.
8. Real trees are increasingly recommended where possible, to minimize the use of plastics. Where artificial trees are the best option (e.g., for conservation reasons), guidance is provided to ensure these are sustainably sourced and reused.

Resources

Chandler, John. *A Country House Christmas*. Sutton Publishing, 1999.
National Trust Manual of Housekeeping. National Trust, 2005.
National Trust. "Christmas Traditions from History." https://www.nationaltrust.org.uk/discover/ history/christmas-traditions-from-history.
National Trust. "Christmas." https://nationaltrust.org.uk/visit/christmas.
National Trust. *Everything Speaks: Seven Working Principles for Interpretation*. National Trust, 2013.
Sandeman, Phyllis Elinor. *Treasure on Earth: A Country House Christmas*. Pavilion Books, 2006.
Slack, Steve. *Interpreting Heritage: A Guide to Planning and Practice*. Taylor & Francis, 2020.

Acknowledgments

The author is grateful for the advice and contributions from the Hanbury Hall, Anglesey Abbey, and Standen property teams and the national Programming and Production Team, particularly Hannah Morgan (project manager) and Richard Grudzinski (experiences and partnerships curator).

CHAPTER 19

Joy to the World

Celebrating Cultural Diversity

Stacia Kuceyeski and Carla Mello

I N THE EARLY 2000S the Ohio History Connection (then the Ohio Historical Society) began considering how we could share the wide variety of immigrant experiences in ways that both celebrate each cultures' uniqueness while highlighting our shared experiences as humans. Through this question, we looked more closely at holiday traditions celebrated in Ohio. One thing that makes holiday traditions so interesting, as well as wonderful teaching tools, is the variety of ways in which we celebrate. Traditions can be very personal to a family or can be part of a collective experience. The richness and diversity of our holiday experiences in the United States is enhanced by and through immigration, and learning about the variety of holiday traditions celebrated in our communities is a wonderful way to engage in global citizenship education and cultural competency.

Immigrants have been a part of Ohio's cultural landscape since the United States opened settlement in the Northwest Territory. Between 1825 and 1847, Ohio constructed over one thousand miles of canals, giving the state an unrivaled transportation infrastructure and creating jobs for thousands of European immigrants, particularly Germans. In the late nineteenth century, the growth of industrialization brought on new waves of immigration and Ohio became home to, among others, communities of Czechs, Hungarians, Poles, Romanians, and Slovaks. Their arrival led to the strengthening of the Roman Catholic, Eastern Orthodox, and Jewish religious communities and social organizations, such as workers groups, gymnastics unions, and social clubs. Not long after, Chinese immigrants arrived from California hoping to leave behind a strong anti-immigrant sentiment caused by an economic recession. World War I and World War II generated yet another wave of immigration coming from Europe and Asia. However, Ohio's immigration story does not

Figure 19.1 During the 2020 pandemic, the Ohio History Connection transitioned the in-person Cultural Traditions program to a virtual learning program. Pictured are presenters (clockwise from top left) Ibrahima Sow (Ramadan and Eid), Yogita Khanal (Diwali), Tony and Aziza West (Juneteenth), and co-author Carla Mello (Carnaval). Courtesy of the Ohio History Connection.

end in the mid-1900s. Currently Ohio's immigrant population is about 5 percent of the total population, with another 5 percent of residents being native-born with one immigrant parent. Ohio's immigrant population is still making its mark on the cultural landscape of the state, with the top five countries of origin currently being India, Mexico, China, the Philippines, and Canada. In addition, there are a variety of immigrants and refugees who have arrived over the past thirty years. Starting in the 1990s, Ohio, particularly Columbus, welcomed a large Somali population of about sixty thousand individuals, making it the second largest Somali population in the United States. Ohio welcomed its first Bhutanese refugees in 2008 and now has the largest population of Bhutanese of any city in the United States.

To reflect this history and diverse community, the first iteration of what is now called the Cultural Traditions program included Christmas, Hanukkah, Chinese New Year's, and Kwanzaa. Targeted to elementary students, the program had interpreters and volunteers discussing the history of each holiday and sharing a special food item. It introduced students, parents, and teachers to traditions they might not know much about but are celebrated throughout the state. This program was offered in person at the Ohio Village, on the campus of the Ohio History Center, over the course of a few weeks between Thanksgiving and Christmas.

Over the years the program shifted and changed based on feedback from teachers. In 2018 we incorporated more authentic voices into the program. While the research around each of the holidays was thorough and well done, our volunteers and staff facilitators were not part of the highlighted communities and did not have personal experience with the holidays.

As a museum, engaging with immigrant and refugee communities is not just a phone call to ask for their help; your organization needs to have nurtured authentic relationships to build trust. The Ohio History Connection's Local History Services Department, now the Community Engagement Department, has done community engagement work for over a decade. In 2017 we hired two full-time community engagement coordinators, one of who brought with him additional contacts in the immigrant and refugee community in Columbus, Ohio. Hiring these two staff members accelerated our community engagement work, particularly with the immigrant and refugee community, resulting in new projects, exhibitions, and programs.

Working with our community partners highlighted where we could do better, which led to our decision to ensure all the holidays in Cultural Traditions were presented by someone who celebrated that holiday. We could collaborate with immigrant communities and organizations to add a layer of authenticity to the Cultural Traditions program. It made the traditions vibrant activities of the present, celebrated by people currently living in Ohio, as opposed to something that only happens in other countries, highlighting the diversity of experiences in Ohio.

The current iteration of the Cultural Traditions program has established clear learning objectives. We want students to discover the diverse ways different cultures celebrate holidays and traditions. They should be able to compare different cultural celebrations and traditions and subsequently describe different customs, traditions, and family celebrations.

The audience of the program are teachers and students in grades K–3. We aligned the program with Ohio's Social Studies, English Language Arts, and Social and Emotional Learning Standards as defined by the state's Department of Education. Exploring traditions and cultures, and connecting them with our local community, allows us to reach social studies standards that explore how "heritage is reflected through diverse cultures and is shown through many culture manifestations" and "how communities may include diverse cultural groups" and change over time. The format of the program allowed students to take part in collaborative conversations and confirm information received orally by asking and answering questions, which are part of the state's English language arts standards.

In addition, connecting students directly to a diverse group of local community members provides opportunities for students to "recognize, identify and empathize with the feelings of others" and "demonstrate an awareness and respect for human dignity, including the similarities and differences of all people, groups and cultures," both competencies defined by the social emotional learning standards.

Although the program has been delivered in the Ohio Village, it can take place in any space or building that would allow for students to be separated into smaller groups (8–15 people) and rotate among stations or rooms where they will learn about the different traditions. The program starts with a general introduction in a physical area that fits all participants and then smaller groups are created. These groups are guided by a staff member or volunteer through the separate rooms or stations. This requires detailed coordination between facilitators and guides to ensure a timely and fluid experience. The time in each station is allotted beforehand and never less than ten minutes. At the end of the program, all groups come together for a conclusion and brief reflection of what they learned. The number of stations, which may vary, defines the duration of the program and the size of the groups.

Our sessions are seventy-five minutes long with a maximum of ninety students per session. There is a cost of $10 per student and $5 per chaperone, which includes the entrance to the Ohio History Center and the Ohio Village. Teachers are admitted free. To facilitate coordination with our community partners' schedules, we offer the program over a condensed period. We choose up to six days in December where we offer the program. During those days we offer up to four sessions each day, which tend to sell out.

In each station, students will either listen to and speak with a community partner or staff member who observes or celebrates the tradition being presented or participate in a hands-on activity that is associated with one of the featured traditions. The latter normally consists of simple handcrafts. For example, students have created red envelopes (or red packets, *hshì* or *lai see* in Cantonese), used during the Chinese New Year to keep money that will be gifted to children and retired seniors, and they have colored a *rangoli* associated with the Diwali celebration.

In one or two stations where students are connecting directly with community partners, they might also try a food or dish that correlates with that specific tradition, like tasting dates when they are learning about Ramadan and Eid al-Fitr. To guarantee food safety, these items are acquired either in sealed commercial containers or through contracted certified local restaurants as caterers. Items are always simple and bite-size to avoid the need of multiple plates and utensils. It is important to mention that the choice of restaurant or caterer is always associated with the tradition in question to guarantee authenticity. If we have a Somali community partner talking about a tradition, we will hire a Somali restaurant to provide the catering.

In 2020, the COVID-19 pandemic shifted Cultural Traditions to a virtual program, which has turned out to be highly successful (see figure 19.1). We prerecorded our presenters from the community and an Ohio History Connection educator facilitated the dialog among students centered on identifying similarities and differences between the holidays depicted and the holidays the students celebrate. The holidays that we offer have shifted over the years based on the availability of partners and teacher feedback. For the 2021–2022 school year we focused on Eid, Carnaval, Juneteenth, and Diwali, widening the idea of traditions to those outside the original winter holidays.

All community partners that are facilitating stations during the program (or presenting in the virtual program) receive an honorarium. Even though some of them may offer to volunteer their time, we think it is important to value the expertise they are bringing into the program and compensate them accordingly. Honoraria are provided according to time spent on engagement and will include any time partners may have provided during planning and co-creation of the stations, plus facilitation times. The pay rate is defined beforehand with partners.

The initial program costs depend on the standard pay rate for your staff and the scope of the program. If you are just targeting three to four traditions, it would be about four staff plus at least one community partner per tradition. Do not forget the staff who welcome and check-in the school groups and any other staff responsible for security or maintenance of your venue. An initial budget should also consider any crafting materials for hands-on activities. We suggest only one or two initially. Traditional foods are certainly a plus but incur additional costs and should not be a priority. All costs considered, this program is not an income-generating program. You can certainly break even, but it will not generate a profit under this format. It is about engagement and mission. Our goal was to make authentic and relevant connections between students and our local diverse community, independent of the cost.

When it comes to experiences that represent our communities, an educational program based on traditions celebrated in and around your community is a wonderful way to introduce global and cultural competency. As museums continue to grapple with issues of diversity and inclusion in interpretation and storytelling, Cultural Traditions reminds us that human stories are an important part of our work. While we might not have the artifacts that highlight the traditions, we have worked extremely hard to develop relationships with cultural partners that are of benefit to our audiences and beneficial to our partners. These authentic voices are an important part of the Cultural Traditions program, providing students with the opportunity to see themselves and their traditions represented at the Ohio History Center and Ohio Village as part of the experience of Ohioans.

CHAPTER 20

A Christmas Card to the Community

West Baton Rouge Museum's Holiday Open House

Jeannie Giroir Luckett

THE WEST BATON ROUGE MUSEUM, established by the West Baton Rouge Historical Association, serves as a pivotal educational resource in south Louisiana. It is devoted to the research, collection, preservation, and presentation of artifacts, documents, and art objects that encapsulate the history and cultural heritage of West Baton Rouge Parish and its surrounding regions. This mission guides all our endeavors. However, there was a time when we introduced holiday programming to our schedule without a clear connection to our core mission—there was no reason for the season.

What began as a spontaneous open house in the mid-1990s aimed at attracting holiday shoppers to the West Baton Rouge Museum's nascent gift shop has blossomed into a beloved community event over the years. Initially, this program was merely a specially advertised weekday shopping event that saw minimal attendance. It's no wonder. There was no special magic or meaning behind the plan. Despite the local garden and civic club beautifully decorating our grounds and interior spaces for the holiday season, and serving festive snacks, the event was devoid of a compelling purpose. What was truly required was an initiative that would invite the community to partake in a genuinely enriching experience.

A young staff member went back to the drawing board and came up with ideas resulting in a figurative "Christmas card" to the community, a free event that welcomes visitors from the very young to senior citizens to celebrate the season. Through trial and error and a good will spirit to grow and change with the community's needs, we have been able to maintain our relevance during the hustle and bustle of competing with events on everyone's holiday calendars.

Soon, this program was renamed Christmas Open House and eventually Holiday Open House, which was held on the first Friday in December. This candle-lit evening event met with much success for years until Louisiana's capital city (located directly across the Mississippi River from the museum) began hosting the downtown tree lighting ceremony featuring a grand fireworks display on the river. Not wanting our audience to choose between the two nor see our visitation drop (as they indeed did; who would want to miss out on the fireworks and walking tours of arts, cultural, and historical sites of downtown Baton Rouge under the night's sky?), it was once again time to grow and change.

Since 2007, Holiday Open House has become a weekend afternoon event filled with some of the same festivities and more. As we evolved and continue to do so year after year, West Baton Rouge Museum is still a place where a multigenerational audience gathers to sip cider, eat homemade gingerbread, tour the museum's current changing exhibits, and see museum theater performances and folk life demonstrations. Visitors can make ornaments and other crafts to keep and enjoy games and the sounds of live music. There's also an opportunity to take a picture with *Papa Noël*, the French version of jolly old Saint Nick, and the gift shop is still open if anyone wants to drop in for that special gift.

The inspiration for the evening program came from various descriptions captured in our research files, oral histories, and general history about nineteenth-century Christmas customs shared with us by other local historic sites. West Baton Rouge Museum's historic structures were used as the backdrop to share history lessons while taking in the sights of the season. We used Victorian-era tableau performances in the circa 1830 Aillet House, a French-Creole-style cottage on our grounds to illustrate the Catholic traditions of the Acadian families living in the home.

Actors include local school students and adult volunteers. Dressed in period attire, actors present still scenes that are described by a narrator. This provides a glimpse of how Christmas was observed as a religious occasion marked with fasting, midnight Mass, and a Réveillon dinner. The narrator explains that because of the sugarcane harvest in Louisiana, New Year's served as a bigger celebration with dancing, music, and the exchange of gifts. These tableaux continue to be a part of Holiday Open House to this day.

At the circa 1850 Allendale Slave Cabin, a structure built from cypress board and batten, interpreters in historical costumes demonstrated open hearth cooking during the "Week of Sundays"—a respite from hard labor, a time for family visits, dancing, and communal meals. However, despite this brief reprieve, the grim reality of impending work, lack of freedom, and the constant fear of family separation were ever-present. The cabin exhibit featured fruits, potentially symbolizing gifts, and a soloist performing spirituals *a cappella*, providing a poignant reminder of the heartrending struggles endured during the era of slavery.

A few years ago, a new exhibitions curator expressed concern over signs of celebration in an enslaved person's cabin. Never wanting to mislead anyone visiting the cabin, it was time to change again for the better. We are a visual culture, and there is always going to be that handful of guests who just like to look. We had to make the setting foolproof for those who prefer to wander and choose not to engage in the interpretive discussion that enlightens and encourages meaningful thought and conversation. Therefore, freshly cut holly and other local greenery, apples, and oranges were removed from the cabin for fear that anyone entering the space would leave with the notion that this was a merry time when indeed it was not. So, this portion of the program now picks up from where it leaves off at the Aillet House with the rest of the story. Visitors are solely led through the sparsely furnished Allendale Cabin by a trained interpreter who can engage in dialog and share information from documented accounts.

Community is the heart of the WBRM's Holiday Open House. To this day, the local garden and civic club still decorates the galleries and grounds giving the museum a festive atmosphere. It is a welcoming environment for the public and participants alike. The evolving event continues to include community choirs and ensembles. Sometimes, opportunities arise where we are gifted with the chance to set the stage with Folk, Cajun, Creole, and Blues musicians. For example, we have been fortunate to provide free performances by artists such as Grammy Award–winner Michael Doucet of BeauSoleil, one of the most well-known bands performing traditional and original music rooted in the folk tunes of Creole Louisiana. Most recently, three artists from the new holiday album, "Joyeux Noël, Bon Chrismeusse," a project translating popular music into Louisiana French, entertained the audience with an outdoor concert.

We also frequently partner with other organizations. Once we partnered with Barnes and Noble when *Elf on the Shelf* hit the market; we hosted a book sale and started a Find the Elves scavenger hunt around the museum and grounds. Families return year after year in search of these whimsical characters. These neighborly efforts provide more opportunities for visitors to enjoy, help to draw more visitors, and place a spotlight on other organizations, which makes for good working relationships throughout the year. We invite local artisans to demonstrate blacksmithing and woodworking in the museum barn, where visitors can leave with a craft or an ornament to keep.

We always tap into themes that tie into current, changing exhibits to offer something new. Other historic buildings on our campus interpreting the 1830s to the 1960s are trimmed with a touch of Christmas appropriate for the decade each space represents. The young and young-at-heart are always excited to see Papa Noël. Sometimes, this Louisiana French Santa Claus is dressed in a long white robe and every once in a while, he arrives clad in Cajun fishing waders and greets guests from an old-fashioned pirogue, a traditional wooden flat-bottom boat made of cypress designed to navigate through the swamps and bayous of south Louisiana's Atchafalaya region. Local lore has it that Papa Noël uses this mode of transportation, pulled by alligators, to reach dwellings along Louisiana waterways, while others still insist he finds his way by traversing in a flying sleigh led by reindeer.

Even though Holiday Open House is filled with whimsical moments and opportunities for visitors to mingle in spaces adorned with a modern-day Christmas tree, we have a great opportunity to provide teachable moments about the past, not all so merry, and how some traditions still practiced today came to be. We have a duty to honor the history of the families who have lived here for generations.

For instance, a visit to the circa 1830 Aillet House on the museum grounds to see the tableau or a step inside the circa 1850 Allendale Slave Cabin gives our guests a look into life almost two hundred years ago. Onlookers can find out what people wore, what they ate, what they looked forward to, and what their worries were. This is partially based on an oral history by Catherine Cornelius, who was enslaved at Smithfield Plantation along the River Road that follows the Mississippi River in West Baton Rouge Parish. She recalls many events including a brief description of Christmastime: "Christmas week we had a week's holiday. Sho, we had gudtimes. We had singin, dancing and visiting among ourselves and on udder plantations."[1]

Memory, as a survival mechanism, can often shield us by obscuring distressing experiences and highlighting perceived good times. However, the fleeting liberties granted during the Christmas week did not erase the atrocities of slavery. In fact, plantation owners frequently exploited the holiday season as a manipulative strategy to extract more labor and foster loyalty among the enslaved, thereby deterring thoughts of escape or rebellion.

As Robert May explains in *Yuletide in Dixie*, regardless of the generosity of gift giving, sumptuous meals, travel passes, and merriment allowed during this period, the deprivation of year-round freedom overshadows these gestures. Furthermore, he notes that the Federal Work Projects' interviews with formerly enslaved individuals were conducted during the Great Depression, a time when securing basic necessities like food and housing was extremely challenging. This time of struggle coupled with the fear of violence in the Jim Crow South certainly could have colored the memory of Christmas past on the plantation as good times.[2]

South Louisiana was largely settled by Catholic French-speaking immigrants from France and by Acadian exiles who today often are referred to as Cajuns. The impact of these cultures is still prevalent. In "Pointe Coupee Holiday Traditions Recalled," Brian Costello notes that Christmas traditions practiced today throughout the United States did not come to French Louisiana until the mid-twentieth century. Prior to that time, Christmas was a Holy Day of Obligation. Also known as *Noël* in French or *Chrismeusse* in Creole, the tradition was to attend Mass, either at midnight on Christmas Eve or on the morning of Christmas Day. After church, families gathered for a meal, and Christmas Day was quiet with the occasional visit from relatives. *Le Jour de l'Année*, or New Year's Day, brought celebration more akin to today's Christmas. Papa Noël, also known as *Père Noël* or *Père Janvier* (Papa Christmas, Father Christmas, or Father January), brought gifts that were found on New Year's morning including "apples, oranges, peppermint stick candy, firecrackers, and small toys ... or a useful gift for the older children, such as a hair ribbon and box of face powder for the girls and a pocket knife for the boys."

New Year's Day also brought visitors with wishes of "Bonne Année" or "Happy New Year." Gifts were exchanged and it was customary then and to this day to feast on cabbage for money and black-eyed peas for luck in the coming year. It was not until "improved mass communication, in the form of national magazines, big city newspapers and mail-order catalogs increasingly brought concepts of American Christmas" that many celebrations transitioned to becoming Christmas traditions.[3] Now Santa visits south Louisiana led by the light of bonfires along the Mississippi River on Christmas Eve and presents and parties are a part of Christmas along with Mass.

With such stories to share, the museum wants to reach as many people as possible. It is important to check local calendars well before the event to ensure no major conflicts will keep crowds away. Contact the tourism department or convention and visitors' bureau to get a bird's-eye view of holiday happenings in the area. This will help determine if proposed dates are good for a stand-alone event or to coordinate schedules to host activities at different times. Better yet, join forces to create a schedule for a day, weekend, or monthlong offering of festivities.

West Baton Rouge Museum had such a meeting set for a date in mid-March 2020 to meet with the mayor's office, the West Baton Rouge Convention and Visitors Bureau, and local business leaders. We were to discuss a holiday stroll through historic Port Allen, a thriving location in the heart of an area designated by the state as a certified Louisiana Cultural District. Visions of visitors pranced in our heads. We imagined them dashing down streets to and from the museum enjoying the arts featured in store fronts. We had hoped to make merry little stops along Jefferson Avenue, the street that runs in front of the museum that was once part of the historic Pine to Palm highway, featuring festive fare, cocktails, or hot chocolate at eateries and at Jack's Place, a gathering space since the early 1900s that served as a speakeasy during prohibition. Alas, the COVID-19 global pandemic laid this plan to rest like a long winter's nap, but this dream will come to fruition when the time is right.

Annually the West Baton Rouge Museum invites church choirs, bands, dance classes, and other performance groups to showcase their talent and to give the public an opportunity to enjoy live performance (see figure 20.1). While not a key aspect, the participation of these groups comes with a distinct advantage. Not only do they add entertainment to the museum's open house program; their participation guarantees attendance. Friends and family will follow their loved ones in support.

Figure 20.1.   Musicians Ashley Orlando and Peter Simon performing at Holiday Jazz and Blues at the West Baton Rouge Museum in Louisiana. Photo courtesy West Baton Rouge Museum.

Ringing out the old and ringing in the new is not necessarily a recipe for success. West Baton Rouge Museum incorporates both to draw a diverse audience. For large, open-to-the-public programs, West Baton Rouge Museum aims to enrich and entertain multigenerational visitors. "Oh, what fun it is" we hear from grandparents accompanied by their adult children and the next generation of little ones who celebrate annually with us in search of tiny elves, who find new hiding places, keeping guests exploring our exhibits and grounds. For some, that along with the cider and gingerbread is what they want, and for others, they leave with a history lesson. Some people don't see themselves as "museum people," but providing a frolic-filled afternoon gets them through the door where they discover that they really do like museums and often come again. Others come expressly to connect with and revel in their history. So, plan for all on your Christmas list.

The magic of the Christmas season comes in many forms. A visit to a historic site or museum can simply be pretty like a ribbon tied into a bow or a happy time chasing down jolly old elves, but if the season's greeting inside the package, card, or program in this case is carefully packed with meaning, the people we serve will walk away enlightened.

Notes

1. Catherine Cornelius, interview by Hazel Breaux and Robert McKinney, Ex-Slave Interview, 1940, Cammie G. Henry Research Center, Northwestern State University, Natchitoches, Louisiana.
2. Robert May, *Yuletide in Dixie* (Charlottesville: University of Virginia Press, 2019), 55–56, 87.
3. Brian J. Costello, "Pointe Coupee Holiday Traditions Recalled," Facebook.com, December 13, 2021, https://www.facebook.com/people/Pointe-Coupee-Parish-Library-II/1000664608 45659/.

CHAPTER 21

The Ghost of Christmas Yet to Come

Placing the Future in Holiday Programs

Anna Altschwager

Traditions mean nothing when they mean nothing to people.

WHEN WE WORK with history, we work for the future. I believe that history, in and of itself, does not matter.[1] When we do our work for the past by centering *content* as priority, we miss what is possible. When we do not account for our guests—their realities and their futures—our stories wither on the vine. Public programs offer a space in which we can shift our priorities and consider what it means to be inclusive and, ultimately, to matter. By reconsidering the motivations for, and outcomes of, our public programs we can do our work not as stewards to the past, but as ancestors. We can be an engaged part of our communities, and a celebrated, much-loved part of the personal lives of those we serve.

Personal and celebrated stories such as those associated with Christmas may seem like a dangerous place to start changing things. Why start messing around with "The Program" that we have done for twenty years that we know everyone loves? Public programs centered around traditions and holidays are the most fertile soil in which to dig and plant these seeds of change. Traditions can trick us into thinking we are doing them exactly as they have always been done, and they are therefore important because of their consistency. But, in the very act of doing them we change them. This natural evolution is why they are even *here* as traditions in the first place. Historians often see this clearly by the grace of well-oiled historical thinking. The real danger is not messing with a popular program but keeping the gift of public history to ourselves.

Traditions are bridges. A bridge works by having things, people, and ideas pass over it. Right now, we are in the middle of that bridge. One side is the past, the other in the future. When we shift the focus of our programs from being *about* "A Tradition" to being about what traditions *are*, we manifest inclusion and can be sustainable and financially sound in the process.

An Old World Christmas Carol

Richard Perrin was dead: to begin with. There was no doubt whatever about that.[2] While he walked this mortal coil, Perrin was one of the visionaries who made Old World Wisconsin come to life.[3] With origins woven within the Works Progress Administration (WPA) oral histories and architectural surveys of the Upper Midwest, and on to the zeitgeist of the bicentennial, Old World Wisconsin was conceived as "a rural village combining buildings of various ethnic groups to portray the distinctive cultural characteristic of Wisconsin's pioneers."[4]

Among the many quirks of Old World Wisconsin, the Wisconsin Historical Society's largest living history site, is the sprawling nature of the grounds. Six hundred acres of rolling landscapes of woods, fields, and prairies dotted with over sixty historic structures from someplace else; picked up and moved stone by stone, board by board, from counties near and far in the place we now call Wisconsin. The buildings were originally constructed between the 1830s and the 1910s and moved to Old World Wisconsin between the 1960s and the 1990s. The idiosyncratic cherry on top is the people—a wonderfully diverse, yet frustratingly not-exactly-historically-complete snapshot of immigrants and migrants: Norwegians, Germans, English, Irish, Bohemians, Finns, Danes, Welsh, Black Migrants from the South, and Yankees from the East who came to call this place home. Wouldn't it be easy if they all celebrated a *homogenous Christmas* so we could do a program?

So here Richard Perrin sat, surrounded by a motley crew of buildings and stories reflecting the complex ethnic hodge-podge of the Upper Midwest in six hundred acres. A farmhouse from Family A, a barn from Family B, an outhouse from Family C—the narrative glue intended to hold this "bicentennial baby" together was composite narratives using several experiences to tell a single, cohesive story. Even before the doors opened, however, this storytelling approach was left by the wayside. There is no smoking gun as to why, but all signs point to an expectation that this composite narrative approach would not be what guests wanted. It seems that it was easier to select *a single* family and place that story onto other families' spaces. So as the decades went along, the focus of each space evolved into a single-family narrative that lived in relative isolation from the other spaces. It was a pretty mosaic, without any grout—consolidated over complete, nostalgic over nuanced.

The First of the Three Spirits

In the last five years, Perrin's vision came back into focus. With a contemporary public history toolkit filled with techniques such as Arc of Dialogue and Essential Questions, our team at Old World Wisconsin found that composite narratives are a powerful way to facilitate exploration of the mosaic of immigrant cultures.[5] With this approach we not only rebuilt an interpretive program but launched the next generation of our public programs. Programs that have demonstrated sustained growth both before and after the impact of COVID-19.

History is just people. Every story we tell is human-scaled and personal. Our homes and barns and businesses are the epitome of the everyman—people living their lives, warts and all. The magic is in finding the universal in the personal. At our 1880s Pomeranian Immigrant Farm (made up of five buildings from five different Pomeranian Immigrant families), our composite narrative may seem to be about what life was like for immigrants from Pomerania in Dodge County, Wisconsin, in the 1880s (the seed Perrin planted). It is in fact about an essential question: *What is it like to live with multiple generations under one roof?*

When we reframe our narratives with essential questions, we give it a heart. A heart brims with inclusive potential. This starting point allows one to explore identity, culture, foodways, gender politics, landscape, transportation—and traditions. All the things that make a specific family story so fascinating, but via a portal with a low threshold. A guest with no interest in history can confidently engage with a question about multiple generations under one roof—as can a family with Pomeranian roots, as can a guest visiting from India, as can a ten-year old, and a seventy-year-old. There is no right or wrong answer to an essential question, only possibility for exploration and shared learning.

As with most things related to the heart, there is always risk. There may be a fear in pulling too far away from the stable foundations of historical fact and becoming too generic. I would ask that you consider your work as a relationship with your public and not as a transaction. In centering dialog and using portals such as essential questions, we give ourselves the gift of that relationship with our guests. We meet them where they are: here and now.

The reason we have taken this detour to a Pomeranian Immigrant Farm on our way to a Christmas Party is to illustrate two things—that we needed to be explicit in our points of view in order for the diversity to be visible, and the real power of the story is not in the specificity but in the *universality*.

The Second of the Three Spirits

In 2015 we began hosting *An Old World Christmas*. The start was simple, opening our doors in December to show off some holiday decorations and bring in some off-season revenue. As the realities of opening historic spaces in a Midwestern Winter became clear, we knew that in order to be worth it, the program needed to be a "real" event and not just public hours.

Over the years the event grew and the identity began to crystallize. At the heart of the work was a desire to have a goal that was *beyond content*. Sharing content is fine—we love

Table 21.1. Home For the Holidays Program Growth

YEAR	ATTENDANCE	REVENUE	RETAIL PER CAP
2017	3,101 (4 days)	$63,594	$3.77
2019	1,237 (4 days)	$63,054	$7.90
2021	3,804 (6 days)	$109,566	$13.00

The first weekend of the program in 2019 included an ice storm that had a significant impact on attendance. In 2021 we implemented online ticketing with required preregistration, which helped maintain attendance numbers even in below-freezing temperatures. Wisconsin *is* beautiful in December.

stories—but we wanted to create community more than "create people who now know a thing." As discussed above, when we can shift the focus of our programs from being *about* "A Tradition" to being about what traditions *are*, we can better serve our communities by being about and for them. Traditions exist due to an intentional cultivation. We, as the institution, do not want to be the cultivators, but rather the facilitators of cultivation by our communities. The centering of inclusive practice puts our public at the heart of the why and how of the program.

Words are powerful things. *An Old World Christmas* was about us, Old World Wisconsin, and about an old-fashioned place, far away in time. In 2021 we applied our interpretive approach from our daily operations to our holiday programs. We moved away from a program about specific content and centered it instead on the *universality* of the concept of home and renamed the program *Home for the Holidays*.

This was the next step in the evolution of a relationship-based program with a goal of ensuring that everyone can show up as they are and find a place at our metaphorical table. They can feel at home. Once around that table, laid with composite narratives of celebrations, places, and generations we ask the essential question: What can traditions mean to people? With this as our north star the program comes into focus: *Home for the Holidays* is a space for exploring this question. The hearth, around which you gather your guests and create a feeling of welcome and home, is the essential question. The content is only fuel for a fire, not the hearth itself. How can each interaction feel like an invitation to our hearth? How can we embody the concept of home for our community?

Home for the Holidays takes place on weekends in December, during daylight hours, which in this part of the world means 10 a.m. to 3 p.m. (see table 21.1). The average guest visit lasts three to four hours, and it consists of self-directed exploration of the Crossroads Village aided by a map and guide to the day's experiences. The Village is a single area of our site, made up of thirteen historic structures arranged across approximately twelve acres. The larger site (several dozen more buildings spread across seven farms, two homes, a small church, and a school) is often inaccessible in the winter months, so the holiday programs are limited to the reliably accessible Village.

Every year we curate a mix of old favorites and new experiences to keep guests engaged and coming back. There are, of course, the nostalgic *musts* including the warm, slightly acrid confines of the Blacksmith Shop, sleigh bells on our horse teams, warm kitchens with the perfect mix of wood smoke, cinnamon, and apple cider in the air.

Holiday characters are a way to both connect to expectations and expand curiosity about the hows and whys of tradition. We are lucky enough to host Mr. Claus himself each year as he transforms our 1890s Wheelmen's Club House into his late nineteenth-century workshop. He dons a leather apron and shirtsleeves and invites good children (of all ages) to join him at the workbench for a photo. From a six-foot-long Nice List streaming down one wall, to a sleigh filled with toys and boxes, and a red wool coat hanging ready and waiting on a nearby chair—guests are treated to a visually rich treat that sparks memories and stories of their own.

Santa Claus is joined by Krampus and Jultomten. Krampus wanders the Village with a large bag, a dry wit, and with a wry smile; he inquires about your behavior this year (see figure 21.1). While interaction with the large, hairy beast is the highlight, Krampus weaves in his story and asks, "Do you believe in me?" And then dares you not to! Jultomten takes a milder approach, welcoming you to the barn where goats bleat, and he laughs with young guests who cannot believe that a goat will bring them presents. He assures them it is possible, *if* you believe *and* you leave him some oatmeal—with butter.

In the historic interiors, we explore traditions like Boxing Day, providing everyone with the *new-to-them-fact* that the day has nothing to do with the sport and inviting them to pack their own charity box as one could in the 1880s. The Bohemian story of St. Nicholas is explored in the Shoe Shop while the Yankee Farm lets guests set the table for the Christmas

Figure 21.1.   Krampus turns his story into a memory for two young guests. Photo by Dean Witter, courtesy of Wisconsin Historical Foundation.

dinner that causes the kitchen to be a world of dishes, half-peeled potatoes, simmering pots, and expectations. The ever-present role of commercialization at Christmas is front and center in the General Store, both meeting the real need to shop, and letting them know that the draw to the shiny and new of the season puts them in good company.

In our Farmers' Club and Church, we host live local music: holiday brass, fiddle songs, and traditional carols. This is a major investment but adds such impact and provides weather-proof, memory-making experiences that proves worth it every year. It is also a highly visible way to showcase our values in action—keeping traditions alive and providing sponsorship opportunities for community supporters.

Home is a feeling, a place, an idea that is powerful, personal, and universal. Holidays are equally dynamic, calling to mid-winter for some, seasonality for others, traditions, or the connections across time. We explore this using the stories of late nineteenth and early twentieth-century immigrants as expressions of our essential question—portals to the ideas but not the end-all-be-all of the experience. The experience will ebb and flow as the program continues to evolve. We are intentionally setting the table knowing that more guests will arrive—will it be mid-winter storytelling from a Potawatomi tribal partner? A local church leading Las Posadas through the village to the church? A high school student creating an 1880s Hanukkah table setting in the boardinghouse? An art installation depicting the Kinara? We have no idea yet, but the program is built to grow and expand as our community needs.

The Last of the Spirits

As we move forward, our wish for *Home for the Holidays* is to set it up for growth rooted in community collaboration—not all at once, but organically over time as funding, partnerships, and needs allow. But we have a north star, and if there is ever a time to follow a star, it is at Christmas.

We are all learners and all teachers. As we gather around the hearth with you to reflect on big ideas like traditions, inclusivity, and how to do the work of public history, we want to be good hosts. Pull up a chair, rest awhile, and partake of some of our lessons learned.

Be Intentional

Why are you doing what you are doing and for whom? What is your north star? What are your outcomes—internally and externally? Start each planning process with this and be disciplined in using your answers as metrics to make decisions. Sometimes the worst idea is the *next* best idea. The goal line cannot keep shifting. Be clear and commit for each planning season. Every single person on your team needs to know *why* you are doing the program, not just what the program is. Having the full team internalize the why and how will make for earnest engagement with your guests, and each other.

Nostalgia as a Portal

Do not ignore it or fight it, it is a reality for your guests even if it is not accurate. An interactive, living history program is not the field of battle for *teaching ALL the history*. It is an opportunity to meet our guests where they are. At the holidays this could well be the nostalgia for a romantic notion of simpler times. Think of these not as roadblocks to the real story, nor as destinations to rest in, but portals—starting points. We train our experience facilitators on the idea of the gracious redirect, taking our guests from where they are, to another place—a new idea, a new experience—with grace. The holidays can be full of grace. Go softly and slowly.

Design Relationships

We create a handful of photo stops at each of our big programs. These are unstaffed, programmatic elements that meet guests where they are—social media. Picture a wagon with our logo and a bench set at a photogenic angle against a pretty forest background. Picture perfect for, well, a picture! The program is about our guests' visit and their stories, so why not meet them there? They get the Instagram-able moment; we get to end up in their feed or on their holiday card. There is minimal cost but big impact. If you have never spent time seeing how people tag your site or post their personal photos of your site, it is well worth the internet rabbit hole. This is literally seeing your spaces through their eyes, and you might be surprised. We also do little things like recipe cards with our logo on them. We are making Bohemian braided bread, but the real experience is *you* making it at home, so grab a card and have at it! Meanwhile, you will think of us and your day here each time you move that card from the fridge door to the countertop back to the fridge; someday you will make it.

Be Iconic

What does your event have that nothing else in your marketplace of holiday experiences has? If your event is trying to be about *this* and *that* and *those* AND *the holiday kitchen sink*, you will start to sound like the teacher from Charlie Brown. Pick two or three icons—your poster children that set you apart. Your icon is both your pre-event tease, and your post-event talisman. *Home for the Holiday's* icons are the Yule Goats, Krampus, and Santa—and some would argue the Wassail made with brandy—but you get my point. Our museum store carries items with these icons as the focus (we cannot keep $10 Krampus Socks in stock!), the images used in marketing are of these elements, and the press release calls these out. Make them human-scaled so that a potential guest says, in the words of Liz Lemon from *30 Rock*, "I want to go to there."

Know Your Hero

If your event is not about your guests, do not bother. The guest is the hero of the day. Be clear in your intentions so that they know that this day is about them and the great experience they are going to have. And they might learn something too—bonus! Education is often the justification, not the motivation, and this is never truer than at the holidays. We double down on our year-round approach to facilitation and clear the decks for stories that guests bring with them. If we do not get to explain what Boxing Day is, but instead a grandparent shares a story of their childhood with their family—BOOM!—that is a win. The program is about the past, present, and future of our holiday traditions. Go beyond content sharing and create spaces for your heroes' stories to be shared. Show up for your community in this way, and they will show up for you.

Tinker Like an Elf

We must listen to our present to ensure the future of our historic program. And then, we keep listening and keep listening. The program is never done. Every year we change things a bit. Not so much that we cannot develop our icons, but enough that we can learn and grow. Find your sweet spot between ritual and innovation. Your guests are more flexible than you know. When their expectations are framed in a sustainable and relevant way such as "We can spend time with our friends and family in a cool/beautiful/fun setting and celebrate the holidays together," you have a lot of room to play and maintain reliable, desirable expectations.

The End of It

Nested within the upcoming 250th commemoration of the Declaration of Independence is a marker of time that likely carries meaning for those who practice public history. The fiftieth anniversary of the 1976 Bicentennial happens in 2026—home to the origin stories of many of our local history and living history spaces. This generation of distance gives us perspective to consider our craft, our intentions, and the evolution of which we are inextricably a part.

When we understand that the dynamism of the history we love so much must be reflected in our *practice* of history, we can challenge ourselves to find our heart. We do our work for people, so we push inclusivity in new ways to make sure people can see themselves in everything we do. Let us do work *for* people, not *about* people. Let us be graceful and share space. Let us know that stories will surprise, challenge, and delight us. Let us walk the bridge of traditions with our communities. And let us be good ancestors.

"Some people laughed to see the alteration in us, but we let them laugh, and little heeded them; for we were wise enough to know that nothing ever happened on this globe, for good, at which some people did not have their fill of laughter in the outset; and knowing that such as these would be blind anyway, we thought it quite as well that they should wrinkle up their eyes in grins . . . and it was always said of us, that we know how to keep Christmas well, if any man alive possessed the knowledge. May it truly be said of us, and all of us!"[6]

Notes

1. Anna Altschwager, "When History Doesn't Matter," *American Association for State and Local History* (blog), 2016: https://aaslh.org/when-history-doesnt-matter.
2. Inspired by *A Christmas Carol* by Charles Dickens.
3. John D. Krugler, *Creating Old World Wisconsin: The Struggle to Build an Outdoor History Museum of Ethnic Architecture* (Madison: University of Wisconsin Press, 2013).
4. Wisconsin Historical Society, "Case Statement for Old World Wisconsin" (Madison: Wisconsin Historical Society, 1973).
5. At Old World Wisconsin, the staff are called *experience facilitators*. This is an intentional shift from the more common *interpreter*. The intention is to make clear their role as a guide-on-the-side, someone to help facilitate the guests' experience; not someone who is required for a translation of the content from the institution to the public, only half-jokingly called a sage-on-the-stage.
6. Inspired by *A Christmas Carol* by Charles Dickens.

Selected Bibliography on the Interpretation of Christmas, Hanukkah, and Kwanzaa

This two-part bibliography includes books and articles on the history and interpretation of Christmas, with additional sources on Kwanzaa, Hanukkah, New Year's Day, and Chinese New Year. With some exceptions, most selections are focused on historic practices in the United States published since 2000. This list is neither comprehensive nor definitive but offers a starting point for historic sites and house museums as they conduct research for enhancing their interpretation of Christmas, Hanukkah, and Kwanzaa.

Part I of the bibliography is comprised of scholarly books and articles along with trade-published books with footnotes and well-documented sources. Most books are available through a local library, bookseller, or online. Most scholarly articles are obtainable through a university library, which offers alumni digital access to library resources. Alternatively, JSTOR offers independent researchers unaffiliated with universities free membership to access most of its online content, up to a hundred articles a month. JSTOR contains more than 12 million journal articles, books, images, and primary sources (https://www.jstor.org/).

Part II of the bibliography focuses on publications for collectors and a general (non-academic) audience. Many sources are richly illustrated with photographs of objects, rituals, and decorations related to winter holidays. We have included several cookbooks and anthologies of music and movies, which may be helpful in thinking about delivering a broad sensory experience for visitors to historic sites, along with several encyclopedias of the holidays. Additionally, this list includes several state or local Christmas histories and collected narratives, memoirs, and primary source material published by state historical societies. Not included in this bibliography are trade press publishers like Arcadia and its imprints the History Press and Pelican Press, which offer many additional titles on local communities worth exploring but are too extensive to list here. Publications written for collectors, which offer bibliographies, and articles focused on Christmas traditions and material culture, are also excluded but for an introduction, we recommend *The Magazine of the Golden Glow of Christmas Past,* https://goldenglow.org/magazine/.

Part I: Scholarly Books and Articles

Abramitzky, Ran, Liran Einav, and Oren Rigbi. "Is Hanukkah Responsive to Christmas?" *The Economic Journal* 120, no. 545 (2010): 612–30.

Adam, Thomas. "From Weihnachten to Christmas: The Invention of a Modern Holiday Ritual and Its Transfer from Germany to England and the United States." In *Approaches to the Study of Intercultural Transfer*, edited by Thomas Adam, 155–78. London: Anthem Press, 2020.

Allen, Reniqua. "Legitimized Blackness? Kwanzaa, Citizenship, and Newark." *Western Journal of Black Studies* 37, no. 4 (2013): 272–84.

Ames, Kenneth L., ed. *American Christmas Cards, 1900–1960.* New Haven: Bard Graduate Center, 2011.

Archer, Melanie. "Xmas Excess." In *The Business of Holidays*, edited by Maud Lavin, 234–41. New York: Monacelli, 2004.

Ashton, Dianne. *Hanukkah in America: A History.* New York: New York University Press, 2013.

Austin, Regina. "Kwanzaa and the Commodification of Black Culture." *Black Renaissance* 6, no. 1 (Fall 2004): 8–18.

Bigham, Shauna, and Robert E. May. "'The Time o' All Times?' Masters, Slaves, and Christmas in the Old South." *Journal of the Early Republic* 18, no. 2 (1998): 263–88.

Bird, William L. *Holidays on Display.* Princeton, NJ: Princeton Architectural Press, 2007.

Bowler, Gerry. *Christmas in the Crosshairs: Two Thousand Years of Denouncing and Defending the World's Most Celebrated Holiday.* New York: Oxford University Press, 2017.

Brewis, Joanna, and Samantha Warren. "Have Yourself a Merry Little Christmas? Organizing Christmas in Women's Magazines Past and Present." *Organization* 18, no. 6 (2011): 747–62.

Brunner, Bernd. *Inventing the Christmas Tree.* Translated by Benjamin A. Smith. New Haven: Yale University Press, 2012.

Carlson, Paul Howard. *Dancin' in Anson: A History of the Texas Cowboys' Christmas Ball.* Lubbock: Texas Tech University Press, 2014.

Cheal, David. *The Gift Economy.* New York: Routledge, 1988.

Connelly, Mark. *Christmas: A History.* New York: I.B. Tauris Publishers, 2012.

Connelly, Mark, ed. *Christmas at the Movies: Images of Christmas in American, British and European Cinema.* New York: I.B. Tauris Publishers, 2000.

Cox-Paul, Lori A., and James W. Wengert. *A Frontier Army Christmas.* Lincoln: Nebraska State Historical Society, 1998.

Davis, Susan G. "'Making Night Hideous': Christmas Revelry and Public Order in Nineteenth-Century Philadelphia." *American Quarterly* 34, no. 2 (Summer 1982): 185–99.

De La Torre, Miguel A. "A Colonized Christmas Story." *Interpretation* 71, no. 4 (2017): 408–17.

Etzioni, Amitai, and Jared Bloom, eds. *We Are What We Celebrate: Understanding Holidays and Rituals*. New York: New York University Press, 2004.

Fine, Steven. *The Menorah: From the Bible to Modern Israel*. Cambridge: Harvard University Press, 2016.

Fisher, Jennifer. *'Nutcracker' Nation: How an Old World Ballet Became a Christmas Tradition in the New World*. New Haven: Yale University Press, 2003.

Flanders, Judith. *Christmas: A Biography*. New York: Thomas Dunne Books, 2017.

Flores-Peña, Ysamur, and Robin Evanchuk. "Kwanzaa: The Emergence of an African-American Holiday." *Western Folklore* 56, no. 3/4 (Summer/Fall 1997): 281–94.

Forbes, Bruce David. *Christmas: A Candid History*. Berkeley: University of California Press, 2007.

Forbes, Bruce David. "Religion Is Like a Snowball." In *Religion and Popular Culture in America, Third Edition*, edited by Bruce David Forbes and Jeffrey Mahan, 127–43. Berkeley: University of California Press, 2017.

Fraser, Rebecca J. "'Every Child Rises Early on Christmas Morning to See the Johnkannaus' [Harriet Jacobs]: The Competing Meanings of Christmas for the Enslaved in North Carolina." *Comparative American Studies: An International Journal* (June 27, 2023). https://doi.org/10.1080/14775700.2023.2229213.

Groff, Sibyl McCormac. "Gothamtide, Christmas Words and Images in Nineteenth-Century New York." *The Magazine Antiques* 162, no. 6 (December 2002): 64–73.

Hahn, Steven. "'Extravagant Expectations' of Freedom: Rumour, Political Struggle, and the Christmas Insurrection Scare of 1865 in the American South." *Past and Present* 157 (Nov. 1997): 122–58.

Hancock, Philip, and Alf Rehn. "Organizing Christmas." *Organization* 18, no. 6 (Nov. 2011): 737–45.

Harris, Moira F. "Season's Greetings from Minnesota." *Minnesota History* 62, no. 8 (Winter 2011–2012): 304–14.

Heinze, Andrew R. "Adapting to Abundance: Luxuries, Holidays, and Jewish Abundance." In *The American Jewish Experience* (second ed.), edited by Jonathan D. Sarna, 165–82. New York: Holmes and Meier Publishers, 1997.

Hill, Miriam G., and Francis Godwin James. *Joy to the World: Two Thousand Years of Christmas*. Portland, OR: Four Courts Press, 2000.

Horsley, Richard A., and James Tracy, eds. *Christmas Unwrapped: Consumerism, Christ and Culture*. Harrisburg, PA: Trinity Press International, 2001.

Joselit, Jenna Weissman. "'Merry Chanukah': The Changing Holiday Practices of American Jews, 1880–1950." In *The Uses of Tradition: Jewish Continuity in the Modern Era*, edited by Jack Wertheimer, 303–25. New York: Jewish Theological Seminary of America, 1999.

Kanellos, Nicolás, ed. *Noche Buena: Hispanic American Christmas Stories*. New York: Oxford University Press, 2000.

Katz-Hyman, Martha B. "It's Not the Jewish Christmas: An Introduction to Jewish Holidays and Their Observance in North America." *ALHFAM Bulletin* XXXV, no. 3 (Fall 2005): 20–26.

Kaufman, Cathy. "The Ideal Christmas Dinner." *Gastronomica* 4, no. 4 (Fall 2004): 17–24.

Lankford, Ronald D., Jr. *Sleigh Rides, Jingle Bells and Silent Nights: A Cultural History of American Christmas Songs*. Gainesville: University Press of Florida, 2013.

Larsen, Timothy, ed. *The Oxford Handbook of Christmas*. Oxford: Oxford University Press, 2020.

Lemish, Peter S. "Hanukkah Bush: The Jewish Experience in America." *Theory into Practice* 20, no. 1 (2001): 26–30.

Li, Mu. "From the Ethnic to the Public: The Emergence of Chinese New Year Celebrations in Newfoundland as Vernacular Cultural Heritage." *Western Folklore* 77, no. 3/4 (Summer/Fall 2018): 277–312.

Mann, Kristin Dutcher. "Christmas in the Missions of Northern New Spain." *The Americas* 66, no. 3 (January 2010): 331–51.

Marling, Karal Ann. *Merry Christmas! Celebrating America's Greatest Holiday*. Cambridge, MA: Harvard University Press, 2002.

May, Robert E. *Yuletide in Dixie: Slavery, Christmas and Southern Memory*. Charlottesville: University of Virginia Press, 2019.

Mayes, Keith A. *Kwanzaa, Black Power, and the Making of the African American Holiday Tradition*. New York: Routledge, 2009.

McCord, Charline R., and Judy H. Tucker, eds. *Christmas Memories from Mississippi*. Jackson: University Press of Mississippi, 2010.

McGreevy, Patrick. "Place in the American Christmas." *Geographical Review* 80, no. 1 (1990): 32–42.

Miller, David, ed. *Unwrapping Christmas*. Oxford: Clarendon Press, 1993.

Moore, Tara. *Victorian Christmas in Print*. New York: Palgrave Macmillan, 2009.

Moore, Tara. *Christmas: The Sacred to Santa*. London: Reaktion Books, 2014.

Nissenbaum, Stephen. *The Battle for Christmas*. New York: Alfred A. Knopf, 1996.

Palmer, Alex. *The Santa Claus Man: The Rise and Fall of a Jazz Age Con Man and the Invention of Christmas in New York*. Guilford, CT: Running Press Adult, 2020.

Penfold, Steve. "The Eaton's Santa Claus Parade and the Making of a Metropolitan Spectacle, 1905–1982." *Histoire Sociale/Social History* 44, no. 87 (2011): 1–28.

Plaut, Joshua Eli. *A Kosher Christmas: 'Tis the Season to be Jewish*. New Brunswick, NJ: Rutgers University Press, 2012.

Pleck, Elizabeth. "Kwanzaa: The Making of a Black Nationalist Tradition, 1966–1990." *Journal of American Ethnic History* 20, no. 4 (Summer 2001): 3–28.

Pritzl, Jody L. *Immigrants, Ornaments and Legacies: A Story of American-Made Glass Christmas Tree Ornaments*. Self-published through Amazon, 2019.

Racine, Laurel A., Gregory R. Weidman, Lenora M. Henson, and Patricia West McKay. "The Curator's Role in Crowd-Pleasing Events: Maintaining Safety, Accuracy, and Sanity in the Excitement of It All." *Collections* 10, no. 1 (March 1, 2014): 47–66.

Restad, Penne L. *Christmas in America: A History*. New York, Oxford University Press, 1995.

Rosen, Jody. *White Christmas: The Story of an American Song*. New York: Scribner, 2002.

Rosewarne, Lauren. *Analyzing Christmas in Film: Santa to the Supernatural*. Lanham, MD: Lexington Books, 2017.

Schmidt, Leigh Eric. *Consumer Rites: The Buying and Selling of American Holidays*. Princeton, NJ: Princeton University Press, 1995.

Seal, Jeremy. *Nicholas: The Epic Journey from Saint to Santa Claus*. New York: Bloomsbury Publishing, 2005.

Shanahan, Madeline. *Christmas Food and Feasting: A History*. Lanham, MD: Rowman & Littlefield, 2019.

Shephard, Diane, and Kenneth C. Turino. "Christmas in Lynn, Massachusetts: The Evolution of a Holiday." *Nineteenth Century* 12, nos. 3 and 4 (1993): 2–8.

Shoemaker, Alfred L. *Christmas in Pennsylvania: A Folk-Cultural Study*. Mechanicsburg, PA: Stackpole Books, 2009.

Silverthorne, Elizabeth. *Christmas in Texas*. College Station: Texas A&M University Press, 1990.

Smith, Thomas Ruys. "*A Christmas Carol* in Nineteenth-Century America, 1844–1870." *Comparative American Studies: An International Journal*, 2023. DOI: 10.1080/14775700.2023.2229214.

Stein, Blair. "'The Charnukah Being Observed Now': Understanding Hanukkah through American Newspapers, 1880–1915." *Journal of Religion and Culture* 23 (2012): 39–61.

Steinberg, Paul. *Celebrating the Jewish Year: The Winter Holidays*. Philadelphia: Jewish Publication Society, 2007.

Stokker, Kathleen. *Keeping Christmas: Yuletide Traditions in Norway and the New Land*. Saint Paul: Minnesota Historical Society, 2000.

Studwell, William E., and Dorothy E. Jones. *Publishing Glad Tidings: Essays on Christmas Music*. New York: Haworth Press, 1998.

Taft, Chloe. "Wishing upon a Star: Christmas Tourism and Urban Renewal in Bethlehem, PA." *Journal of Planning History* 12, no. 2 (2013): 154–78.

Taylor, Judith M., Roberto G. Lopez, Christopher J. Currey, and Jules Janick. "The Poinsettia: History and Transformation." *Chronica Horticulturae* 180, no. 3 (September 2011): 23–28.

Theobald, Mary Miley, and Libbey Hodges Oliver. *Four Centuries of Virginia Christmas*. Richmond: Dietz Press, 2000.

Thomas, Nancy Smith. *Moravian Christmas in the South*. Winston-Salem, NC: Old Salem Museums and Gardens, 2007.

Tigchelaar, Jana. "The Neighborly Christmas: Gifts, Community, and Regionalism in the Christmas Stories of Sarah Orne Jewett and Mary Wilkins Freeman." *Legacy: A Journal of American Women Writers* 31, no. 2 (2014): 236–57.

Toles-Patkin, Terri. "Hallmarking Hanukkah: Flawed Attempts at Diversity in Cable Television Christmas Movies." *Journal of Popular Culture* 54, no. 5 (2021): 917–40.

Towne, Douglas C. "Maybe Christmas Wasn't Meant to Last Forever: The Rise and Fall of Santa Claus, Arizona." *Journal of Arizona History* 49, no. 3 (Autumn 2008): 233–54.

Waits, William B. *The Modern Christmas in America: A Cultural History of Gift Giving*. New York: New York University Press, 1994.

Wenger, Beth S. *History Lessons: The Creation of American Jewish Heritage*. Princeton: Princeton University Press, 2012.

White, J. P. "American Eye: Christmas at the Plantation." *The North American Review* 278, no. 6 (November–December 1993): 4–9.

Whiteley, Sheila, ed. *Christmas, Ideology and Popular Culture*. Edinburgh: Edinburgh University Press, 2008.

Yeh, Chiou-ling. *Making an American Festival: Chinese New Year in San Francisco's Chinatown*. Berkeley: University of California Press, 2008.

Part II. Sources for a General Audience and Collectors

Albers, Henry H., and Ann Kirk Davis. *The Wonderful World of Christmas Trees*. Parkersburg, IA: Mid-Prairie Books, 1997.

Allen, Linda. *Decking the Halls: The Folklore and Traditions of Christmas Plants*. Minocqua, WI: Willow Creek Press, 2000.

Allen, Moira, ed. *A Victorian Christmas Treasury II*. Scotts Valley, CA: CreateSpace Independent Publishing Platform, 2014.

Apkarian-Russell, Pamela E. *Postmarked Yesteryear: Art of the Holiday Postcard*. Portland, OR: Collectors Press Inc., 2001.

Archer, Sarah. *Midcentury Christmas: Holiday Fads, Fancies, and Fun from 1945 to 1970*. New York: Countryman Press, 2016.

Armstrong, Nancy. *The Rockefeller Center Christmas Tree*. Kennebunkport, ME: Cider Mill Press, 2009.

Arnold, Jeremy. *Christmas in the Movies: 30 Classics to Celebrate the Season*. Philadelphia: Running Press Adult, 2018.

Ballowe, James, ed. *Christmas in Illinois*. Champaign: University of Illinois Press, 2015.

Beauchamp, Monte. *Krampus: The Devil of Christmas*. San Francisco: Last Gasp, 2010.

Belanger, Jeff. *The Fright before Christmas: Surviving Krampus and Other Yuletide Monsters, Witches, and Ghosts*. Newburyport, MA: New Page Books, 2023.

Bellamy, Gail G. *Cleveland Christmas Memories: Looking Back at Holidays Past*. Cleveland: Gray & Company Publishers, 2012.

Bennett, William J. *The True Saint Nicholas: Why He Matters to Christmas*. New York: Howard Books, 2018.

Bowler, Gerry. *Santa Claus: A Biography*. Toronto: McClelland & Stewart, 2005.

Bowler, Gerry. *The World Encyclopedia of Christmas*. Toronto: McClelland & Stewart, 2000.

Brenner, Robert. *Christmas 1940–1959: A Collector's Guide to Decorations and Customs*. Atglen, PA: Schiffer Publishing Ltd., 2007.

Brenner, Robert. *Christmas through the Decades: A Guide to Christmas Antiques*. Atglen, PA: Schiffer Publishing Ltd., 1997.

Cafferata, Patty. *Christmas in Nevada*. Reno: University of Nevada Press, 2014.

Canfield, Kaylene. *Christmas Advertisements: 1859–1912*. Scotts Valley, CA: CreateSpace Independent Publishing Platform, 2016.

Chipps, Cindy, and Greg Olson. *Collector's Encyclopedia of Electric Christmas Lighting: Identification and Values*. Paducah, KY: Collector Books, 2004.

Collier-Thomas, Bettye, ed. *A Treasury of African-American Christmas Stories*. Boston: Beacon Press, 2018.

Colonial Williamsburg Foundation. *A Colonial Williamsburg Christmas: Celebrating Classic Traditions and the Spirit of the Holiday*. Essex, CT: Globe Pequot Press, 2021.

Copage, Eric V. *Kwanzaa, An African-American Celebration of Culture and Cooking*. New York: William Morrow, 1991.

Crump, William D. *The Christmas Encyclopedia*. Jefferson, NC: McFarland, 2022.

Crump, William D. *Encyclopedia of New Year's Holidays Worldwide*. Jefferson, NC: McFarland, 2008.

Deekens, Donna Strother, and Doug Riddell. *Virginia's Legendary Santa Trains*. Mount Pleasant, SC: Arcadia Publishing, 2013.

Demarest, Janet Emily. *A Merry, Very Victorian Christmas!: Trivia, Tales and Traditions from 19th Century America*. Scotts Valley, CA: CreateSpace Independent Publishing Platform, 2016.

Earl, Brian. *Christmas Past: The Fascinating Stories behind Our Favorite Holiday's Traditions*. Guilford, CT: Lyons Press, 2022.

Eckstein, Bob. *The Illustrated History of the Snowman*. Lanham, MD: Globe Pequot, 2018.

Edworthy, Niall. *The Curious World of Christmas: Celebrating All That Is Weird, Wonderful and Festive.* London: Doubleday, 2007.

Elliott, Jock. *Inventing Christmas: How Our Holiday Came to Be.* New York: Harry N. Abrams, 2002.

Foley, Michael P. *Why We Kiss under the Mistletoe: Christmas Traditions Explained.* Washington, DC: Regnery History, 2022.

Forsyth, Mark. *A Christmas Cornucopia: The Hidden Stories behind Our Yuletide Traditions.* London: Viking Books UK, 2018.

Gant, Andrew. *The Carols of Christmas: A Celebration of the Surprising Stories behind Your Favorite Songs.* Nashville: Nelson Books, 2015.

Gifford, Daniel. *American Holiday Postcards, 1905–1915: Imagery and Context.* Jefferson, NC: McFarland Publishing, 2013.

Goodman, Rabbi Philip, ed. *The Hanukkah Anthology.* Philadelphia: Jewish Publication Society, 2018.

Gray, Annie. *At Christmas We Feast.* London: Profile Books Ltd., 2021.

Gulevich, Tanya. *Encyclopedia of Christmas and New Year's Celebrations.* Detroit: Omnigraphics, 2003.

Harrell-Sesniak, Mary. *Dear Santa: Children's Christmas Letters and Wish Lists, 1870–1920.* San Francisco: Chronicle Books, 2015.

Harris, Jessica B. *A Kwanzaa Keepsake: Celebrating the Holiday with New Traditions and Feasts.* New York: Simon & Schuster, 1995.

Haydon, Sharon A. *The Games of Christmas: Images of Christmas Past.* Haworth, NJ: Saint Johann Press, 2012.

Johnson, George. *Pictorial Guide to Christmas Ornaments and Collectibles: Identification and Values.* Paducah, KY: Collector Books, 2003.

Kall, Vickey. *The Boomer Book of Christmas Memories.* Torrance, CA: Kalambakal Press, 2014.

Kaplan, Tsadik. *Jewish Antiques: From Menorahs to Seltzer Bottles.* Atglen, PA: Schiffer Publishing, 2014.

Karas, Sheryl Ann. *The Solstice Evergreen: The History, Folklore and Origins of the Christmas Tree.* Fairfield, CT: Aslan Publishing, 1998.

Karenga, Maulana. *Kwanzaa: A Celebration of Family, Community, and Culture.* Los Angeles: University of Sankore Press, 1998.

Kissinger, Barbara H. *Christmas Merrymaking.* New Orleans: Pelican Publishing, 2007.

Marsh, Dave, and Steve Propers. *Merry Christmas, Baby: Holiday Music from Bing to Sting.* Boston: Little, Brown and Co., 1993.

Matthews, John, and Caitlin Matthews. *The Winter Solstice: The Sacred Traditions of Christmas.* Wheaton, IL: Quest Books, 1998.

McMillan, Patricia Hart. *Christmas in America's Landmark Houses.* Atglen, PA: Schiffer Publishing, 2022.

McMillan, Patricia Hart. *Delicious Christmas Decorations at Historic Houses and Your Home.* Atglen, PA: Schiffer Publishing, 2011.

McMillan, Patricia Hart, and Katherine Kaye McMillan. *Christmas at Historic Houses.* Atglen, PA: Schiffer Publishing, 2014.

Menendez, Albert J., and Shirley C. Menendez. *Christmas Songs Made in America: Favorite Holiday Melodies and the Stories of Their Origins.* Nashville, TN: Cumberland House Publishing, 1999.

Mole, Rich. *Christmas in the Prairies: Heartwarming Legends, Tales, and Traditions.* Calgary: Altitude Publishing, 2004.

Monahan, Sherry. *Tinsel, Tumbleweeds, and Star-Spangled Celebrations: Holidays on the Frontier from New Years to Christmas.* Essex, CT: Globe Pequot Press/TwoDot, 2017.

New York Public Library. *100 Christmas Wishes: Vintage Holiday Cards from The New York Public Library.* New York: St. Martin's Griffin, 2018.

Oliver, Libbey Hodges, and Mary Miley Theobald. *Williamsburg Christmas: The Story of Decoration in the Colonial Capital.* New York: Harry N. Abrams, 1999.

Palmer, Alex. *The Atlas of Christmas: The Merriest, Tastiest, Quirkiest Holiday Traditions from around the World.* Philadelphia: Running Press, 2020.

Pinsky, Nina. *Celebration: The Christmas Flower Book.* New York: Red Rock Press, 2006.

Raedisch, Linda. *The Old Magic of Christmas: Yuletide Traditions for the Darkest Days of the Year.* Woodbury, MN: Llewellyn Publications, 2013.

Rätsch, Christian, and Claudia Müller-Ebeling. *Pagan Christmas: The Plants, Spirits, and Rituals at the Origins of Yuletide.* Rochester, VT: Inner Traditions, 2006.

Rawlings, Kevin. *We Were Marching on Christmas Day: A History and Chronicle of Christmas during the Civil War.* Glen Burnie, MD: Toomey Press, 1995.

Reed, Robert M., and Claudette Reed. *Christmas Postcards: A Collector's Guide.* Atglen, PA: Schiffer Publishing, 2007.

Richliano, James A. *Angels We Have Heard: The Christmas Song Stories.* Chatham, NY: Star of Bethlehem Books, 2002.

Ridenour, Al. *The Krampus and the Old, Dark Christmas: Roots and Rebirth of the Folkloric Devil.* Los Angeles: Feral House, 2016.

Rountree, Susan Hight. *Christmas Decorations from Williamsburg.* Williamsburg, VA: Colonial Williamsburg Foundation, 2006.

Schiffer, Margaret. *Christmas Ornaments: A Festive Study.* Atglen, PA: Schiffer, 1995.

Smith, Thomas Ruys, ed. *Christmas Past: An Anthology of Seasonal Stories from Nineteenth-Century America.* Baton Rouge: Louisiana State University Press, 2021.

Smith, Travis. *Kitschmasland! Christmas Décor from the 1950s to the 1970s.* Atglen, PA: Schiffer Publishing, 2008.

Spain, Tom, and Michel Shohl, eds. *I'll Be Home for Christmas: The Library of Congress Revisits the Spirit of Christmas during World War II.* New York: Delacorte Press, 1999.

Standiford, Les. *The Man Who Invented Christmas: How Charles Dickens's* A Christmas Carol *Rescued His Career and Revived Our Holiday Spirits.* New York: Crown Publishers, 2011.

Stubbs, Carol, and Nancy Rust. *A Louisiana Christmas: Heritage Recipes and Hometown Celebrations.* New Orleans: Pelican Publishing, 2014.

Svehla, Gary J., and Susan Svehla. *It's Christmas Time at the Movies.* Baltimore: Midnight Marquee Press, 1998.

Thomas, Andy. *Christmas: A Short History from Solstice to Santa.* London: Ivy Press, 2019.

Tichi, Cecilia. "A Dry Christmas." In *Jazz Age Cocktails: History, Lore, and Recipes from America's Roaring Twenties,* 130–35. New York: New York University Press, 2021.

Waggoner, Susan. *Christmas Memories: Gifts, Activities, Fads, and Fancies, 1920s–1960s.* New York: Stewart, Tabori, and Chang, 2009.

Waggoner, Susan. *It's a Wonderful Christmas: The Best of the Holidays, 1940–1965.* New York: Stewart, Tabori and Chang, 2004.

Weintraub, Stanley. *Pearl Harbor Christmas: A World at War, December 1941*. Cambridge, MA: Da Capo Press, 2011.

Werts, Diane. *Christmas on Television*. Westport, CT: Praeger Publishers, 2006.

Wheeler, Joe, and Jon Rosenthal. *St. Nicholas: A Closer Look at Christmas.* Nashville: Thomas Nelson, 2005.

Ziebarth, Marilyn, and Brian Horrigan. *Christmas in Minnesota: A Celebration in Memories, Stories, and Recipes of Seasons Past*. Saint Paul: Minnesota Historical Society Press, 2019.

Index

Pages for figures are italicized.

About the Editors

Kenneth C. Turino is manager of community partnerships and resource development at Historic New England and a faculty member at Tufts University's museum studies department, where he teaches courses on exhibition planning and reimagining historic house museums. As a council member of the American Association for State and Local History, Ken's expertise spans various roles including author, consultant, curator, director, educator, and producer. His award-winning films have been featured on PBS and several of his edited books have garnered national recognition.

Ken frequently consults and contributes writings on LGBTQ+ interpretation, interpretive planning, and community engagement projects at historic sites, most recently at Frank Lloyd Wright's Fallingwater. He coedited *Reinventing the Historic House Museum: New Approaches and Proven Solutions* in 2019 with Max van Balgooy. A renowned lecturer on the history of Christmas, Ken has written extensively on the subject for the past three decades. He was honored with Salem State University's Outstanding Educator Award in 2008 and the New England Museums Association Excellence Award in 2023.

Max A. van Balgooy is president of Engaging Places, a design and strategy firm that connects people and historic places. He has worked with a wide range of historic sites on interpretive planning and business strategy, including the Mercer Museum, Betsy Ross House, Thomas Jefferson's Monticello, and Andrew Jackson's Hermitage. He is an assistant professor in the museum studies program at George Washington University and regularly leads workshops for the American Association for State and Local History.

He is a frequent contributor to professional journals and books, including *Interpreting African American History and Culture at Museums and Historic Sites* (2015) and *Reimagining Historic House Museums: New Approaches and Proven Solutions* (2019) with Ken Turino of Historic New England. These experiences provide a rich source of ideas for EngagingPlaces.net, where he blogs regularly about the opportunities and challenges facing historic sites and house museums.

About the Contributors

Anna Altschwager is a storyteller. From gemstones to plants, Ancient China to chamber pots, Anna has worked for numerous institutions overseeing experience design, program development, exhibits, and education. She is experienced in leading engaging, improv-based training sessions that align daily work with institutional strategy. Anna is passionate about curiosity, exploration, and putting stories in the hands of citizens—fostering critical thinking and stronger communities. Anna holds an MA from the Cooperstown Graduate Program (2007) and a BA in art history and material culture from the University of Wisconsin, Madison (2004). She is a maker, a Mama, and a fifth-generation Wisconsinite.

Sara Bhatia is a historian and an independent museum consultant. She has worked on projects and written articles on museums including Petersen House (the House Where Lincoln Died), the National Building Museum, the Newseum, and Osborn Oldroyd's Lincoln Museum. She holds a master's degree in museum studies from George Washington University and history degrees from Columbia and Princeton Universities. She can be reached at sarabhatia2@gmail.com.

Emmanuel Dabney is a public historian. After completing high school, Emmanuel graduated magna cum laude with an associates of arts from Richard Bland College; graduated magna cum laude with a bachelor of arts in historic preservation from the University of Mary Washington in Fredericksburg, Virginia; and completed a master's degree in public history at the University of North Carolina at Greensboro. Emmanuel has given many programs on the issues facing African Americans in antebellum, Civil War, and immediate postwar America as well as how to portray these experiences within professional museum settings.

Andrew R. Dunn grew up in Twin Falls, Idaho, twenty-five minutes from the Minidoka site. He dedicated his studies to learning about the camps and interned for Minidoka National Historic Site while pursuing a graduate degree through Idaho State University. Dunn joined the Friends of Minidoka board of directors in 2017 and received his MA in historical resources management in 2018. Dunn's specific research areas related to Minidoka include cultural impacts, agricultural production, food, sports, and military contributions of incarcerated Nikkei. For more information regarding Minidoka or ways to get involved, please visit www.Minidoka.org or reach out to Dunn directly at dunnandr@isu.edu.

Susan Fletcher is a historian, writer, and artist. She has served as the director of History and Archives at the Navigators for fifteen years. She is the author of *Exploring the History of Childhood and Play through 50 Historic Treasures, Light and Life: First Presbyterian Church at 150*, and the coauthor of *Dawson Trotman in His Own Words* and *The Glen Eyrie Story*.

Barbara Franco is a past chair of AASLH Council and current member of the AASLH Religious History Affinity Group. Her broad interest in the cultural and intellectual history of the nineteenth century has included research on communal societies, fraternal organizations, and the role of religion. She coedited *Interpreting Religion at Museums and Historic Sites* with Gretchen Buggeln and serves as president of the Advent Historical Society, preserving and interpreting an 1849 Millerite chapel in Centre County, Pennsylvania.

Erik Greenberg is a public historian, educator, and scholar with over twenty years of experience in museum work, public programming, written works, and in the university classroom. He holds a PhD in American history from UCLA, and he is currently the manager of development and membership for the Rhode Island Black Heritage Society.

Andrew W. Hahn began his career as an intern at the historic house museum on his college campus. Since 2003 he has worked as director of the Campbell House Museum, an 1851 townhouse in downtown St. Louis. Initially he oversaw the planning and completion of a $3 million restoration effort. More recently he has directed the expansion of the museum's research efforts and in 2020 the completion of an accessibility expansion. Hahn has served on the AASLH Historic House Committee and on the board of the Saint Louis chapter of the Victorian Society in America.

Lenora M. Henson oversaw and facilitated twenty-three and a half iterations of the Victorian Christmas decorating/de-decorating process during her tenure as curator of the Theodore Roosevelt Inaugural National Historic Site. She believes in the power of history to provide inspiration and insight that help us navigate the complexities of the contemporary world.

Martha B. Katz-Hyman has worked for many historical organizations, including Colonial Williamsburg and the Jamestown-Yorktown Foundation and is now an independent curator working with historic sites on the East Coast. She is the coeditor of *The World of a Slave: Encyclopedia of the Material Life of Slaves in the United States*, as well as numerous articles on various aspects of historic house furnishing. In 2013 she received the John T. Schlebecker Award from the Association for Living History, Farm and Agriculture Museums for her many contributions to the organization. She can be contacted at martha.katzhyman@gmail.com.

Katie Knowles is assistant national curator for engagement for the National Trust for England, Wales, and Northern Ireland. She specializes in interpretation and collections, working with a huge range of heritage sites to inspire and engage visitors. Recent publications include *100 Curiosities and Inventions from the Collections of the National Trust* (September 2022). Katie has held previous heritage roles as a research manager and communications advisor. She can be contacted at katie.knowles@nationaltrust.org.uk.

Stacia Kuceyeski is the chief operating officer at the Ohio History Connection (OHC). Having served in a variety of capacities at OHC over the past twenty years, Stacia was most recently the director of outreach where she managed a large-scale overhaul of all K–12 programming, as well as transitioned the division's work to have an added emphasis on community engagement and partnerships. Stacia received both her BA in history and her MA in cultural policy and arts administration from Ohio State University.

Karen Trahan Leathem, a historian at the Louisiana State Museum, has developed a broad range of exhibitions on Louisiana history and culture. Her publications include essays in *New Orleans Cuisine: Fourteen Signature Dishes and Their Histories* and *Louisiana Women: Their Lives and Times*. A native of southwest Louisiana, Leathem holds a PhD in American history from the University of North Carolina at Chapel Hill.

Jeannie Giroir Luckett, a graduate of Louisiana State University in art education, is director of programs and partnerships at West Baton Rouge Museum where she has worked since 1994. Prior to that, she was a classroom art teacher and workshop instructor at area museums. While at West Baton Rouge Museum, she has worked alongside a talented team of museum professionals. Through this support, she has been able to help design and implement festivals, school tours, history camps, teacher institutes, Blues enrichment programs, museum theater programs, lecture, documentary, and concert series, workshops, bus trips, and community partnerships. Contact her at Luckett@wbrmuseum.org.

James McKay is a retired National Park Service (NPS) professional who served with the agency for thirty-seven years, most recently as chief ranger at Martin Van Buren National Historic Site in Kinderhook, New York. Previous assignments included the Statue of Liberty and Ellis Island National Monuments, Lowell National Historical Park, and Saint-Gaudens National Historic Site. Throughout his career he was responsible for the full spectrum of NPS ranger duties, but his passion has always been American history and interpretation. He holds a BA in history from the University of Massachusetts and an MA in American history from Pace University–Gilder Lehrman Institute of American History.

Carla Mello has a BS in biological sciences and a BA in education from the University of Sao Paulo, Brazil, and has worked in the museum education field for more than thirteen years. She has successfully participated in the implementation of a brand-new education department and created and facilitated hundreds of demonstrations and activities for visitors of all ages. At Ohio History Connection, she is using all her accumulated experience with outreach, community engagement, and program management to bridge the gap between informal and formal education environments. She is part of the AASLH Educators and Interpreters Affinity Community committee. Contact her at https://www.linkedin.com/in/carla-mello/.

Kelly Elaine Navies is the Museum Specialist in oral history at the National Museum of African American History and Culture (NMAAHC). Navies' oral history projects are located at the Southern Oral History Program, The Reginald F. Lewis Maryland Museum of African American History and Culture, the Washington DC Public Library *Peoples' Archive*, and at NMAAHC's Oral History Initiative. Her writing may be found in several publications, including *Musical Crossroads: Stories Behind the Objects of African American Music* (2023) by Dwandalyn Reece and the upcoming, *Affrilachia: Testimonies* (2024) with photographer Chris Aluka Berry. Navies, a graduate of UC Berkeley and the Catholic University of America, is originally from the California Bay Area, but has resided in Washington, DC, for the past 20 years.

Laurel A. Racine has an MA from the Winterthur Program in Early American Culture at the University of Delaware and a museum studies certificate from Tufts University. She has held a variety of positions at private museums and with the National Park Service (NPS). During her tenure with the NPS she has served as a senior curator with the Northeast Museum Services Center, cultural resource manager at Lowell National Historical Park, and currently is supervisory historian/program manager for the Northeast Region's history and preservation assistance team. Laurel specializes in historic furnishings in historic houses but leaves the Christmas decorating at home to her daughter.

Melody Smith is an emerging professional in the museum and nonprofit sectors. She earned an MA in museology from the University of Washington, where she focused on rural heritage. She is a member of AASLH's Religious History Committee.

Sandra Smith has spent more than two decades working with a variety of history museums and historic sites. While her roles have ranged from collections management to museum administration, the majority of her work has focused on developing programs for community engagement along with strategies for mission-driven revenue generation. After receiving her BA in classical studies from the College of William and Mary and her MA in museum studies from George Washington University, Sandra went on to work for the National Trust for Historic Preservation and the Senator John Heinz History Center, among other organizations.

Mary A. van Balgooy is an award-winning public historian and accomplished nonprofit executive who has worked in a variety of institutions, including archives, associations, botanic gardens, historic houses, historic societies, museums, preservation organizations, universities, and agencies at city, county, and national levels with major responsibilities for administration, awards, collections, education, fellowships, fundraising, interpretation, preservation, and public relations. She is a recognized researcher, author, and speaker on interpreting women's history at historic sites, museums, and historical societies. Mary received a BA in history from the University of California, Irvine, and an MA in history from Claremont Graduate University. She currently lives in the Washington, DC, area and is vice president of Engaging Places, LLC, where she can reached at mary.vanbalgooy@ engagingplaces.net.

Gregory R. Weidman has been the National Park Service curator of Hampton National Historic Site and Fort McHenry National Monument and Historic Shrine since 2008. For eleven years prior, she had worked for Historic Hampton Inc. as a consultant on historic interiors. From 1978 to 1998 she served on the staff of the Maryland Historical Society as a leading authority on Maryland furniture and historic interiors. She has written several books and numerous articles and essays.

Patricia West, PhD, is the recently retired curator of Martin Van Buren National Historic Site in Kinderhook, New York, and author of numerous works about historic house museums including *Domesticating History: The Political Origins of America's House Museums*, published in 1999 and still widely used in public history classrooms. Well known for her groundbreaking work to foreground the lives and labors of domestic servants in historic house museums, she teaches public history at the University at Albany and is a lifelong resident of New York's Hudson Valley.